JACKSONVILLE AND THE ROOTS OF SOUTHERN ROCK

UNIVERSITY PRESS OF FLORIDA

Florida A&M University, Tallahassee
Florida Atlantic University, Boca Raton
Florida Gulf Coast University, Ft. Myers
Florida International University, Miami
Florida State University, Tallahassee
New College of Florida, Sarasota
University of Central Florida, Orlando
University of Florida, Gainesville
University of North Florida, Jacksonville
University of South Florida, Tampa
University of West Florida, Pensacola

University Press of Florida

Gainesville · Tallahassee · Tampa · Boca Raton

Pensacola · Orlando · Miami · Jacksonville · Ft. Myers · Sarasota

JACKSONVILLE
AND THE
ROOTS OF SOUTHERN ROCK

Michael Ray FitzGerald

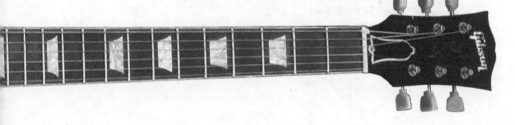

First cloth printing, 2020
First paperback printing, 2023

28 27 26 25 24 23   6 5 4 3 2 1

Library of Congress Control Number: 2020938175
ISBN 978-0-8130-6665-3 (cloth) | ISBN 978-0-8130-8035-2 (pbk.)

The University Press of Florida is the scholarly publishing agency for the State University
System of Florida, comprising Florida A&M University, Florida Atlantic University, Florida
Gulf Coast University, Florida International University, Florida State University, New College
of Florida, University of Central Florida, University of Florida, University of North Florida,
University of South Florida, and University of West Florida.

University Press of Florida
2046 NE Waldo Road
Suite 2100
Gainesville, FL 32609
http://upress.ufl.edu

CONTENTS

Preface: Jacksonville Blues vii

Introduction: What Is Southern Rock? 1

1 | Gram Parsons: A Walking Contradiction . . . 16

2 | The Bitter Ind/31st of February 31

3 | The Allman Brothers Band 39

4 | Cowboy 66

5 | Lynyrd Skynyrd: Bad-Boy Chic 75

6 | Blackfoot: Southern Metal 106

7 | 38 Special: Holding on Loosely 118

8 | Molly Hatchet: Southern Spinal Tap 132

9 | Derek Trucks: Channeling Duane 145

10 | Conclusion 152

Notes 159

Bibliography 185

Index 199

PREFACE

Jacksonville Blues

IN 1968, my father was transferred from Naval Air Station (NAS) Lemoore, California, to NAS Jacksonville, Florida. A high-school friend and fellow music lover who had lived in Jacksonville told me I would really dig it. It was "really happening," he said.

My family arrived on April 4, the day Martin Luther King was assassinated. My parents had gone to nearby Orange Park to look for a house. I was sitting in the bathtub in the hotel on the base when the news from Memphis came over the radio.

Ensconced at Orange Park High School (OPHS), I was amazed to discover there were young bands all over the place. There were a half dozen rock groups at OPHS alone: the Daybreakers, the Nu-Sounds, the Six Teens, the Sound Vibrations, and more. The Daybreakers even had a local hit on 50,000-watt WAPE-AM. Coincidentally, the group recorded at the same Edgewood Avenue studio where the Classics IV of "Spooky" fame—a number-three hit earlier that year—had begun their careers.

Being a rock musician in Jacksonville had its hazards, though. Packs of rednecks cruised around town in "muscle cars," looking for longhairs to terrorize. There was one area where you could be left alone: Riverside, Jacksonville's answer to Greenwich Village, where rents were low and people were open-minded.

My dad had taken me to Paulus Music downtown and cosigned for my first professional guitar, a cherry-red Gibson SG Standard, which we bought for the princely sum of $348.40—I'd wanted a Les Paul, like my buddy Page in the Daybreakers had, but it was out of our price range. I was to make the twenty-two-dollar monthly payments with wages I earned busing tables at the enlisted men's cafeteria on the base for $1.65 an hour. The marines constantly hassled me about my hair, which was maybe an inch over the tops of my ears.

Things were getting tense between my dad and me. He didn't object when I moved in with my grandmother, who had come down from rusty old Roxbury, a district in Boston, to get away from the gray slush. She bought a trailer and rented a lot in Freeman's Trailer Park, close to school. She wound up making most of the payments on my guitar, God bless her.

In the trailer park lived another local legend: Paul Glass. His black, stringy hair was already almost to his shoulders. He had quit school a year before to become a rock musician with a band called Doomsday Refreshment Committee, which included future 38 Special guitarist Jeff Carlisi.

Glass spent most of his days in the trailer, shades drawn, practicing his Epiphone ES-335. I brought my new SG by one day, hoping for some pointers. Never one for niceties, Glass lovingly fondled it as he sneered, "You don't deserve this guitar." He wanted to borrow it, but of course I wouldn't let it out of my sight. So we struck a bargain: He'd bring me along on his gigs, I would let him use the guitar, and, in return, I would get to meet his bandmates and other Westside musicians like Carlisi and Leon Wilkeson (later with Lynyrd Skynyrd). I might even get to "sit in" and gain some experience. This connection did eventually lead to my being invited to audition for a group called Sweet Rooster, which evolved into 38 Special.

As part of my instruction in guitar lore, Glass took me to see a Riverside band called the Second Coming, which featured a virtuoso picker from Bradenton by the name of Dickey Betts, whose group had recently relocated to town. If Clapton was God, as the saying went, then Betts was Jesus—he could play Clapton's solo on "Crossroads" note for note.

Forrest Richard "Dickey" Betts had been performing on and off in Jacksonville for years. He had come here in the mid-1960s with a Bradenton group he led called the Jesters, who served as the house band at Jacksonville's Normandy Club. Back in the Tampa Bay area in 1967, Betts met Berry Oakley, a guitarist and bassist from Chicago, who had recently relocated to Sarasota. Psychedelic blues, or "acid-rock," was

Paul Glass (*left*) with Jeff Carlisi, ca. 1967. Photo courtesy of Jeff Carlisi.

the next big thing, and Oakley wanted to get in on it. Oakley and Betts would form the Blues Messengers along with Betts's wife, Dale, on keyboards, guitarist Larry "Rhino" Reinhardt, and drummer/vocalist John Meeks.

The band, now known as the Second Coming, came to Jacksonville at the invitation of club owner Leonard Renzler. They quickly became the toast of the town, garnering a substantial following, myself and Glass included.

Betts's guitar playing was our drug. Glass and I would go almost anywhere to get it. We hitchhiked all over northeast Florida—as far as Ravine Gardens in Palatka—to hear Betts at every possible opportunity. One night, the two of us set out on a hitchhiking excursion into one of Jacksonville's toughest blue-collar neighborhoods. This was a risky proposition for semi-longhairs, but we braved our way to the Woodstock Youth Center on Beaver Street to get our dose of Betts's magic. This must have been mid-March 1969.

It was not the band's best performance. The group had a mystery guest sitting in: Betts stood by as most of the solos were taken by a diffident young man who looked like the Cowardly Lion and spent most of the show staring down at his Fender guitar, blond stringy hair draped over his face.

Glass and I were outraged. We couldn't understand why Betts was letting this guy hog the solos. "We came to hear Dickey!" we heckled. "Dickey can play circles around this dude!" It would be months before we found out that *this dude* was Duane Allman, and that he was already famous—well, sort of.

It just so happened that *this dude* was from Daytona Beach, about ninety miles south of Jacksonville, and had been playing around our vicinity for years. Allman and his younger brother Gregg, with their band the Allman Joys, had been semi-regulars at a downtown joint called the Comic Book Club. Glass had mentioned the Allman Joys once or twice, but he didn't recognize the mostly obscured face onstage that evening.

Already signed to a recording contract with Alan Walden's new Macon-based Capricorn Records—as well as a management deal—Allman, needing a bassist, got in touch with Berry Oakley, whom Allman had met while performing with the Hour Glass at the Comic Book Club. After getting a new band together at the Gray House in Riverside, Allman rang brother Gregg in LA and told him to hustle back to Florida because he now had a smokin' new band *and* a new record deal. Gregg Allman arrived in Jacksonville on March 26. On March 29 the new group, unannounced, shared the bill with the Second Coming at the Beaches Auditorium and on March 30 did the same at the Cedar Hills National Guard Armory on Normandy Boulevard. Betts and Oakley performed with both acts.

A day later they were gone. Just as Betts and his compadres had bolted Tampa for Jacksonville, they upped and left as quickly for Macon.

In November, another musician friend and I were browsing at Hoyt Hi-Fi in Roosevelt Mall, right next to the site of the old Scene, the nightclub where the Second Coming had served as house band. In a display you couldn't miss was an album bearing a figure that looked a lot like Berry Oakley doing his best Jesus imitation. Here he was in a dark robe, in an outdoor church niche, both arms outstretched, as if he were blessing a group of sinners below him—most of whom looked familiar.

"Is that—?" I stammered as I pointed to the album. The store clerk, who had obviously been asked this question many times, interjected, "It sure is!"

There they were, the Second Coming, reincarnated as the Allman Brothers Band. My friend and I shot looks at each other. Suddenly anything was possible. Success in the music biz for local dudes was a reality, not just some pipe dream, as my dad had declared. The parents were wrong!

A band of Westsiders called the One Percent was able to pick up a lot of loose fans after the Second Coming and its spinoffs left town. That band would later be known by the name Lynyrd Skynyrd. Many more Jacksonville bands, such as Blackfoot, Cowboy, 38 Special, Johnny Van Zant, Molly Hatchet, and others would follow the trail blazed by the band of brothers.

JACKSONVILLE AND THE ROOTS OF SOUTHERN ROCK

Introduction

What Is Southern Rock?

IT SEEMS ESSENTIAL TO DEFINE the term "southern rock" before one can write about it. This is necessary in order to plan what goes into the text and what gets left out. So what exactly *is* southern rock?

Trying to define it is tantamount to going down the proverbial rabbit hole. It's a slippery, nebulous term that can mean almost anything. On its face it appears to imply rock music from the 1970s that came from the South, but that could include anything from Wet Willie to Marshall Tucker to Lynyrd Skynyrd, acts that have little in common stylistically or sound-wise.

Author Scott B. Bomar states that the term "southern rock" was first used in the early 1970s by Mo Slotin, a writer for the Atlanta underground paper *Great Speckled Bird* in a review of an Allman Brothers Band concert.[1] But the phrase didn't come into broad usage until Al Kooper incorporated the concept into the name of his Atlanta-based record label, Sounds of the South, *before* he signed Lynyrd Skynyrd. Kooper was one of the first—along with Phil Walden of Capricorn Records, founded in 1969—to realize that southern talent was something that might be codified and commodified. It happened that Skynyrd fit nicely into Kooper's concept.

Some people argue that southern rock is an amalgam of rock, blues, and country, dominated by electric guitars. However, applying this definition, the early "rockabilly" acts out of Memphis—Elvis, Carl Perkins, Jerry Lee Lewis—along with Chuck Berry, Buddy Knox, and Buddy Holly might also qualify as southern rockers. One might go so far as to assert that rockabilly was an earlier *wave* of southern rock. There have been others. When you start digging, you never know what you'll find down there. Variations of R&B-influenced country music go back to the 1940s with Hank Williams's "Move It on Over" and even further, with a style called "hillbilly boogie." Someone so inclined could probably dig even deeper.[2]

Country and rock 'n' roll may *seem* dissimilar, but they actually spring from the same Celtic roots, with rock 'n' roll containing African-ized and Native elements, specifically drums—traditional country or bluegrass bands eschewed drums. Rock 'n' roll was *always* a hybrid of country and blues, an admixture of black, white, and Native elements. Cut in Memphis in 1954, Elvis Presley's first record was a revved-up version of Bill Monroe's bluegrass standard "Blue Moon of Kentucky." Elvis added African American rhythmic flourishes (that is, a gospel-style backbeat) to his interpretation.

There is a big semantic problem, however, with the term "rock." Rock is not the same thing as rock 'n' roll, even though the two terms are often used interchangeably. Rock refers specifically to the music of the hippies and "freaks" emanating from California during the Summer of Love (1967), with the movement heading eastward. Rock culture was based on rejection of middle-class values, the use of "mind-expanding" recreational drugs (mostly pot and LSD), sexual freedom, and bizarre clothes. Rock, then, was the soundtrack of the so-called counterculture. It was never monolithic to begin with and in fact embraced *any* style, from Hindu ragas to psychedelic "acid" guitars to blues to bluegrass along with anything and everything in between. Hence the term "rock" as a designation for a musical sound or style has no musical meaning—it was simply the sound of the countercul-ture, whatever that happened to be at any given moment. Hence there could be no such thing as "southern rock" or "country-rock" prior to 1967. *Southern* rock, then, was music made by southern longhairs. The hair element is important, as noted in Charlie Daniels's anthem "Long-Haired Country Boy." Southern rock tended to have more blues and country in it, simply because that was closer to home for southern musicians.

Southern Rock Versus California Country-Rock

Something very similar if not parallel was happening out West with the "California country-rock" sound, which was usually lighter in tone and more traditional than what came to be called "southern rock." California country-rock was based more on traditional styles such as folk and bluegrass than the contemporaneous country style then called "honky-tonk" or "the Bakersfield sound." It often featured kitschy three-part harmonies. One could say that the early 1960s folk boom—spearheaded by the likes of the Kingston Trio, the New Christy Minstrels, and Peter, Paul and Mary—had been a *point of entry* for these young players, bringing them first to folk, then to bluegrass, and then to country. This amalgam was primarily developed in 1967 by a Los Angeles–based group called Hearts and Flowers, led by former Waycross, Georgia, resident Larry Murray on Dobro and including Bernie Leadon (who had moved to San Diego from Gainesville) on banjo and guitar. This style was further developed—and electrified—by groups like the Byrds, whose 1968 incarnation included former Waycross resident Gram Parsons and former Byrds member Chris Hillman; the Flying Burrito Brothers, founded by Parsons, along with Hillman and Leadon; Poco; Linda Ronstadt; and the Eagles, of whom Leadon was also a founding member. The lineage can be traced back to a San Diego folk/bluegrass group that included Murray and Leadon. Clearly, then, a good portion of the inspiration for California country-rock came from Georgia and Florida by way of Murray, Leadon, and Parsons.

It's difficult to draw a dividing line between California country-rock and southern rock, as they can at times seem quite similar, but it is clear that country-rock came first, so it could be argued that southern rock is a *subset* or a variation of country-rock—perhaps simply another branch of the same tree. The differences seem to be:

California country-rock contains traditional country and/or bluegrass instruments such as pedal steel, fiddles, mandolins, and banjos, which are rarely heard in southern rock (with the exceptions of Charlie Daniels and Dickey Betts's group Great Southern, both of whom occasionally used fiddles).

In keeping with country-rock's overall adherence to country techniques, country-rock's guitar tones are generally clean (usually played on Fender Telecasters), whereas southern rock is dominated by louder, thick-sounding—and often distorted—electric guitars (such as Les Pauls, which are renowned for their "sustain"), more suggestive of hard rock. This seems to be the basic difference between the two styles.

Country-rock often features gleeful-sounding three-part harmonies derived from faux-folk acts like the Kingston Trio and Peter, Paul and Mary, whereas southern rock more often focuses on one main singer, sometimes adding a single harmony vocal, rarely more (with exceptions being the Outlaws and Cowboy, who both sound quite folkish).

Country-rock, generally speaking, seems to be about 40 percent folk, 40 percent country, and 20 percent rock—if even that much. Southern rock seems to be about 60 percent hard rock, 15 percent country, 15 percent blues, and the rest miscellaneous influences like jazz, soul, folk, and what-have-you.

The dividing line between country-rock and southern-rock is fuzzy because country music came from the South, so country-rock already had a southern component.[3]

However, as California country-rock was taking shape in the late 1960s, the South reacted with a harder, more rock- and R&B-influenced country hybrid.

Early Southern Rock

Out of Memphis, a place where black and white styles—if not people—mingled freely, came the oddball proto-rap (or "talking blues") of "Let It All Hang Out" by psychedelic country-rockers the Hombres (their debut album was produced in Memphis by Houston's Huey P. Meaux, who had worked with the Sir Douglas Quintet). Also in Memphis, Delaney and Bonnie and Black Oak Arkansas (under the name the Knowbody Else) had recorded music that could be categorized as southern rock for Stax Records in 1968 and 1969 respectively. In Nashville in 1967, Louisiana singer-guitarist-songwriter Tony Joe White signed to Monument Records. White was clearly a seminal southern rocker, although his sound was heavy on the funk/R&B side (not unlike Wet Willie's would be later) and was referred to at the time as "swamp rock." It sounds like it was recorded in Muscle Shoals, but his 1969 breakout hit, "Polk Salad Annie," was recorded in Nashville at RCA's illustrious Studio B. Nashville artist Jerry Reed, from Atlanta, was working on his own swamp-rock sound, very much reminiscent of White's—replete with references to Louisiana swamps and alligators—releasing his breakout "Amos Moses" in 1970. Stylistically, it's only a short step from this to Lynyrd Skynyrd's 1974 song "Swamp Music." The point here is that what came to be called "southern rock" was already a fully fledged form—without a name—by the time the Allman Brothers Band (ABB) released its first album in 1969.

Allman Brothers as Pioneers of Southern Rock

A case could be made that Duane and Gregg Allman, under the name the Allman Joys, had pioneered a blues-based southern-type rock with their September 1966 album recorded for Nashville-based Dial Records (that album went unreleased until 1973, when the ABB hit it big). However, what the Allman Joys were doing was really not much different from what blues-based bands like the Rolling Stones, the Yardbirds, and the Animals had been doing in Britain since 1962 (Duane and Gregg Allman even wore English-style "pageboy" hairdos like Brian Jones and Keith Relf). So it seems Britain might have been the actual home of "southern rock." But of course the music had to be made by real southerners to be seen as authentic.

Many fans assume the style we now call southern rock began with the ABB's 1969 debut on Atco Records. There is little on this album that evinces a direct country influence. The ABB's debut album is a gumbo of psychedelic rock, blues, soul, and jazz. However, Gregg Allman did experiment with country-rock on the ABB's second album, 1970's *Idlewild South*, with his song "Midnight Rider," which he had written while living in Los Angeles during his tenure with the Hour Glass.

In 1972, ABB guitarist/vocalist Dickey Betts began adding his own style of country-rock to the band's mix with the song "Blue Sky" (from *Eat a Peach*) on which he implemented his unique style of what sounded like mandolin licks played on a Les Paul through a humongous Marshall amplifier (Betts had played mandolin in a bluegrass band as a youth). In 1973, he contributed the song "Ramblin' Man" (on

Brothers and Sisters), which sailed to number two on *Billboard*'s Hot 100 singles chart. Betts's breezy paean to wanderlust was hardly representative of the ABB's overall sound or style. "Ramblin' Man" wasn't appreciably different from what the Eagles were already doing in California. "Ramblin' Man" and "Take It Easy" are so similar they could be made into a medley.[4] In actuality all that really separated these two ostensibly disparate styles was geography.

Whereas blues were commonly associated with uneducated blacks, country music was associated with uneducated rural "rednecks." First of all, neither of these stereotypes holds true, and second, this division itself is a false dichotomy: In fact, both styles had much in common—as did the people themselves—and borrowed generously from each other.[5] As Ray Charles, who spent his youth in St. Augustine and Jacksonville, told music historian Peter Guralnick, "You take country music, you take black music, you got the same goddamn thing." Charles's gift, according to author Tom Moon, was "erasing artificial divisions between genres to uncover the common heart and soul lurking underneath."[6]

The Allman Brothers Band tried to disassociate itself from the southern-rock tag, largely because, after the arrival of Lynyrd Skynyrd, this tag would become a liability, often equated with rednecks and racism, an inference ABB members disdained.[7] Southern rock, as exemplified by Skynyrd, was music for "redneck hippies": crude, simplistic, it celebrated drinking, juking, and fighting, whereas the music of the Allman Brothers Band was sophisticated, complex, and cerebral.

Tom Petty, Southern Rocker?

Tom Petty, mostly known as a pop-rocker, did briefly flirt with a southern-rock image in the mid-1980s.[8] Journalist Darianne Schramm writes, "Though he's often thought of as a southern rocker, Tom Petty actually shied away from that label as much as he could."[9] Petty himself has said, "We're an L.A. band," since the Heartbreakers were formed in Los Angeles.[10] However, three of the group's five members had been in a previous band, Mudcrutch, formed in Gainesville. In 1985 Petty was writing and singing about the South, even displaying a rebel flag at his shows. However, he later expressed remorse for this gesture.[11]

One song in particular that embodied Petty's nostalgia for an imagined South was "Rebels":

> Even before my father's fathers
> They called us all rebels
> Burned our cornfields
> And left our cities leveled
> I can still feel the eyes
> Of those blue-bellied devils[12]

Others

Another hard-to-categorize act is contemporary singer JJ Grey from Jacksonville, who heads up a band called Mofro that is essentially—like Derek Trucks's group, the Tedeschi Trucks Band—an R&B act. Grey himself might disagree with categorizing Mofro as a "southern-rock" act, but there is room—as well as precedents—in this broad rubric for his style. Mofro's music is sometimes described as "swamp funk," which might put it in a category pioneered Tony Joe White. There have been other groups oddly categorized as southern rock—such as Delaney and Bonnie or Wet Willie—whose sound was almost entirely R&B. Mofro, formed in 1999, signed with San Francisco's Fog City label in 2001, releasing two albums: *Blackwater* that same year and *Lochloosa* in 2004. Both are replete with geographical references to north Florida. In 2007 Mofro signed with Chicago-based blues label Alligator Records and released *Country Ghetto*. After six albums on Alligator, the group, now known as JJ Grey and Mofro, signed with Dutch label Provogue Records in 2015 and continues its heavy touring schedule with many European performances.

Another group sometimes included in the swamp-rock category is Swamp Cabbage, which looks and sounds a bit like ZZ Top. Both Swamp Cabbage and Mofro record at Jim DeVito's Retrophonics Studio in St. Augustine, Florida. DeVito has also performed with Swamp Cabbage both in the studio and onstage.

It's in the Subject Matter

Ultimately the term "southern rock" defies attempts at a logical definition. In the final analysis, all that can be said is that southern rock, like today's country music, has no discernible sound or musical character; it can primarily be recognized by its *subject matter*, which has to do with the provincial men—and occasionally women—of the so-called heartland: the common man, the workingman, in short, the *folk*.[13] Lynyrd Skynyrd's Ronnie Van Zant, whose writing style would come to epitomize southern rock, wrote about what he knew. Simple folk, *his* people, could relate. His stories created a community of sorts, based around the music. Van Zant's story-songs told tales of everyday people struggling to get by and wringing every ounce of pleasure obtainable whenever possible from their short, brutish lives. Seen in this light, then, one can grasp how similar the subject matter of songs in vastly disparate styles, such as Wet Willie's "Keep on Smilin'" and Skynyrd's "Down South Jukin'," have in common.

Another popular theme of southern rock is *rambling*, a theme taken from blues. "Rambling" is more than just a taste for unfettered travel: It has much to do with sexual conquest and the rejection of middle-class morals such as marriage and monogamy—and how well-suited the traveling musician's life is to these endeavors. Musicologist Travis D. Stimeling writes: "At their worst, men's blues boasted about the ability to attract and have sexual and perhaps economic power over several women without having responsibilities to any of them. . . . That approach to gender relations sounds a good deal like the perspective of the southern-rock movement, and the ramblin' blues man cut off from his community was an appealingly dramatic image to many young white men."[14] Van Zant celebrated this theme in one of Lynyrd Skynyrd's earliest songs, "Free Bird," and it becomes even more explicit in the band's remake of J. J. Cale's blues-based "Call Me the Breeze":

> Well, now, I dig you Georgia peaches
> Makes me feel right at home
> Well, I don't love me no one woman
> I can't stay in Georgia long[15]

This theme also becomes apparent in the third verse of Dickey Betts's "Ramblin' Man":

On my way to New Orleans this morning
Leavin' out of Nashville, Tennessee
They're always havin' a good time down on the bayou, Lord
Them delta women think the world of me[16]

A Boys' Club

Much like country music, southern rock's most salient feature may
be its inherent—and incessant—*maleness*. Rock 'n' roll in general has
always been a boys' club, beginning with Elvis, Carl Perkins, Gene Vincent, Little Richard, Chuck Berry, and continuing with the Beatles,
the Rolling Stones, and so forth; nonetheless rock music occasionally
produced a Grace Slick, a Janis Joplin, a Suzie Quatro, a Joan Jett, a
Chrissie Hynde.[17]

I would argue that Joplin meets most if not all the criteria to be
categorized as a southern rocker except perhaps for the fact that the
term did not exist in 1967, when she and her band, Big Brother and
the Holding Company, became nationally prominent. There is also the
issue of her gender: are *any* females recognized as southern rockers?
The term itself is practically synonymous with maleness. The few female voices one can find in so-called southern rock are Bonnie Bramlett, who broke out with Delaney & Bonnie in 1972; Ruby Starr, who
first claimed national attention with Black Oak Arkansas in 1973; and
Dale Krantz, a backing singer for 38 Special who was brought in as lead
singer for the short-lived Rossington Collins Band featuring former
members of Lynyrd Skynyrd in 1980. Krantz was rerelegated to the position of backup singer with a reconstituted version of Lynyrd Skynyrd
in 1987.

Brief Cultural and Musical History of Jacksonville

Originally called Cow Ford by early English settlers because it was located in a shallow spot on the St. Johns River where cows could cross,
the City of Jacksonville was platted in 1822 and incorporated ten years
later.

From the beginning the city was a regional distribution hub, mostly
thanks to its ports' proximity to the Atlantic. Railroads began appearing in 1899, which connected New York with Miami—such as Seaboard

Coast Line's Orange Blossom Special—and the Atlantic seaboard with west Florida. Warehouses and appurtenant distribution infrastructure multiplied predictably; transportation, warehousing, trucking and logistics have nearly always been a major source of employment, which attracted many workers from south Georgia and lent a blue-collar character to the area.[18] In fact, some observers, culturally speaking, consider Jacksonville not only part of south Georgia but the virtual capital of south Georgia.[19] Jacksonville even has the largest Georgia Bulldogs football-team supporters' chapter, founded in 1946.[20]

North Florida is not like the rest of the state: record producer Tom Dowd said, "Florida is the only place in the world where you have to go north to get the South."[21]

Much like south Georgia, Jacksonville never had a multitude of cultural activities, although Jacksonville eventually established a couple of decent museums as well a symphony. Even if there *had* been a plethora of cultural outlets, much of the city's largely blue-collar populace could not afford to attend such events; many relied instead on the tradition of creating their own entertainment. Making music was one such diversion, and it was often a family affair, passed down through generations.[22] This was a common practice throughout rural areas of the Deep South, where other forms of live entertainment were usually scarce. Television did not even arrive until 1949.[23]

However, as in the rest of the nation, the cinema was quite popular.[24] In fact, starting in 1907, Jacksonville became the southern capital of the motion-picture industry. More than thirty studios, including Kalem, Selig, Edison, Lubin, Vim, King Bee, Encore, Eagle, and Metro, were based in the city, and the industry attracted people from all over the region looking for work. A few film stars even emerged. Perhaps the earliest was Oliver Hardy, who came to Jacksonville from Milledgeville, Georgia, in 1913 and became a ticket-taker at a local cinema, moonlighting as a drummer in Pablo Beach bars. Hardy used his film connections to score his first acting role at Metro Pictures (as in Metro-Goldwyn-Mayer), whose studio was located on the riverfront site of what is now Metro Park, named after the company.[25]

Jacksonville has long evinced a puritanical streak that has hindered its pop-culture contributions. Its film-industry personnel were not especially welcome, particularly among the religious factions who dominate city government. To be fair, film crews did create a bit of mayhem, often blocking downtown streets without garnering permits, using passersby as movie extras without their permission, and generally behaving like "carnies," a view espoused by local attorney John W. Martin, who in 1917 ran for mayor on a platform promising to expel the film industry. Martin won, and the city did exactly that. By 1920 the film industry had relocated to Los Angeles.[26] Martin went on to become governor.

Despite all this, the city's large African American populace managed to make the downtown LaVilla district a popular entertainment destination that nearly rivaled New York's Harlem.[27] African American promoter and theater owner Pat Chappelle, who became one of the richest residents of the city, started out as a minstrel singer, eventually opening his own five-hundred-seat Excelsior Hall on Bridge (now Broad) Street in 1899, the first black-owned theater in the South.[28] The district eventually became host to top African American entertainers and was where Ray Charles first plied his trade after leaving the Florida School for the Deaf and Blind in St. Augustine in 1945.[29] Another very important figure was James Weldon Johnson, who in 1900 along with his brother J. Rosamond Johnson, wrote "Lift Every Voice and Sing," sometimes referred to as the Negro national hymn. Johnson moved to Harlem, where he became a cofounder of the National Association for the Advancement of Colored People (NAACP). Another famous African American performer was Billy Daniels, who made a huge name for himself on Broadway as well as on London's West End and on television. Jacksonville songwriter Charlie "Hoss" Singleton wrote many hits, including the lyrics for Frank Sinatra's number-one "Strangers in the Night."

Jacksonville also hosted a great many insurance and financial companies that brought in educated people from all over. Another countervailing factor to Jacksonville's provincialism was the U.S. Navy, which brought a somewhat cosmopolitan element to the city during and after World War II. The navy brought the Axtons to town from Oklahoma in 1945, including mama Mae Axton and son Hoyt, both of whom would achieve significant success in the music world.[30]

Jacksonville began to explode as a music city when local media started to feature regional entertainers, perhaps beginning with city-owned WJAX-AM in the 1940s, which featured Savannah transplant Connie Haines, who went on to sing alongside Sinatra in both Harry James's and Tommy Dorsey's orchestras. She also had hits of her own and appeared in many movies.

There are many reasons Jacksonville developed as a notable music town, but radio was surely the primary catalyst. Stations such as former Georgia farm boy Marshall Rowland's country-flavored WQIK-AM, established in 1957, and Alabamian Bill Brennan's WAPE-AM, established in 1958, began hosting concerts that brought in national headliners with local acts as openers. These stations took a chance on playing recordings by local acts, and a firecracker was lit. WAPE was a 50,000-watt "blowtorch" that could be heard from Daytona to Virginia Beach, so airplay given to local acts practically launched them into the stratosphere, even though this practice often flouted FCC regulations.[31] Television stations, too, jumped on the bandwagon, creating live-music programs for teens with Dick Clark's *American Bandstand* as the model. With such media saturation, live, local music was soon in high demand; so many gigs materialized in the 1960s that a musician could book a date first and then throw a band together to play it; indeed, this practice was fairly common.

Jacksonville's music boom lasted more than thirty years, starting—more or less—with Mae Axton's involvement in Elvis Presley's first million-selling single, "Heartbreak Hotel," in 1956.[32] Since Jacksonville's Arthur Phelps, aka Blind Blake, signed with Paramount Records in 1926, Jacksonville has produced more than one hundred national acts.[33] Following are just a few of the big names to emerge from Jacksonville:

Blind Blake	1926
Ray Charles	1947
Connie Haines	1949
Johnny Tillotson	1960
Hoyt Axton	1962
The Classics IV	1967
Allman Brothers Band	1969
Lynyrd Skynyrd	1974
38 Special	1977
Molly Hatchet	1978

Marcus Roberts.	.	.	.	.	1988
95 South	.	.	.	.	1993
Quad City DJs	.	.	.	.	1996
Limp Bizkit	.	.	.	.	1997
Derek Trucks Band	.	.	.	.	1997
Yellowcard	.	.	.	.	2001
Mofro	.	.	.	.	2001
Red Jumpsuit Apparatus	.	.	.	2006

There seem to have been no significant developments since 2006 except perhaps the signing of singer-songwriter Yuno by Sub Pop Records in 2018. For all intents and purposes, the glory days of Jacksonville music appear to be irrevocably in the past. Yet the story of how it all happened is surely worth telling.[34]

However, this book focuses on the so-called southern-rock acts that began with the Allman Brothers Band, which formed in Jacksonville's Riverside district in March 1969. Here is a listing of acts that are often—loosely—categorized as "southern-rock" groups:

Allman Brothers Band
Cowboy
Lynyrd Skynyrd
Blackfoot
38 Special
Molly Hatchet
Alias
Johnny Van Zant Band
The Rossington Collins Band
The Allen Collins Band
Derek Trucks
Van Zant
Mofro

Is Jacksonville the Birthplace of Southern Rock?

Jacksonville is sometimes called "the birthplace of southern rock." This is, strictly speaking, hyperbole and is erroneous for the following reasons:

1. Musical styles are not *born*; rather they evolve and emerge slowly, often before they even have a name. Hence musical styles generally do not have a single birthplace.

2. In order to know when and where this music purportedly began, one must first define the term "southern rock." There really is no definition that holds water. As near as I can figure, it's music for "redneck hippies," which can combine a profusion of styles. Hence the term seems to describe the audience more than the music itself.

3. Finally, southern rock—to the extent it can be defined, which is pretty much an impossible task—was *already* happening in other cities before the Allman Brothers Band, who are often—erroneously—credited as the originators of the style in 1969 (although a case could be made that the brothers pioneered the style in 1966 as the Allman Joys on Dial Records).

Jacksonville was neither the home nor the birthplace of southern rock, but it surely was a motherlode. Why were there so many successful southern-rock groups from Jacksonville? In an interview with writer Colin Escott, Rickey Medlocke, former lead vocalist and guitarist for Blackfoot and later member of Lynyrd Skynyrd, opines: "The only answer I can come up with—and I've thought about this—[is that] Jacksonville was a transient town. There [were naval bases], shipyards, an Anheuser-Busch brewery, and a lot of other industries that attracted a transient workforce. They came from everywhere. They brought their families. Then, all of a sudden, in the 1960s, there was a rock-music scene: teen clubs, bars. It just grew."[35] Jacksonville musician Scott Sisson expounds on Medlocke's hypothesis: "All these navy kids and other transient types were bringing in influences from all over, along with their enthusiasm for playing music. This meshed with the southern tradition of making your own entertainment."[36]

Indeed, many of the southern-rock musicians who emerged from the Jacksonville scene, such as Skynyrd pianist Billy Powell and bassist Leon Wilkeson, 38 Special's Jeff Carlisi, Molly Hatchet's Dave Hlubek, and others, were "navy brats" who seemed to fit right in with the goings-on. In an interview with writer Steve Houk, 38 Special singer-guitarist Don Barnes offers, "Being a navy town, Jacksonville was full of venues the sailors would frequent on leave, and it gave budding young southern rockers ample opportunities to play live and hone both their performing and songwriting chops."[37] Barnes adds, "There were [three] navy bases, so all of us—I mean everybody from Duane and Gregg Allman to Ronnie Van Zant—played the sailors' clubs."[38] Barnes mentions another ingredient, that of raw determination: "Coming from the [predominantly working-class] Westside—it's pretty much no-man's land—you either end up driving a truck or going to prison. I really think there's a thread of that underdog spirit that comes from not being from New York or Los Angeles. . . . [The music carries an] underlying aggression, with the big, strong guitars. . . . You're scream-ing at people to pay attention because you're not fashionable, you're not from a hip place."[39]

Following Barnes's line of logic, part of this desperation was gener-ated by the fact that there weren't many—if any—so-called legitimate bookings for musicians. There were few "sweet gigs" such as cruise ships, casinos, tony nightclubs, musical theaters, session dates, etc., as there would be in a cultural center like New York, Chicago, or Los Angeles, where a skilled musician might make a decent living and per-haps become complacent. Jacksonville's rock, pop, country, and R&B musicians had to scuffle, compete, and perform in some rough places. Hence Jacksonville musicians had to be especially tough and deter-mined. Those who weren't got weeded out soon enough.

It seems necessary to include a chapter on Gram Parsons, not only because he spent his formative years in Waycross and in Jacksonville, but because he is widely considered one of the pioneers of country-rock, which could be seen as a precursor or progenitor of southern rock. Perhaps southern rock was the South's *answer* to soft, creamy California country-rock.

Gram Parsons

A Walking Contradiction

SCRATCH A JACKSONVILLE NATIVE and you will likely find someone whose parents came from south Georgia, probably to escape working in the fields or some other form of farm labor.

Jacksonville is often considered the economic and cultural hub of south Georgia. In the early 1900s, folks from all across south Georgia relocated to Jacksonville to look for work in such booming industries as transportation, warehousing, and construction. Some got lucky and found jobs brewing Budweiser at the regional Anheuser-Busch plant or wrapping cigars at Swisher. Oliver Hardy came to town from Milledgeville to become a ticket-taker at a local cinema and, after signing with Jacksonville-based Metro Pictures, left a movie star.

Ingram Cecil Connor III came to Jacksonville in 1958 at age twelve from Waycross, about seventy-five miles northwest of Jacksonville. His parents weren't looking for jobs. In fact his parents—his mother at least—were extremely wealthy. Rather, they were looking to instill some discipline in their only son by enrolling him in military school, Jacksonville's Bolles Academy. Or perhaps they were just looking for a way to get him out of their hair so they could continue partying.[1] In any case, he didn't last long at Bolles, at least not this first stint. He would return in 1965 when the school ditched its military-style program and became a prestigious prep school.

His biological father, Ingram Cecil "Coon Dog" Connor Jr., from Tennessee, had been a World War II aviator who met debutante Avis Snively while stationed at Bartow Field, near Winter Haven, where Avis Snively was raised. Her father was a massively successful citrus grower, real-estate developer, railroad magnate, and banker. He also owned a 20 percent share in Cypress Gardens, which was situated in the middle of his property.[2] John Snively also happened to own two box factories—one in Waycross and one in Baxley, Georgia—that manufactured boxes for packing oranges. Avis Connor also kept a beach home in Ponte Vedra, Florida, about forty minutes from Jacksonville in adjacent St. Johns County.[3]

Gram (short for Ingram) was born in his mother's hometown of Winter Haven. She wanted to be near her family during and after the birth on November 5, 1946. She soon returned to her husband and their nice but not exclusive neighborhood, Cherokee Heights. Young Gram went to Ware County public schools for his first years of schooling.[4]

Gram was exposed to many southern styles of music at a young age, including the sacred hymns. He was raised in his mother's Episcopalian church, where the singing—if indeed there was any—might have been staid and sedate, yet he developed a taste for gospel songs. "It was something he absorbed with his southern culture," James E. "Jet" Thomas, his adviser at Harvard, told Parsons biographer David Meyer in 2005.[5] Gospel music was ubiquitous on Sunday-morning radio programs all over Georgia if not all across the Deep South. "It was everywhere; you couldn't get away from it," said Billy Ray Herrin, a Waycross music-store owner and musician. Herrin, a Parsons historian and booster, grew up around people who knew the Connors, including box-factory foreman Claude Goble, a pallbearer at Coon Dog's funeral. Goble, a part-time musician, led the Starlite Ramblers, a bluegrass and gospel group who rehearsed at the Snively plant. As a child, Gram listened in on the Ramblers' sessions, and this, Herrin said, set the stage for his lifelong musical pursuits. As in many small southern towns that lacked entertainment options, south Georgia folks often entertained themselves by making their own music. "Making music was [generally] a family tradition, passed down," Herrin adds. Gram may have inherited his musicality from his father's family in Columbia, Tennessee, about fifty miles southwest of Nashville.[6]

Waycross also spawned another very influential figure, Larry Murray, who joined the U.S. Navy in 1955 and was stationed in San Diego as a diver. In 1962 Murray formed folk-bluegrass band the Scottsville Squirrel Barkers, in which he played guitar and Dobro. Murray soon added future Byrds member and future country-rock superstar Chris Hillman on mandolin and also brought in another country-rock pioneer, Bernie Leadon, who would later join Hillman (and Gram Parsons) in the Flying Burrito Brothers. After his stint in San Diego, Murray relocated to Los Angeles, where he presided over "hoot nights" at the Troubadour and formed the seminal folk-country-psychedelic trio Hearts and Flowers. That group signed with Capitol's Folk World division in 1966 and later added Leadon. A strong argument can be made that Murray and Hillman are the real architects of the California-country-rock sound. But as Murray himself said, "To be ahead of your time is to be wrong."[7] The country-rock baton would be picked up and carried by the International Submarine Band, the Byrds, the Flying Burrito Brothers, Poco, and the Eagles, the latter of whom also included Leadon and went on to become one of the biggest acts the music business has ever seen.

A ten-year-old Gram had a flash when some family friends took him to the Waycross City Auditorium on February 22, 1956, to see a busting-out Elvis Presley opening for Little Jimmy Dickens. This was only a few weeks prior to Presley's nationwide eruption on RCA Records with "Heartbreak Hotel," a song that had emanated from Jacksonville. Gram waited outside the stage door for Presley's autograph and was not disappointed. Inspired by Presley, Gram instantly decided being a singer and pop star was his calling in life.[8] Presley would appear the next night in Jacksonville's Gator Bowl as part of Hank Snow's Jamboree. Mae Boren Axton, a Jacksonville high-school teacher, was a part-time publicist and copromoter for the show. A few months prior to these shows, she seized the opportunity to cowrite Presley's first million-seller, "Heartbreak Hotel." She had personally delivered a demonstration record to Presley at his hotel during a disc-jockey convention in Nashville.[9]

Another huge influence on Gram was Ray Charles, who also happened to be from the north Florida–south Georgia region.[10] Living in Jacksonville in 1946, he had briefly worked in a so-called hillbilly band, the Florida Playboys. Charles was an incorrigible genre-bender;

musical boundaries meant nothing to him. He was mixing country with blues, gospel, Afro-Cuban, jazz, and pop as early as 1959, when he remade Hank Snow's "Movin' On." After making his mark on the West Coast with Los Angeles–based Swingtime Records and then New York–based Atlantic Records, Charles went over to ABC-Paramount, where he scored a huge pop hit with Don Gibson's country chestnut "I Can't Stop Loving You." The single rocketed to the number-one position on *Billboard*'s Hot 100 in 1962 and was followed by a landmark album titled *Modern Sounds in Country and Western Music.*

It was this album, along with Charles's 1965 *Country and Western Meets Rhythm and Blues* that became the primary influence on Gram's concept of a "cosmic American music," which blended country, gospel, soul, and rock. Parsons's compatriot in the International Submarine Band told biographer Ben Fong-Torres, "That [album] was the thing that broke the barriers, getting into this amalgam of a truer country music but with a rock or rhythm-and-blues treatment."[11] "Soul" music would become a large component of Parsons's style.[12] Soul and country can easily be combined due to the simple fact that both derived largely from gospel music. In fact, country has often been called the white man's soul music. Parsons himself explained, "I was brought up in the South, and I never knew the difference between Negro gospel music and country music—it was all just music to me."[13]

Gram Connor left Bolles Academy after less than two years. His parents were having marital issues, to put it mildly. His life would change irrevocably in 1958: After putting his family on a train to Florida for a Christmas visit, Coon Dog went home and shot himself in the head. After his father's death, Gram would move with his mother and younger sister to the Snively family's enclave in Winter Haven, where he continued his public-school education. In 1960 his mother married Robert Parsons, who adopted young Gram.

In Winter Haven young Parsons befriended many area musicians, including Jim Stafford, Kent "Lobo" Lavoie, Jon Corneal, and Bobby Braddock, all of whom became successful. Parsons and Stafford formed a teen rock band named the Legends. However, around 1962, Parsons jumped on the burgeoning folk-music bandwagon, forming the Village Vanguards. He switched to acoustic guitar and began performing commercialized folk in the style of the Kingston Trio, the Journeymen (featuring John Phillips), and Peter, Paul and Mary. In 1963, with help from a family friend who became his first manager, Parsons joined a Greenville, South Carolina, trio, the Shilos, as its fourth member.

During one of many trips to Greenville during 1963 and '64, Parsons may have heard local singer-songwriter Sylvia Sammons performing "Hickory Wind." A few years later the song would become Parsons's calling card, released during his brief tenure with the Byrds on their 1968 Columbia album *Sweetheart of the Rodeo*. Sammons, who went blind at six, said she wrote the song in 1963, when she was sent off to boarding school in Spartanburg. The song was her expression of homesickness: "I was listening to a lot of country music in those days. Still do." She sent herself a tape-recorded copy in the mail: "I had heard that you could establish copyright by mailing yourself a tape, so I did. But I stupidly tore it open when it arrived, so I had to do it all over again." Sammons had been working in local pizza joints for five dollars a night, during the period Parsons had been in Greenville with the Shilos. She has never heard the Byrds version, she said—she first heard it on the radio, as recorded by Joan Baez in 1971. "Needless to say, I was flabbergasted." She approached the song's publishers, Tickson Music, co-owned by Parsons (and Byrds) manager, Eddie Tickner, who offered a three-thousand-dollar cash settlement (worth about twenty-five thousand dollars today) with the proviso that she hand over the tape. She agreed: "I was happy to get the money because I didn't have a pot to pee in, and I didn't think the song was good enough to really go anywhere." Sammons said she had written two verses, but the Byrds version has three, one of which is generally credited to Bob Buchanan. Sammons did not insist on a credit because relinquishing it was part of the deal, she said. She is satisfied with her decision, she adds.[14] Sammons's story has been corroborated in a letter to author David W. Johnson from former professor Bea Hutzler. Hutzler states in the letter that she heard Sammons performing the song years before it was recorded by the Byrds.[15]

In 1964, Parsons returned to Bolles, often spending weekends at his mother's beach house in Ponte Vedra. He was what some Bolles colleagues characterize as one of many "throwaway kids" whose parents just didn't want them around.[16] Throwaway kids cramped their parents' social scene—which in the Parsons' case involved a lot of alcohol. Parsons was by most accounts a popular guy on campus who cut a flashy figure. Parsons "was a swashbuckler, a real magnet," roommate

Gram Parsons at the Bolles School, 1964. Photo courtesy of the Bolles School.

Gram Parsons
941 Piedmont Drive
Winter Haven, Florida

Gram came to Bolles in the eleventh grade after taking a vacation from us for a couple of years . . . .is Bolles' noted singer and song writer. . . . plans to go to Harvard and study psychology. . . . noted for his prolonged stays on campus over the weekends. . . .best course at Bolles has been Advanced Composition. . . .one of his hobbies is arranging "social functions."

Parsons blurb from the Bolles yearbook, 1965. Courtesy of the Bolles School.

James Mallard told the *Florida Times-Union*. "When he was around girls, you could hear their skivvies hit the floor. And his voice was beautiful."[17] Parsons gave frequent impromptu acoustic performances around campus.[18] He even appeared on WJAX-AM, a city-owned station located downtown. Tom Williams, a retired Jacksonville teacher, performed on the same program. In 2005, he told the *Florida Times-Union* that Parsons was already a dedicated performer: "He was really serious backstage while everybody else was goofing around."[19]

During his junior year at Bolles, Parsons and members of the group determined they would spend a summer in New York to try to make connections in the Greenwich Village folk scene. They had already met the Journeymen at a concert in Greenville, and John Phillips had given them his number. The other members of the Journeymen were Scott MacKenzie, a Jacksonville native whose real name was Philip Blondheim, and Dick Weissman. However, by this point the Journeymen had split up, and Phillips was in the process of starting the Mamas and the Papas. When the boys arrived in the Village, they crashed on John and Michelle Phillips's floor.[20] Parsons also got in touch with another of his idols, St. Petersburg, Florida, native Fred Neil, who was a brilliant singer and songwriter but already a notorious junkie.[21]

Bill Conrad, like Parsons, was a class of 1965 Bolles graduate. A native of Jacksonville, Conrad, who was a "day student" (that is, he lived at home instead of in the dorms), said Parsons was a gentle soul who came off like a regular guy. Parsons had taken piano lessons in Waycross and played well: "He taught me some cool boogie-woogie licks." Conrad, who went on to enjoy some success in the music business, ran into Parsons in London three years after graduation, when Parsons was performing at Royal Albert Hall with the Byrds. But even at Bolles he had demonstrated an addictive personality, Conrad said. "He was doomed from the start—both his parents were hard-core alcoholics." Parsons would do almost anything to escape the tedium of sobriety. "I walked into the dorm room one time and they [Parsons and his pals] were all sniffing glue."[22] Parsons exhibited no interest in country music at that time, Conrad adds. Most students listened to Jacksonville's 50,000-watt pop powerhouse WAPE-AM.[23] "The Big Ape," as it was nicknamed, had an extremely eclectic playlist, presenting a mix of pop, R&B, a smattering of country, occasional oldies, and anything else that might interest young listeners.

Parsons may have been a spoiled preppie, but he'd already had a rough life. In addition to his father's suicide, his mother died from cirrhosis on what should have been a joyful occasion—his graduation day. Another Bolles classmate, Hugh Simpson, coeditor with Parsons at the school newspaper, remembers his own mother delivering the sad news to Parsons: "Her heart was breaking as he laid his head on her lap and cried."[24] Parsons seems to have been able to sublimate his pain into his singing. He could suffuse ordinary songs with deep meaning with his poignant renditions. In a 1974 posthumous review of Parsons's second solo album, *Grievous Angel*, *Rolling Stone* reviewer Bud Scoppa—who later erroneously dubbed Parsons the "inventor of country rock"—wrote that Parsons was "the most convincing singer of sad songs I ever heard."[25]

Parsons was not a particularly assiduous student yet was bright enough to get good grades without really trying.[26] With recommendations from faculty members, Parsons was accepted into Harvard as a divinity student. He was already getting out of his head and exhibiting a reckless streak. By the summer of 1965, the Shilos had split up, with the members going to separate universities. Parsons spent another summer in the Village, where he got in touch with Dick Weissman. Weissman produced two sets of demos for Parsons, one in his house on Twentieth Street, which has been issued by Sierra Briar Records, and another at a downtown studio, the tapes of which have been recorded over. Weissman played guitar on some of the tracks, one of which might have been "Hickory Wind," but Weissman is not sure.[27] Gram's stepfather, Robert Parsons, came to New York and took Weissman and Gram out to dinner. Weissman said the elder Parsons embarrassed everyone by sending back the wine. One day Weissman walked into his brother-in-law's apartment, where Parsons was staying, and caught him cooking up heroin. That was the end of their relationship.[28]

Soon after Parsons graduated from Bolles, the Byrds attained astronomical success with their merger of folk and Beatlesque pop-rock with a cover version of Bob Dylan's "Mister Tambourine Man." The single rocketed to number one. Dylan himself went electric that summer. Suddenly acoustic-based folk music seemed *passé*.

Parsons, too, was searching for a new direction. He had seen the Beatles—who were dabbling in country stylings at the time—at Shea Stadium on August 23, 1965. During a brief visit to Winter Haven,

Parsons visited former Legends bandmate Jim Stafford, who suggested Parsons should reinvent himself as a "country Beatle." Stafford told biographer Bob Kealing he was just looking for a gimmick that would help Parsons get noticed in a glutted marketplace. He told Parsons: "Why don't you let your hair grow long and do country music? . . . You could be the first long-haired country guy."[29] Parsons apparently pooh-poohed the idea at first. His former Legends bandmate Jim Carlton told biographer Jason Walker that "he was not into country music at all back then." Parsons had heard Carlton singing some country songs and asked "what the hell I was doing playing 'that stuff.'"[30]

Enrolled at Harvard—but only for little more than one term—Parsons was spending a lot of time getting out of his head and ignoring his studies.[31] A friend from Bolles, Judson Graves, visited Parsons there. Many years later Graves told biographer David Meyer that Parsons was so out of it he "could barely string a sentence together."[32] Another Bolles visitor, Paul Broder, told writer David W. Johnson of the *Harvard Journal*, "He [Parsons] got fucked-up a lot" and that Parsons would drive his Austin-Healy convertible at more than 100 miles per hour on back roads.[33]

Parsons soon began looking around Boston for musicians to start a new band. Yet even at this point he was not committed to a country-rock fusion. He recruited fellow Harvard student Ian Dunlop on bass, who brought in guitarist John Nuese. Nuese had already been gigging professionally in the Boston area with some prominent musicians. He claims credit for Parsons's transformation from folkie to country-music aficionado. Nuese, who died in 2012, told biographer Sid Griffin that Parsons was at that time neither interested in nor knowledgeable about country and that he was the one who had turned Parsons on to the real deal.[34] Nuese's claim, however, is mitigated by former Harvard freshman adviser Jet Thomas, who told biographer David Meyer that both he and Parsons liked old-timey country stuff like Faron Young, gospel songs, and hymns.[35] Meyer explains, "[Parsons] liked Ernest Tubb and Webb Pierce, but when Nuese played Buck Owens for him, Gram had been immersed in folk music for years" and hence was hardly knowledgeable about the current state of the music.[36] Parsons himself in 1973 credited Nuese and Dunlop for reintroducing him to country music "after I had forgotten about it for ten years."[37]

The group recruited hard-hitting R&B drummer Mickey Gauvin, re-naming itself the International Submarine Band (ISB), and took off for New York, where Parsons somehow finagled a connection with Barbra Streisand's manager, Marty Erlichman. Parsons—who was the benefi-ciary of a hefty trust fund—used his family's largesse to rent a house in the Bronx as band headquarters. The group soon dropped Erli-chman and hired new managers who duly garnered the ISB a deal with Ascot Records, distributed by United Artists (UA). The ISB's first and only Ascot single was an instrumental rendition of Johnny Mandel's theme for the film *The Russians Are Coming, the Russians Are Coming*, a UA film. But it was the B-side that reflected the spirit of the band, a remake of Buck Owens's recent hit "Truck Drivin' Man." The ISB's second single, a Parsons-Nuese collaboration titled "Sum Up Broke," released on Columbia (Streisand's home label), however, contains not one iota of country.

While in New York, Parsons met neighbors Stephen Stills and Richie Furay, who were already working on bringing country stylings into their musical concoction that, after their leaving for Los Angeles, would become Buffalo Springfield. Parsons, too, continued to dabble in country-rock but would not make the leap to full-time country-rock until forming the Flying Burrito Brothers with Chris Hillman in 1968. Three Burrito Brothers, Hillman, Parsons, and drummer Michael Clarke, had all been members of the Byrds.

Inventor of Country-Rock?

The ISB was hardly the first group to experiment with fusing country and rock. The Beatles had been doing it—very successfully—for nearly two years before Parsons got into it. They had in turn been inspired by such rockabilly artists as Presley, Perkins, Holly, and Berry as well as fellow Capitol artist Buck Owens. Some of Lennon and McCartney's own songs, such as "I'm a Loser," and "Baby's in Black," both released in December 1964, stand as seminal moments in the development of what later came to be called country-rock, although at the time it was scarcely recognized as such. It's clear that the Beatles understood and appreciated the commonalities between their Irish-Celtic roots and American country music; the Celtic influence in "Baby's in Black" could not be more obvious. In 1965, the Beatles had even gone so far as to cover Owens's country hit "Act Naturally." They in turn influenced the Byrds, who that same year recorded a Dylanesque rendering of Porter Wagoner's 1955 country hit "A Satisfied Mind." The ISB followed this trend in April 1966 with a remake of Owens's "Truck Drivin' Man." This was the B-side of the International Submarine Band's first single, "The Russians Are Coming, the Russians Are Coming!" Parsons's vocal rendition of "Truck Drivin' Man," however, sounds like a burlesque, like a teenager doing a send-up of country music, which might have been what it was: Parsons during this period had been known to poke fun at country music.[38]

Frustrated by what he felt was a lack of appreciation for what he was doing, Parsons set off for greener pastures. Parsons and his band left New York for LA in 1967, whereupon the ISB was signed by producer Lee Hazlewood to his LHI label, which released the landmark country-rock album *Safe at Home*. However, contrary to Bud Scoppa's claim that Parsons was the "inventor of country rock,"[39] this style had already been gaining traction in Los Angeles with acts like the Dillards and Hearts and Flowers. Larry Murray from Waycross was there. So was Bernie Leadon. Parsons was hardly the first to explore the country-rock style, but he may have been the first to cut an *entire album* in the genre. By 1967, many groups, including Hearts and Flowers, the Monkees, Buffalo Springfield, the Grateful Dead, and the Rolling Stones, had incorporated country sounds into their repertoires—but they were all dabblers. Even the Beatles had been dabblers. Few if any groups were willing to gamble their careers on country-rock. Most hedged their bets. What would set Parsons apart is the fact that he decided to dedicate his career to developing this hybrid.[40]

However, before the ISB album was even in the can, Chris Hillman recruited Parsons to join the Byrds, who were seeking a new direction. The Byrds and the ISB had the same manager, Larry Spector. Parsons abruptly quit his own band, leaving his partners to carry on as they saw fit. But who could blame him? The Byrds had been unbelievably successful.

Nevertheless, Parsons's tenure in the Byrds was brief. Using the Byrds as a stepping-stone, Parsons would try to ingratiate his way into the Rolling Stones, another group that, like the Byrds, had dabbled in country-rock in 1965; they had, for example, recorded Hank Snow's

"I'm Movin' On" in Los Angeles. Parsons's name had been suggested as a possible replacement for Brian Jones, who would soon be dismissed.[41] Parsons's burgeoning relationship with Keith Richards proved influential on the Stones' sound and style. Backstage at a 2004 tribute concert to Parsons, Richards told reporters that Parsons taught him the "finer points of country music . . . the difference between Bakersfield and Nashville, for example."[42] Parsons was reportedly involved—in some manner—with such Stones songs as "Wild Horses," "Country Honk," and "Torn and Frayed." Rumors persists that Parsons himself may have cowritten one or more of these. Mick Jagger's brother Chris has gone on record saying "Wild Horses" was indeed a Parsons composition, "not that he ever got credit for it."[43] Parsons certainly sings the song more convincingly than Jagger: Parsons *owns* it, whereas Jagger sounds like he's reading it.

If Parsons did dream of joining the Stones, those dreams were dashed when Jagger sent him packing. There were several reasons, one of which was that the Stones could hardly get any work done with Parsons and Richards engrossed in drugs. Parsons could get better drugs than the Mafia, Richards once quipped.[44] However, Bill Conrad speculates there was more to it than that: Parsons was too good a singer: "Jagger would never have let anyone with that much talent anywhere near the Stones"—for fear of being upstaged.[45]

As bright a future as he had, Parsons took a path of self-destructive behavior, becoming an unapologetic drug addict and an alcoholic to boot. Parsons died of drug toxicity—morphine, barbiturates, and alcohol—in a motel near the Joshua Tree National Park in California. His Jacksonville friend Margaret Fisher was with him. She and her female friend tried to save him, to no avail.[46] His corpse, slated to be buried in his stepfather's home state of Louisiana, was hijacked by his former road manager, Phil Kaufman, and set ablaze in the Joshua Tree park. This undertaking was to honor Parsons's personal request to Kaufman should he meet an untimely fate, which he of course did. His death came as no surprise to those who really knew him.[47] "[Parsons] set out to become legendary by dying young," Bernie Leadon told Parsons biographer David Meyer. "He saw that it worked for James Dean and Hank Williams. I think he thought it was a great idea, to live a tragically excessive life, *die* a tragic hero and become immortal."[48]

Parsons's legacy has assumed iconic status in the music world.

There have been several all-star tributes to his memory and his work, which have included the likes of Keith Richards, Emmylou Harris, Elvis Costello, Lucinda Williams, and many other important figures who eagerly acknowledge his influence. Many if not most modern "Americana" and "alternative-country" acts owe major debts to his vision and style. And all this goes without even mentioning how much money the Eagles—whose original lineup included Leadon—made by launching their careers with what Parsons described as a watered-down version of his style.[49]

Parsons was clearly *not* the inventor of country-rock, but he may have been the godfather of "alternative country," a term that didn't even come to play until decades after his death—but it is a good description of his music. A more accurate term might be "hippie country." Still, even in this he shares the billing with former bandmate Chris Hillman along with fellow Waycross native Larry Murray. Murray himself said Hillman actually deserves most of the credit for many of the accomplishments people normally assign to Parsons: "Gram rode on Chris's shoulders," Murray said. Hillman was the real deal, a diligent trooper, and he had his head screwed on straight, unlike Parsons, Murray adds.[50]

The biggest accomplishment Parsons deserves credit for is bridging the gap between hippies and rednecks, or, in the slang of the day, "longhairs" and "greasers."[51] It's difficult now to fathom the enmity between these two factions in the late 1960s and early '70s. Hippies were considered dirtier than animals by many if not most country fans. What really galled the uberpatriot country fans was the hippies' antiwar stance, which they saw as inherently un-American. Hippies, on the other hand, eschewed all types of violence and smoked pot to cool out, while rednecks got drunk or high on speed and actually enjoyed getting into fights. Merle Haggard poured more fuel on the fire that same year when he released "Okie from Muskogee." Meyer writes, "'Okie from Muskogee' was the national anthem for anyone who wanted to beat up longhairs and feel righteous about it."[52] And if "Okie" hadn't been hostile enough, Hag's 1970 follow-up, "The Fightin' Side of Me," in which the Hag told protestors to "love it [the United States] or leave it," was a virtual declaration of war.[53] The two warring parties would eventually come to an uneasy truce and learn to appreciate each other somewhat, partly thanks to Parsons and his evangelical efforts. Nonetheless, tensions remained. Even as late as 1972, when the Nitty Gritty Dirt Band seemed to have actually realized Parsons's vision of bringing together country folks with hippies with *Will the Circle Be Unbroken*, its landmark, Grammy-winning album of country and bluegrass standards recorded in Nashville, Bill Monroe refused to participate—because he hated hippies.[54]

Parsons took a brave stance in 1967 with the ISB. He loved country music and wanted to turn his hippie brethren on to it. "When I say that the long-hairs, short-hairs, people with overalls and people with their velvet gear can all be at the same place at the same times for the same reason, that turns me on."[55] He risked an ass-whipping more than once, showing up and performing his renditions of country songs in redneck dives where he was not always welcomed, yet he soldiered on in service to his vision. The final irony is that the country crowd would—over the course of the next three or four decades—completely absorb country-rock and claim it as their own. It would take credible country-music figures like Willie Nelson, Waylon Jennings, and Hank Williams Jr.'s imprimaturs to make the music—and the hair—acceptable. Nelson hired former Burritos bassist Chris Ethridge in 1978 and even recorded a version of Parsons's "One-Thousand-Dollar Wedding" in 2006.

Parsons had—directly or indirectly—an influence on what came to be called southern rock. I have argued elsewhere that southern rock is actually another iteration or perhaps simply a variation of country rock—a branch off the same tree—but with more rock: grittier guitars, harder drums.[56] It would seem likely that Dickey Betts of the Allman Brothers Band, who emerged from the Jacksonville music scene in 1969, would have been at least acquainted with Parsons's music in the late 1960s or early '70s. Country-rock, however, was not the ABB's forte. The group was reluctant to record his song "Ramblin' Man" when he first presented it to them around April 1971.[57] "We all thought 'Ramblin' Man' was too country to even record," Butch Trucks told ABB biographer Alan Paul. "It was a good song, but it didn't sound like us. "Ramblin' Man" sounds like something Parsons himself might do—with the exception of the long Les Paul guitar solo at the coda. The song became a number-two hit for the ABB in October 1973. It's quite likely that the success of the Eagles' "Take It Easy" in May 1972 paved the way for the success of "Ramblin' Man" a year later. The two songs are similar in structure, tempo, time signature, and key.

With regard to Lynyrd Skynyrd, there is little or no evidence to suggest that the group was directly influenced by Parsons.[58] However, Billy Ray Herrin of Hickory Wind Music in Waycross points out that bandleader Ronnie Van Zant's wife, the former Judy Seymour, was from Waycross, only a couple of years younger than Parsons.[59] Although the two did not run in the same circles, she would likely have heard about Parsons—or might even have met him at some point— and later mentioned him to Van Zant. By 1975, when drummer Artimus Pyle replaced Bob Burns in the group, the members of Skynyrd certainly knew Parsons by reputation.[60] It's even possible they had gotten the idea of using the Confederate flag as a stage backdrop from Parsons, who had employed it in his final tour in 1973.[61] In addition, both Parsons and Van Zant were major Merle Haggard fans. The Burritos covered Hag's "Sing Me Back Home" and "Tonight the Bottle Let Me Down" in 1970 (with Parsons singing lead); Skynyrd recorded Hag's "Honky-Tonk Nighttime Man" in 1977.[62] Van Zant, however, had taken his own style of country-rock in a harder-edged, more aggressive turn—far more rock than country.

One Jacksonville group that was clearly influenced by Parsons was Cowboy, formed in 1969 by Binghamton, New York, native Scott Boyer and prominent Orlando musician Tommy Talton. Boyer and future ABB drummer Butch Trucks had previously been in the Bitter Ind (later called the 31st of February) along with bassist David Brown. The Bitter Ind, a virtual clone of the Byrds, was well acquainted with Parsons's work. In fact, "[Parsons] was on our radar before he joined the Byrds," Brown said. "We were also well aware of Gram's roots in Jacksonville."[63] Indeed, some of Boyer's work with Cowboy—especially "Please Be with Me," recorded in 1971 with accompaniment from Duane Allman on Dobro (and later recorded by Eric Clapton)—sounds positively Parsonsesque.

2

The Bitter Ind / 31st of February

A YEAR BEFORE THE soon-to-be-legendary Allman Brothers Band (ABB) put Jacksonville on the southern-rock map—around the same period Jacksonville's Classics IV were striking gold with "Spooky"— three local boys, including future ABB drummer Butch Trucks and two Southside schoolmates, Scott Boyer and David Brown, were carving out a comfortable niche gigging around the region and blazing a path for other bands, including the ABB itself. This group was the folk-rock trio the Bitter Ind, who would record for Vanguard Records under the moniker 31st of February. This group had been very much influenced, directly and indirectly, by former Bolles School student Gram Parsons. All three had been big Byrds fans and were familiar with Parsons's music before his groundbreaking work on that group's seminal country-rock outing *Sweethearts of the Rodeo*.[1]

Drummer-singer Claude Hudson Trucks Jr., nicknamed "Butch," was born in Jacksonville in 1947, the son of an optician who ran a shop in the Riverside district. Trucks and family lived in Jacksonville's Northside, where Butch attended Jean Ribault High School (named after the leader of the first Huguenot settlement, Fort Caroline, a few miles east of what later became Cow Ford). His parents were active in the North Jacksonville Baptist Church, where Butch served as youth director.[2]

Trucks began playing percussion in the eighth grade. A year later he joined the Ribault High band and showed so much promise he was quickly promoted to first chair. Just as he was entering his senior year, the Trucks family abruptly moved across the river to the Glynlea/ Southside area, whereupon he transferred to Englewood High. Besides performing with the school's orchestra, Trucks worked with the Jacksonville Symphonette, a junior version of the symphony, playing tympani. In his senior year, Trucks later joined a Beatles-tribute combo called the Echoes.[3]

Fellow aspiring musicians David Brown, who had come to Jacksonville from Shreveport as an infant with his parents, and Scott Boyer, who had recently moved from Binghamton, New York, lived in the neighborhood and attended Englewood. Brown's household was steeped in music, his father being a part-time musician. Brown took piano lessons as a child and began playing clarinet in the seventh grade. Guitarist and singer Boyer came to Englewood in the tenth grade. Like so many boys, all three had gotten bit by the music bug after seeing the Beatles on the *Ed Sullivan Show*. However, although they went to the same school and knew each other fairly well, they were not friends at this point. In fact, Trucks told biographer Randy Poe, "we hated each other's guts."[4]

Trucks began begging his parents to buy him a drum kit. Strict Southern Baptists, they feared he might wind up playing rock 'n' roll in juke joints. They relented and bought him a set on the condition that he would never perform in places that served alcohol.[5] While playing with a teen band called the Vikings, Trucks first ran into Brown, who lived on the Southside, while playing at Northside's Tredinnick Youth Center at Forty-Second and Pearl Streets.

Trucks met Boyer, who, aside from playing violin in the high-school orchestra, played acoustic guitar and sang with a folk group called the Travelers. Boyer was a Bob Dylan fan, learning about him by way of Peter, Paul and Mary's hit recordings of his songs. Despite the fact that they disliked each other, the three boys performed together during their senior year at a 1965 high-school talent contest, playing Dave Brubeck's jazz standard "Take Five," with Brown on alto saxophone, Boyer on upright bass, and Trucks on drums.[6]

Later that year, all three were accepted at Tallahassee's Florida State University, where Trucks majored in "staying out of Vietnam."[7] By sheer coincidence all three happened to be assigned to the same floor in the same dormitory, Kellum Hall. By this point Brown, seeing little future in the saxophone, switched to bass guitar. Trucks and Brown, who had been jamming, approached Boyer, who was officially studying the viola, and convinced him to switch from acoustic to electric guitar. The three quickly formed a group. "The impetus was folk-rock," Brown said, "especially the Byrds' first album," which rocketed to the top ten in June 1965.[8] The group also borrowed from the Lovin' Spoonful. The three named their group the Bitter Ind, short for "individual," and started playing frat parties. It wasn't long, however, before they dropped out of college and returned to the coastal region to seek fame and fortune.

They bypassed Jacksonville. Most groups in north Florida and south Georgia at this time were either playing teen-style garage-rock or lame imitations of R&B or a blend of both. Being a big fan of folk music, Boyer had been following Gram Parsons's progress since Parsons had joined the Shilos while at Jacksonville's Bolles School.[9] He also felt that the Byrds' hybrid of folk and rock had great commercial potential, and it surely did. But the headquarters of the folk-rock scene was Los Angeles, which was 2,700 miles away. Searching for hipper audiences, they had a hunch they might do better in Daytona Beach, a famous spring-break resort for students from all over the East. To their disappointment, however, they garnered pretty much the same reception they would have gotten in Jacksonville: "You can't dance to it."[10] Ironically, it might have pleased Trucks's fundamentalist parents to know they didn't have to worry about people dancing to his music.

Trucks, Boyer, and Brown packed up their station wagon and headed to a club called the Martinique, where the favorite band was Daytona's own Allman Joys. During their audition, in walks a blond guy who really likes their music. It was Duane Allman. The Bitter Ind members had been in town for ten days and were broke, homeless, and hungry. Allman put them up at his mother's house on Van Street, but the three decided their chances in Daytona weren't any better than they would be in Jacksonville. So they went home.

A couple months later, the Allman Joys were doing a house gig in Jacksonville at the Beachcomber Lounge, which would later become the Comic Book Club, when Trucks got a call from Allman. The Allman Joys needed a substitute drummer that very night; Trucks agreed to fill in. This would lead to a lucky break thanks to Allman's quick thinking: Since the Allman Joys would be leaving the club in a few weeks,

The Bitter Ind, ACP Records publicity photo, 1967. *Left to right*, David Brown, Butch Trucks, and Scott Boyer.

he suggested the Bitter Ind should come in and audition for the manager, who happened to be a Dylan fan. The Bitter Ind then took over as house band, a gig they held onto for eighteen months.

After working six nights a week at the Beachcomber for a long stretch, the Bitter Ind were polished and professional and had built up a sizable following. This got them noticed, Brown said.[11] The group was approached by Jacksonville impresario Don Dana. Dana had already managed Palatka, Florida–based band the Illusions, who after releasing their debut single on his ACP (Atlantic Coast Productions) label, had garnered some regional airplay and successfully negotiated that group's one-off deal with Columbia Records. Dana aimed to do more or less the same with the Bitter Ind. This success impressed the members. Dana arranged for the young men to travel to Memphis, where they recorded at Ardent Studios with producer/arranger/keyboardist Jim Dickinson.

Taking a page from the Byrds, whose first record had been an electric adaptation of Dylan's "Mister Tambourine Man," the Bitter Ind fashioned a similar treatment of Dylan's "It's All Over Now, Baby Blue," which the group performed in cloying three-part harmony. It was duly released on ACP. This did not lead to any major-label signings, but it did get the group noticed by producer Finlay Duncan, whose Valparaiso, Florida–based Minaret label was distributed (and later acquired) by Shelby Singleton's SSS International label in Nashville. The Bitter Ind's 1967 version of Dino Valenti's "Let's Get Together" was produced by Duncan at the famous Bradley's Barn studio in Nashville. Anticipating complaints from the Greenwich Village folk club the Bitter End, the label changed the group's name to Tiffany System. The song was also erroneously credited to Boyer, Brown, and Trucks.[12] "Let's Get Together" seemed like a perfect follow-up to the group's recording of "Baby Blue" but was blown out of the water by the Youngbloods' competing version on RCA.

Undeterred, the group continued to play up and down the Southeast. They played a Young Republicans convention at the Fontainebleau Hotel in Miami Beach. In nearby Hialeah, record distributor/label owner Henry Stone had heard good things about the group. Stone assigned producers Bradley Shapiro and Steve Alaimo to work with the group at Criteria Studios with engineers Ron and Howie Albert. The Bitter Ind cut an entire album's worth of material in about two weeks. "Alaimo's name was on the record [as co-producer], but he wasn't there," Brown said. Brown was not thrilled with the album's quality. "We were writing songs in the van on the way to the studio," he admits. "It [the resulting album] was a little embarrassing." Nonetheless, Stone used his connections in the industry to land the group a deal with New York's Vanguard Records, home to Buffy Sainte-Marie, Joan Baez, and Country Joe & the Fish. The trio again changed its name, this time to the 31st of February, a phrase taken from an episode of *The Alfred Hitchcock Hour.*

Once again commercial success eluded the band. Its 1968 Vanguard debut was widely overlooked. The members thought a harder, more rock-oriented approach might be the ticket and brought in a lead guitarist. On the way home to Jacksonville, they stopped in Daytona to see their friends Duane and Gregg Allman. It just so happened that the Allmans' group, the Hour Glass, who had been signed to Liberty Records in Los Angeles to little avail, had broken up. Duane Allman spotted an opportunity and asked the three if they'd like to join forces with the two brothers. "Hell, yes!" came the reply.[13] The guitarist they'd hired only four days earlier was quickly dispatched. "We went back to Miami and recorded a whole bunch of songs with Duane and Gregg and started playing shows," Trucks told biographer Randy Poe.[14] Gregg Allman contributed two songs to the proceedings, "God Rest His Soul," which he dedicated to Martin Luther King, and an early version of "Melissa," a ballad that would be rerecorded by the Allman Brothers Band in 1972. Again the tracks were recorded at Criteria with Shapiro producing and the Albert Brothers engineering. However, this set failed to garner a green light from Vanguard or any other label. They languished in Steve Alaimo's vault for four years—until he was able to capitalize on the ABB's meteoric success in 1972, when they were finally released on Alaimo's own Bold label under the title *Duane and Greg [sic] Allman*.

Seeing no future in this new project, however, Gregg Allman decided to return to Los Angeles and pick up the pieces of the Hour Glass's deal with Liberty, using studio musicians to back him as a solo artist. Duane Allman, after spending some time in Jacksonville jamming and living with members of the Second Coming, decided to move to Muscle Shoals to pursue a new career as a studio musician. The 31st of February broke up after this fiasco, but the time spent in Hialeah led to other opportunities, at least for Brown.

Producer Shapiro hired Brown as part of his new, in-house studio band, the Zoo, which recorded regularly at Alaimo's tiny studio in an attic above a garage at Tone Distributors in Hialeah. Trucks played on a few sessions but decided to head back to Jacksonville, where he planned a return to college to become a math teacher. Brown would go on to work with many of Alaimo's top acts, such as Betty Wright, whose first album was produced by Alaimo and Brad Shapiro and released on Atco (Trucks had played on a couple of Wright's songs). Brown got a chance to meet some very influential people at this point: "I would see Ahmet Ertegun and Tom Dowd [of Atlantic Records] quite a bit—they would come to that tiny studio above the garage."[15]

After Trucks and Boyer returned to Jacksonville, Trucks was visited at his Arlington home by Duane Allman, who wanted to recruit him as the second drummer in his new project, the Allman Brothers Band. Allman had managed to parlay his fame as a session player into a recording contract with Phil Walden's Macon-based Capricorn label, distributed by Atco. Scott Boyer got together with Orlando musician Tommy Talton and formed a group in Jacksonville they called Cowboy. Duane Allman recommended the new group to Walden, who signed them after sending Johnny Sandlin to Jacksonville to hear them. Sandlin, who had been in the Hour Glass and also played with Brown in the Zoo, was by this time ensconced in Macon as house drummer and producer.

Brown was living in Miami's Coconut Grove district, helping Alaimo build a new, bigger studio at Tone, when Boz Scaggs, a former member of San Francisco's Steve Miller Band, called. Scaggs, now a solo artist managed by Phil Walden, was living in Macon. Brown went with Scaggs to Muscle Shoals to record his second solo album, on which Duane Allman contributed a searing solo on the gospel-infused R&B workout "Loan Me a Dime." Scaggs also recorded one of Brown's songs, "Slowly in the West."

Brown relocated to San Francisco with Scaggs but left Scaggs's group in 1972. He moved back East, to a cabin outside Macon nicknamed "Idlewild South," where he roomed with Tuscaloosa, Alabama, keyboardist Chuck Leavell. When Gregg Allman cut his 1973 solo album *Laid Back* for Capricorn, Brown, along with Leavell, Boyer, Talton, and Sandlin, performed on it. Allman recorded one of Scott Boyer's songs, "All My Friends," on that same album. That same year Brown rejoined Scott Boyer, this time in Cowboy.

Brown returned to San Francisco in 1976, where he worked with RSO Records act Mistress for five years and then went with Commander Cody and His Lost Planet Airmen. He joined blues band Norton Buffalo and the Knockouts in 1985 and stayed with that group until he retired in 2009. He lives in Marin County.

Boyer and Talton kept Cowboy going, on and off, for many years. After spending some time in Los Angeles, Boyer moved to Muscle Shoals in 1988, where he worked with Sandlin in the Decoys. He died in 2018 of peripheral artery disease.

Trucks spent most of his career with the Allman Brothers Band, although he did participate in side projects from time to time, including a short-lived Jacksonville-based jazz-fusion group dubbed Trucks. He moved to Tallahassee in the late 1980s, where he built a state-of-the-art recording studio, Pegasus, which he later sold to FSU's film school. He brought his young nephew, Derek Trucks, into the ABB in 1999. That same year he and his wife bought a $1.3 million home near West Palm Beach, which he later sold for $2 million. The ABB broke up for the third and final time in 2014. Trucks, a recovering alcoholic, was undergoing severe financial problems, including owing the Internal Revenue Service $540,000 in back taxes, when he put a gun to his head, killing himself, in 2017.[16] He was nearing seventy. His father, in his late nineties, still lives in Jacksonville.

3

The Allman Brothers Band

DICKEY BETTS, with his Bradenton-based band, the Jesters (formerly
the Jokers), had been making sorties to Jacksonville since the mid-
1960s to find work. He snagged a gig as the house band at the Normandy Club on Jacksonville's rough-and-tumble Westside. Betts also
advised his younger friend, guitarist, and singer Mack Doss, to come
to Jacksonville, because there were lots of gigs to be had.[1]

Forrest Richard Betts, born 1943 in West Palm Beach and raised
near Bradenton, had come from a musical family and took for granted
that being a musician would be his calling. Reared on WSM's Nashville's *Grand Ole Opry*, as a child he had briefly taken up the ukulele,
mandolin, and banjo: "When somebody said, 'What are you going to
do when you grow up?' [I answered,] 'I'm gonna play on the *Grand Ole
Opry*.'"[2]

In 1965, while leading the Jesters, Betts had run into a pair of musical brothers who led a rival combo based in Daytona Beach, the Allman
Joys. At first Betts and guitarist Duane Allman did not hit it off: "My
girlfriend took me to Daytona to see the Allman Joys and introduced
me. . . . I thought they were stuck-up, and they thought I was some
hillbilly hayseed."[3] A couple years later, the brothers came out to a club
in Winter Haven where Betts's band was performing: "Duane came
up onstage to play. . . . It was hard to see, so as he was plugging in, I
tried to help him, saying, 'This here is the bass and treble, and here's
the volume,' and he looked at me and said, 'Man, I *know* how to run an

Mack Doss (*left*) with Dickey Betts, ca. 2015. Photo by
Gail Grimm Gerdes, BOSK Photo. Used by permission.

amp by now, I think!' . . . So I said, 'Okay, well, fucking have at it then.'
So we didn't get along that time either."[4]

Duane and Gregg Allman, both born in Nashville, also came from a
musical family.[5] "The first stuff I heard was Hank Williams and Flat &
Scruggs on my grandma's old 78 player," Duane said.[6] It was Gregg, one
year younger than Duane, who started the love affair with the guitar.
In 1957, they had moved to Daytona Beach, where their mother had
relocated a few years after their father, a U.S. Army recruiter, had been
killed by a hitchhiker in a robbery near Norfolk, where he had been
stationed. By the time the boys were fourteen and fifteen, they had
begun forming a succession of local bands. Gregg Allman also played
alto saxophone in the freshman band at Seabreeze High School.[7] Besides playing guitar and riding his motorcycle, one of Duane Allman's
favorite pastimes was sniffing airplane glue.[8]

Florida was a fertile spawning ground for teen bands, largely because there were dozens of youth clubs catering to baby boomers and
their leisure pursuits. The kids of this era (and region) preferred dancing to live bands instead of to discs played by DJs at "record hops."[9] At
first the boys were playing the Ventures and other surf music, Gregg
Allman told biographer Alan Paul.[10] They soon discovered rhythm and
blues on Nashville's WLAC (AM 1510), which on a clear night could
be heard from Miami to Canada. "We listened to WLAC a lot," Gregg
Allman told biographer Randy Poe.[11] WLAC's nighttime programming

featured R&B targeted to a black audience but also became popular with a certain segment of white listeners. One of its famed jocks was John R (Richbourg), a white guy doing a bad blackface impression who was nonetheless a key figure in turning white teenagers on to this music. In an interview with Dennis Elsas, Gregg Allman recollected these years: "[WLAC's R&B programs] didn't come on until nine or ten, and I stayed up 'til five [a.m.]. They had different shows, and they played Howlin' Wolf. They played Muddy [Waters]. They played B. B. [King]. I got turned onto Little Milton. . . . Herman Grizzard had a jazz show, and that's when I first heard Hammond organ, first heard Jimmy Smith. . . . [This music] enriched our repertoire, that's for sure."[12]

About this time, the pair also met a group of African American teenagers in Daytona Beach through Daytona musician Bob Greenlee, another R&B fanatic who listened to WLAC on a nightly basis. Greenlee formed an all-white R&B group, the House Rockers, who worked with a black vocal quartet, the Untils, one of whose members was Floyd Miles. Both Gregg and Duane Allman worked occasionally with Greenlee's group. Greenlee told interviewer Jas Obrecht:

I'd known Duane, but it was just getting together and playing blues. . . . I'd started [putting the band together] in '61, and Duane would come in and sit in. . . . [The House Rockers' guitarist Jim] Shepley's out of town. So I called over to Duane and Gregg's house. I didn't know Gregg at this time. I said, "I'm trying to get a hold of Duane Allman because I need somebody to play guitar down at the Pier." He said, "He's out of town." . . . So this guy, who turned out to be Gregg, said, "Listen, I'd like you to let me play some guitar." . . . So I said, "Sure, Gregg, come on." He had his own drummer and his own bass player. Gregg came over and we started gigging. We had a blind singer who was an influence on Gregg too, named Charles Atkins. If anything, he was more of an influence than Floyd [Miles], because he sounds more like Bobby Bland, who I think obviously influenced Gregg.[13]

Gregg Allman himself recalls: "When I was thirteen or fourteen, Floyd started taking me across the tracks. . . . It wasn't cool for me to be hanging out with him, and it wasn't cool for him to bring me there. We both caught hell from our families.[14] Guided by Miles, Gregg went record-shopping in stores catering to African Americans. Back home,

Duane would pick out the guitar parts on Gregg's Silvertone electric guitar.

In the spring of 1965, their group, the Escorts, recorded some demos at a local studio and landed a prestigious gig opening for the Beach Boys at the City Island Ball Park. Another Daytona group, the Nightcrawlers, who had enjoyed a national hit with the goofy "Little Black Egg" (the Nightcrawlers at this point included Jacksonville guitarist Jimmy Pitman) also performed on this show.

This appearance got the Escorts noticed. They soon evolved into the Allman Joys. The group snagged the services of an Atlanta booking agent, Toby Gunn, and the minute Gregg graduated from high school, the group hit the road.[15] The agency had them gigging all up and down the Southeast, and even as far as Trude Heller's nightclub in New York's Greenwich Village.[16]

At an early Allman Joys gig at Jacksonville's Beachcomber club downtown, Butch Trucks had filled in on drums. Trucks had met the Allmans during an unscheduled, unsuccessful tour of Daytona Beach in 1966.[17] That same year, the group was working at the Briar Patch in Nashville, when George Hamilton IV heard the group and introduced the members to prominent songwriter John D. Loudermilk.[18] Loudermilk took the Allmans under his wing, put them up, and even cowrote a couple of songs with Gregg. Loudermilk signed the group to recording, publishing, and management contracts and then put them in Bradley's Barn recording studio at his own expense. No one was interested. However, on a return trip to Nashville, songwriter John Hurley recommended them to Buddy Killen of Tree Music, the company that had published Mae Axton's and Tommy Durden's "Heartbreak Hotel."[19]

Killen also ran Dial Records, a small, Atlantic-distributed label that had had a couple hits with R&B singer Joe Tex. Killen acquired the tracks Loudermilk had produced for the Allman Joys and then took the group into RCA's Studio B in Nashville to record an album with Hurley engineering and cowriting a couple of songs. "They were terrible songs, just awful," Gregg Allman wrote.[20] A single, a remake of Howlin' Wolf's "Spoonful" (whose arrangement borrowed from the Paul Butterfield Blues Band), backed with a Loudermilk country-rocker, "You Deserve Each Other," was issued on Dial in August to no noticeable acclaim. Plans for an album release were quietly scuttled.

Duane Allman used to tell the story that Killen told the members they were the worst he'd ever heard and that they should quit the business and get day jobs.[21] Killen denied ever saying this. He told this author that, in the first place, he'd never spoken to anyone that way, and in the second place, why would he have spent a lot of money recording them if he'd thought they weren't any good?[22]

Also in 1966, Leon Russell and Thomas "Snuff" Garrett wrote and produced a single, "Batman and Robin," designed to cash in on the superhero craze fomented by the ABC-TV series. The record was released on Mercury's sister label, Smash, which was run by producer Shelby Singleton, who would later work with the Bitter Ind/Tiffany System. David Brown of the Bitter Ind wrote that the Allman Joys had sheepishly agreed to pose as the group in order to get some extra work; however, they did not play on the recording. It was performed by session musicians led by Russell.[23]

Despite the fact that they were working feverishly and going places, the brothers found they could not hold onto musicians due to the low pay and grueling nature of road work. Other players did not seem to have the level of dedication that Duane and Gregg did and would often drop out and return home. With the Allman Joys broken up and stranded in Pensacola, the brothers got in touch with the remnants of the Five Men-Its, a group from Decatur, Alabama, who had also been performing in Pensacola. The Men-Its had lost their own lead singer, Jacksonville-born Eddie Hinton, and were back in Decatur trying to recoup. Hinton left the Men-Its to move to Muscle Shoals, where he would become a session player and producer.[24] Both groups at loose ends amalgamated and began working under various names as deemed necessary: the Allman Joys, the Five Men-Its, Almanac, and eventually the Hour Glass. The new group picked up where the two previous bands had left off: touring like crazy.[25]

Back in the Tampa Bay area, Dickey Betts met Raymond Berry Oakley, a guitarist and bassist from Chicago. Oakley had previously worked with a couple of Chicago-based teen groups as well as with the ABC Records act the Roemans, whose members, including drummer Bertie Higgins, were from New Port Richey, not far from Tampa Bay. Oakley joined the Roemans at a gig in Chicago and went with the group back to Florida, where he ran into Betts.

Tired of bubblegum music, Oakley talked Betts into gambling on a new act that would specialize in the burgeoning "underground" music emanating from California, which consisted in large part of psychedelic adaptations of blues. Although Betts was skeptical, Oakley managed to convince him that their future lay with this new sound. Betts and Oakley formed the Soul Children, which they renamed the Blues Messengers. The band included Betts's wife, Dale, on keyboards and vocals. Bradenton guitarist Larry Reinhardt, for whom Betts had subbed in the Thunderbeats, was added along with drummer John Meeks, sometimes known as Nasty Lord John, whom Dale Betts had met when he was playing at a club called the Scene in Atlanta.[26] The Blues Messengers specialized in the latest psychedelic sounds including numbers by Jefferson Airplane, Steppenwolf, Grateful Dead, Cream, Jimi Hendrix, and of course a bunch of blues.

While performing at a bar in Tampa, a nightclub owner from Jacksonville, Leonard Renzler, heard them and offered them a house gig at a new club he was opening. The club was to be called the Scene, and like its sister operation in Atlanta, would spare no expense in creating a psychedelic milieu with sensory-pounding lights and sound. He offered the band twice what they were earning in Tampa. There was one hitch, however: Renzler, who thought Oakley looked like Jesus, insisted the group change its name to the Second Coming.[27] By April 1968 the Second Coming was ensconced at the new club, formerly the Forum, on Roosevelt Boulevard (U.S. Highway 17) about four miles north of Naval Air Station Jacksonville.[28] Drummer Meeks recalls: "Now the Scene in Atlanta was nice, but the Scene in Jacksonville was *really* nice! It had been built to be an upscale dinner theater [that] failed. . . . There was not a bad table in the whole place. The stage was really a stage, and right in between the front-row tables and the stage was a Plexiglas dance floor with flashing colored lights underneath."[29]

Guitarist Reinhardt had played in a band called Bittersweet with classically trained keyboardist Reese Wynans and drummer Ramone Sotolongo.[30] When Dale Betts got pregnant, Wynans came up from Bradenton to replace her. After the baby was born in July, Dale returned to the group strictly as a singer (although she did play some percussion); Wynans remained on keyboards.[31] Wynans described the Second Coming's sound to biographer Randy Poe: "The Second Coming played six nights a week at the Scene. Our repertoire was about half rock and half blues. Dickey played most of the blues, and Larry

Dickey Betts with the Second Coming, 1968. Photo by Alan Facemire; used by permission.

Berry Oakley with the Second Coming, 1968. Photo by Alan Facemire; used by permission.

Gray House on Riverside Avenue. Photo by the author.

Reinhardt did most of the rock. . . . Dickey sang [numbers like] 'Born in Chicago' and 'Born under a Bad Sign.' Berry Oakley sang 'Oh, Pretty Woman' and 'Hoochie-Coochie Man.' Larry Reinhardt did a bunch of Hendrix covers. . . . Dale sang some Jefferson Airplane."

Jacksonville had a reputation for being the unofficial capital of red-neck south Georgia, and the members of the Second Coming at times regretted the move. The hostility toward hippies was palpable: "We were the only [guys] in town with long hair," Betts told interviewer Andy Aledort of *Vintage Guitar*. "We'd be driving around and people would throw shit at us."[32] At first the band stayed in some apartments Renzler had rented for the musicians.[33] Soon, however, they collectively rented an old Victorian house at 2799 Riverside Avenue (the "Green House") in the heart of Jacksonville's burgeoning bohemian district, a few blocks from Willow Branch Park, not far from the Scene.[34] When this got too crowded, some members moved down the street to larger digs at 2844 (the "Gray House"), which had been divided into five apartments.

The grand, old Riverside area was platted in the early 1900s as what urban designers now call an "inner-ring" suburb or a trolley-car suburb. It was a short trolley ride from downtown, and there are still one or two streets that have visible remnants of the trolley tracks. The area, as its name suggests, sits along the banks of the massive St. Johns, peppered with stately mansions and many parks with giant live oaks dripping Spanish moss. The neighborhood was in a period of slow decline from the 1960s to the 1980s as Duval County schools were disaccredited and middle-class parents fled to the outer 'burbs. There was a racial element to this flight as the area is adjacent to a couple of black neighborhoods, and the local high school, Robert E. Lee, was undergoing the throes of integration. To make matters worse, the river was polluted.

Some of the old houses had been carved up into tenements or had garage apartments that attracted long-haired types thanks to the area's cheap rents. The area became the center of bohemian life—Jacksonville's version of New York's Greenwich Village. Everything was close at hand; you didn't need a car—you could walk, ride a bike, or take a bus almost anywhere you needed to go. People would gather on Sundays, play volleyball or sunbathe in beautiful Memorial Park on the riverfront, and afterward walk over to a head shop called Edge City in Five Points where they could buy underground comics or get an ice-cream cone at the Baskin-Robbins next door or catch a flick at the venerable Five Points Theatre. Jacksonville resident and Allman Brothers Band historian Rick Whitney writes: "This is old Jacksonville at its visually stunning best. From Gothic and Queen Anne to Art Deco and Georgian revival, it is a mighty collection of classic residential masterpieces representing just about every architectural style known. Many of these nearly century-old homes rival the best southern mansions we often associate with cities such as Savannah, Charleston and Atlanta."[35]

One of the attractions of Jacksonville in general is that housing was, and still is, a bargain. An actual Riverside home could be bought—not that any hippies were buying in those days—for a tenth of what they go for now that the area has been regentrified. Cheap housing, good vibes, and abundant gigs brought musicians from all over Florida and south Georgia.

Attendance at the Scene, however, was not as busy as expected. Apparently the Second Coming was a bit ahead of its time, at least in Jacksonville terms. In 1968, most of the audience for the new music was simply too young to drink in bars. Oakley assured Betts that the fans were out there; the band just had to find a way to bring the music to *them*. He suggested the group begin performing free outdoor concerts, dubbed "be-ins" (after San Francisco's famous Human Be-In during the 1967 Summer of Love). The strategy worked.

Sometime in late 1968, the group began performing for free on Sundays, their only day off, at the Forest Inn, about three miles west of the Gray House. Duane Allman dropped by a few times and sat in. He had already begun hanging out in Jacksonville as often as possible. Attendance grew so large that these jam sessions had to be moved to Riverside's Willow Branch Park.[36] Other bands were showing up too, and these began to attract hundreds of hippies, just as Oakley had predicted. Soon the Second Coming outgrew the Scene.

The Second Coming's growing reputation and professionalism drew the attention of newscaster and part-time WAPE disk jockey Allen Facemire. A former musician and cameraman for WJXT-TV, Facemire hosted a Sunday-night radio show called *The Underground Circus*.[37] He became the Second Coming's manager, scoring the group a deal with a New York–based reggae label, Steady Records, formed in 1968 and purchased a year later by International Tape Cartridge Corp.[38] Steady released a single that comprised Betts's off-key rendition of Cream's "I Feel Free" backed with Dale Betts's version of Jefferson Airplane's "She Has Funny Cars."[39] Facemire proceeded to play the record on his radio show, which boosted the Second Coming's regional profile sky-high. Steady saw enough potential in the group to option an album, but that plan went south in March 1969.[40] When its gig at the Scene ran out, Facemire, whose position was as a sixth member of the group, guided the band in promoting its own shows at venues such as national-guard armories.

Before Facemire came aboard, Larry Reinhardt, who had been itching to front his own "power trio," had returned to Sarasota to form the Load with bassist Richard Price and drummer Monty Young. The Load landed a steady gig at Dub's Steer Room in Gainesville. They were playing a date at University of Florida with the Second Coming when Facemire had the idea that he could sell both bands as a package and invited the members of the Load to come to Jacksonville and move into the Green House.[41]

The Jacksonville underground-music scene was exploding, and these two groups practically had the market all to themselves. Of course the local teen-group garage-rockers, the Noble Five and the rest, would fight to get in on the action, but they couldn't hold a candle—not only in terms of popularity but in terms of musicianship—to these interlopers from Tampa Bay. The Second Coming was the best band in northeast Florida, and everybody knew it. "Dickey Betts was the hottest guitar player in the area," Reese Wynans told Alan Paul. "[He was] the guy everyone looked up to and wanted to emulate." [42] Bassist Richard Price of the Load agreed: "Dickey was already considered one of the hottest guitar players in Florida. He was smokin' in the Second Coming."[43]

Meanwhile, big things were happening for Almanac. In April bassist Mabron McKinley had been at the airport picking up his wife and had run across a group of longhairs who turned out to be the members of the Nitty Gritty Dirt Band coming to town for a three-night stand at Kiel Auditorium. Keller struck up a conversation and invited the Dirt Band members to Pepe's a Go-Go, where Almanac was performing.[44] Several members of the Dirt Band turned up along with their manager, Bill McEuen, all of whom were reportedly astounded by the group's talent and musical prowess. McEuen quickly offered to manage the band and make it the "next Rolling Stones."[45]

The group took him up on his offer—some members reluctantly—and moved into the Dirt Band's communal house in Los Angeles. With McEuen representing the group, the Dirt Band's label, Liberty Records, signed the act, soon to be renamed the Hour Glass. The group's first Los Angeles gig was opening for the Doors at the Hullabaloo. "Man, that scared me to death," Gregg told biographer Scott Freeman. "There must have been 2,000 people in that place, and my knees were knocking together."[46] They also appeared on ABC-TV's *Pat Boone Show*.[47]

However, this tale did not have a happy ending. The group opened for many big-name acts in Los Angeles and San Francisco but were not allowed to play out too often for fear of overexposure.[48] Even worse, the suits at Liberty hadn't a clue what the Hour Glass was all about—their producer, Dallas Smith, whose main claim to fame was producing teen idol Bobby Vee, also signed to Liberty, characterized the group as a "Motown band."[49] He was almost right insofar as they *were* an R&B act, but their sound was far closer to Memphis than Detroit, with a hefty helping of down-home blues. Gregg had been writing a few songs at the time, but the group's repertoire—although some of it was quite good—had been forced on them by Smith and the label execs. Gregg Allman was actually rooming with one of Liberty's staff songwriters, Jackson Browne.

It was during this period in Los Angeles that Duane Allman heard

Jesse Ed Davis playing slide guitar with blues singer Taj Mahal. Mahal and his band had been performing Blind Willie McTell's 1928 "Statesboro Blues" in an arrangement fairly similar to the one Duane and Gregg later adopted in their own band.[50] According to Gregg Allman, he bought Taj Mahal's debut album and left it on Duane's doorstep, along with a Coricidin bottle (to use as a slide), on Duane's birthday, November 20, 1967. Duane learned the solo "note-for-note" from Mahal's album.[51] The problem with this story is that Taj Mahal's debut album was not released until January 1, 1968.

The Hour Glass's October 1967 debut was anything but promising. The album stiffed. A second album, *Power of Love*, was released in March 1968. By this point Daytona Beach guitarist Pete Carr, now on bass, had come on board. The band members were happier with this effort to some extent as Gregg was allowed to write more songs and the band had more input with arrangements. But it, too, failed to dent the charts, and the members, especially Duane, were getting frustrated. Duane in particular did not like working with Dallas Smith, felt his talents were being underutilized, and stormed out during the sessions. Carr, who was more a guitarist than a bassist, wound up overdubbing Allman's unfinished parts.[52]

Hour Glass drummer Johnny Sandlin, from Decatur, Alabama, who had done some session work for Rick Hall at FAME (Florence Alabama Music Enterprises) studios in Muscle Shoals, convinced the band members they could get a great sound there that would showcase their talents to the utmost because the staff at FAME understood and appreciated the kind of music they were doing. The band members, who included keyboardist Paul Hornsby, also from Alabama (Elba), used what money they could scrape together to record some demos at FAME. These tracks were produced (that is, supervised) by none other than Eddie Hinton, the Five Men-Its' former singer. In an interview with Dave Kyle, Sandlin recalls:

> We got to FAME, and Eddie [Hinton] was there. Jimmy Johnson engineered the session. We recorded the "B.B. King Medley," along with "Ain't No Good to Cry" and "Been Gone Too Long," songs we were doing in our live set. We got the tape and were really happy about it. We sent it to our manager [Bill McEuen] in L.A., and he took it to Liberty Records. They thought it was

terrible. They weren't interested in us if that's [the kind of music] we wanted to do.[53]

Disgusted and downhearted at the reception to this music by Liberty's execs, Duane Allman went AWOL. He returned to St. Louis with the other members except Gregg, who decided to stay in Los Angeles and record what was essentially a solo album with session musicians. "Gregg Allman and the Hour Glass" released a remake of Tammy Wynette's "D.I.V.O.R.C.E." on Liberty in July.

In July 1968, a new group called Pogo (renamed Poco) was being assembled in Laurel Canyon by former members of Buffalo Springfield, for whom the Hour Glass had opened at the Fillmore Auditorium in San Francisco. Gregg Allman was one of the musicians who auditioned. He came to rehearsals at Furay's, but his style and his material was deemed unsuitable for the band's country-rock sound. Bandleader Rusty Young told author John Einarson: "Gregg was going to play piano and sing in our band. He had a great voice. But we were more into country, and he was into a blues-based music." Member Jim Messina recalls: "Gregg showed up at my house on his motorcycle. He'd had a few drinks. Before I know it he was playing away and having a good time, but it didn't have much to do with what we were doing."[54]

Gregg probably realized as much when he rejoined the Hour Glass for a gig in St. Louis. Then the members returned to northeast Florida, where they did a gig at Jacksonville's Comic Book Club (formerly the Beachcomber) downtown on July 12, 1968, for which the opening act was Larry Steele's group the Male Bachs. Steele recalls: "I looked around for [Lynyrd Skynyrd singer] Ronnie [Van Zant], who was now standing alone at the center of the room, arms folded across his chest. . . . 'Better than the Bitter Ind, huh?' I teased. . . . 'Best in the business,' he said."[55]

Berry Oakley's wife, Linda, who had already seen the Allman Joys and who had heard about the Hour Glass's upcoming gig at the Comic Book Club, told Berry he had to hear these guys. Oakley, not expecting much, went to the Comic Book to catch their act and was floored. He invited Duane over to his house, and the two stayed up all night talking about music.

For the most part, however, the Hour Glass's lukewarm reception on their home turf seemed less than gratifying after opening for the likes of the Doors, Buffalo Springfield, and other big names on the West Coast.[56] Hour Glass keyboardist Paul Hornsby told Randy Poe that audiences back home "wanted to hear 'Mustang Sally.' . . . We didn't get the respect we'd gotten in L.A."[57]

In August Gregg and the rest of the Hour Glass left for a last spate of gigs in St. Louis, where they opened for Big Brother and the Holding Company and Iron Butterfly at Kiel Auditorium. The next day they did a concert at Forest Park World's Fair Pavilion as well as a club date at the Castaway in Ferguson. Then they broke up. Hornsby and Sandlin returned to Tuscaloosa.

At loose ends, Duane and Gregg Allman moved back in with their mom at Van Avenue in Daytona. In a letter to a relative dated September 25, mother Geraldine Allman wrote that Duane and Gregg were "on the outs" with Hour Glass keyboardist Paul Hornsby and that Hornsby had been "let out" while the others sought to keep Johnny Sandlin on board.[58] Whether out of loyalty to Hornsby or just plain road rash, Sandlin would not agree to stay. Duane Allman himself announced in a letter to Donna Roosmann, Duane's girlfriend and mother of his daughter Galadrielle: "We got rid of Paul [Hornsby] and the Duck [Johnny Sandlin]. We tried to get the Duck to stay, but he wouldn't have it without Paul."[59] Looking for work, Duane and Gregg began hanging out in Jacksonville—there was always work to be found—and sitting in with the Second Coming at the Scene.[60]

It was at this point Butch Trucks came to the brothers' aid, as they had done for him a couple years earlier. Trucks's group, the 31st of February, which included guitarist/lead vocalist Scott Boyer and bassist/vocalist David Brown, had released an album on Vanguard Records, produced in Hialeah by Brad Shapiro and Steve Alaimo. That album went nowhere, but there was a slim chance the group could land a second album if the material and musicianship were strong enough—at least Alaimo and company thought enough of the prospect to "spec out" the act (that is, advance studio time and services on the speculation that a deal would be forthcoming). Gregg and Duane Allman joined forces with drummer Trucks, bassist David Brown, and guitarist-songwriter Scott Boyer in 31st of February. The new lineup played its first gig at the Scene in Jacksonville on September 25 and then another in Fort Pierce.

The Allmans went with Trucks, Brown, and Boyer to Hialeah to record an album's worth of demos with producer Brad Shapiro at the helm. This set included two songs written by Gregg Allman: the earliest recording of "Melissa," which would be rerecorded by the Allman Brothers Band in 1972 on the Capricorn album *Brothers and Sisters*, and "God Rest His Soul," a tribute to Martin Luther King, who had been assassinated five months earlier. Nothing happened for the fledgling group. Its album was rejected by Vanguard but released four years later, by Alaimo's label, Bold Records, not long after the Allman Brothers Band had broken into the big-time.

Apparently, unbeknownst to Trucks, Boyer, and Brown, the brothers' participation had been contingent on the group's landing a new deal with Vanguard. Gregg Allman recalls: "Butch Trucks had some kind of an idea about forming a band by combining his group, the 31st of February, with Duane and me, but he was the only one thinking that. I was planning to go back to L.A. to fulfill the deal with Liberty. . . . Butch may still hold a bit of a grudge to this day. He thought this was the beginning of the Allman Brothers Band."[61]

Gregg sold half his songwriter's credits on his two songs—which he would later buy back for a small fortune—to Steve Alaimo in order to buy plane fare to Los Angeles where he would to try to salvage his abortive career as Gregg Allman and Hour Glass. When he left, the 31st of February threw in the towel. Brown stayed in Hialeah, where he would work for TK Records' house band, the Zoo. Brown initially brought Trucks to the studio with him, but Trucks decided to chuck it in and returned to Jacksonville, thinking of a new career as a math teacher.[62] Johnny Sandlin replaced Trucks in the Zoo before heading up to Macon to join Phil Walden's burgeoning operation.

Recalling his all-night reverie with Berry Oakley, Duane Allman headed to Jacksonville, where he stayed with Berry and Linda at the Gray House. Perhaps he was hoping to *join* the Second Coming at this point. After staying with the Oakleys for a spell, Duane moved in downstairs with Ellen Hopkins, a graphics artist who lived in a separate apartment.[63]

It was while staying at the Gray House that Allman cooked up a plan to go to Muscle Shoals and get work as a session player at FAME, which Eddie Hinton, Johnny Sandlin, and Paul Hornsby had already done. This would turn out to be a clever move indeed. Despite some initial resistance from FAME owner Rick Hall, Allman would in a matter of weeks find himself playing on records by several top R&B artists, beginning with Clarence Carter, for whom he played slide.[64]

Allman was still living in Jacksonville, shuttling back and forth to Muscle Shoals. He reported to Donna Roosmann that the Second Coming had been hosting "these huge gatherings of freaks [hippies] in Jacksonville, Florida, every Sunday for the past few weeks. Millions of bands play, and it's really fun; I wish you could be here to see it—it's a miracle. . . . I've been living there for quite a while with friends, and I'll probably stay until move to Muscle Shoals."[65]

He also indicated to Roosmann that he intended to leverage his newfound recognition into snagging himself a deal as a solo artist.[66] In November, Allman returned to FAME to work with Wilson Pickett, who nicknamed Allman "Sky Man" because he was always high.[67] It was during these sessions that Duane Allman's big opportunity presented itself.

While the other musicians at the session went to lunch—in Alabama it would not do for a black man *or* a long-haired hippie to accompany them—Allman talked Pickett and producer Hall into doing a remake of the Beatles' current hit "Hey, Jude." At first everyone thought he was nuts, but when he showed them the rhythm he had in mind, they thought it just *might* be a clever twist on the song. Hall dug it: "He [Allman] started plunking on his guitar like Chet Atkins playing one of those country-funk things," Hall told Alan Paul. "And I said, 'Hey, that sounds pretty good.'" Allman also contributed a searing guitar solo on the song's out-choruses, which blew everyone's minds: "When I sent it to [Jerry] Wexler [vice president of Atlantic Records], he called and said, 'A fucking stroke of genius, Rick.' I said, 'Really? Well, it wasn't my idea; it was Duane Allman's idea.' He said, 'Whoever's idea it was, you produced a great record. I do believe it's going to Number One.'"[68] Wexler's enthusiasm convinced Hall that Allman indeed had star potential, and Hall, to his later regret, signed him to a recording contract as a solo artist—exactly the deal Duane had hoped for.

Phil Walden, who had managed several acts who had recorded at FAME, including Clarence Carter, Percy Sledge, and Arthur Conley, heard the Pickett record and was impressed. Walden told Hall that this guitarist and his music would make him a million dollars. Hall remained skeptical. "That's bullshit," he retorted.[69] Walden was eager to sign Duane to a management deal, but there was the issue of his already being signed to Bill McEuen in Los Angeles. McEuen magnanimously gave Allman a release from his contract.

Allman would be needing a band to back him. He recruited his old cohorts from the Hour Glass, Johnny Sandlin on drums and Paul Hornsby on keyboards, to play on his upcoming demos, which Hall was planning to take to Atlantic.[70]

Since by all accounts Duane was no singer, he also hoped to talk his brother into coming back from Hollywood to sing in this new outfit and kept calling Gregg, only to be repeatedly rebuffed.[71] Duane was obviously trying to get Hour Glass back together, and he wasn't fooling anyone. However, Sandlin and Hornsby, while willing to play on his sessions, wanted no part of the road or of being in a full-time situation with the brothers. "I didn't want to do it," Hornsby told Randy Poe. "[Neither did] Sandlin or Pete [Carr]—none of us. We just didn't want to go through it again."[72]

Hall, who suspected Allman and his hippie pals were smoking a lot of pot—they were—got tired of waiting around for them to record.[73] However, Johnny Sandlin, who played drums on Duane's demo sessions, disputes Hall's account.[74] Frustrated, Hall was ready to unload Allman. The perfect pigeon was Jerry Wexler at Atlantic, who had egged the whole thing on in the first place. Hall called Wexler and asked if he wanted to buy Allman's contract along with tracks for the eight songs they had cut. Wexler said he would. Hall sold the package to Atlantic for ten thousand dollars.[75] Wexler said it was fifteen thousand dollars.[76]

Wexler didn't know exactly what to do with Allman either, since Allman had no band, didn't write, and didn't sing well. "Ostensibly [buying his contract] wasn't a very good move," Wexler said.[77] There was good deal of developmental work to be done just to get an act together. Phil Walden was just the man for the job. "It was with Phil's encouragement that I did this, because Phil was going to build a band around him."[78]

Walden wanted to start his own Macon-based recording studio and assemble its own house band. Wexler agreed to lend him the funds. Walden's new operation, a recording studio *and* a label, would enter into a joint venture with Atlantic by which Atco, an Atlantic subsidiary, would assume marketing and distribution costs while Walden would pay studio and production costs. All this would be deducted from the proceeds of record sales, if any were to be had.

Suddenly Walden was president of Atco-distributed Capricorn Records. This deal with Wexler drastically altered Walden's relationship with Allman: not only was he Allman's manager, he would henceforth be his executive producer and owner of Allman's recordings. This effectively put Walden on both sides of the table. A manager, like a lawyer, must suborn his or her own interests to the interests of the client. A manager cannot conduct business with *himself* on behalf of his client. This is a breach of fiduciary duty to the artist, one that unfortunately would become fairly common in the 1970s. Not only that, Walden sold himself the band's publishing rights *and* he owned their booking agency. He had fingers in every pie. It wouldn't be surprising if he'd owned the properties he'd rented for them to live in. He even owned the liquor store where they bought their booze.[79]

None of this mattered at this point. The only thing Duane Allman seemed to care about was the fact that he was being encouraged to make the music *he* wanted to make, the way *he* heard it in his head.

On January 3, Duane Allman moved into a cabin on Lake Wilson near Muscle Shoals, but he would not stay long.[80] On January 5 he flew to New York, along with the other members of the FAME rhythm section—who would soon form their own studio with financial assistance from Wexler—to work with Aretha Franklin. While in the city, Allman and rhythm guitarist Jimmy Johnson went to see Johnny Winter at the Fillmore East. Johnson told interviewer Jas Obrecht of *Guitar Player*:

> I'll never forget what he said—this was about midway through: "Johnny is really good, but I can cut him." . . . He looked over at me. "Jimmy," he said, "Do you see that stage down there? Next year by this time I'm going to be down there." I looked at him and kind of did one of them double-takes, and I said, "You know, I think you will." And he was.[81]

Walden recommended a black drummer from Ocean Springs, Mississippi, who had worked with Otis Redding and Percy Sledge, both Walden clients. Walden got hold of Duane and said, "Listen, I've got this drummer over here in Macon who plays so weird nobody knows if he's any good or not."[82] Johnson, who went by the nickname Jaimoe, had been planning to move to New York to play jazz; however, at the urging of a mutual friend, songwriter Jackie Avery, Johnson made the trip from Macon to Muscle Shoals to meet Allman on January 10. The two hit it off, with Jaimoe settling into Allman's cabin. But they still needed a bass player. Naturally Allman thought of Berry Oakley. Oakley arrived in Muscle Shoals two days later, and the trio worked on a few songs. Jaimoe did not play on any recordings, however, as he had no studio experience; Sandlin was the session drummer.[83] Allman had approached Sandlin with the idea of using two drummers, but Sandlin nixed it: "I didn't understand the two-drummer thing, and I didn't want to do it."[84]

Oakley stayed long enough to get some tracks in the can and then left for his Jacksonville home. He would return to Muscle Shoals in February to finish the recordings. Meanwhile Allman was getting fed up with studio work and starting to resent Rick Hall's authoritarian manner. He hated when Hall overrode his decisions on how and what to play. The fact is Allman couldn't stand *anyone* telling him what to do. He needed to get back to leading his own troupe and playing live. Writing again from Jacksonville, he told cousin Jo Jane Pitt: "I quit my staff position at [FAME] because all these people up there keep telling me how rich I was gonna be in a few years [by] kissing the boss's ass and playing *exactly what the boss wants* [emphasis in original]. I told the motherfuckers that I was the boss in that department and would they excuse me but I hear the highway calling me."[85] Now that they had a record deal practically in the bag, it was time for Duane and Jaimoe to make another trip to Jacksonville. This time Allman wasn't taking no for an answer.

After a side trip to St. Louis to visit Donna Roosmann, Duane and Jaimoe arrived in Jacksonville on March 5. Allman had been considering the prospect of using double drummers—he got the idea from James Brown—so when he and Johnson landed in Jacksonville he got in touch with Butch Trucks, with whom he had played in the 31st of February. Allman moved in with Ellen Hopkins at the Gray House. He began sitting in with the Second Coming at every available opportunity—it was almost as if he were a new member of the band.

"Me and Jaimoe eased on down to Jacksonville, and Berry met us there," Allman said. "We all got together in a big house in Jacksonville,

Duane Allman and Butch Trucks (on drums behind Allman) at the Forest Inn, early 1969. Photo by Charlie Faubion; used by permission.

and Santa Claus came and brought us a band."[86] Allman was intent on prying Oakley out of the Second Coming, but Oakley was steadfastly loyal to Dickey Betts. Allman dug Betts's playing and decided to add him to the mix. He was thrilled with the results of the first jam session, the now-famous "Jacksonville Jam," as were the others: Oakley, Betts, Wynans, Johnson, and Trucks. Second Coming drummer John Meeks wasn't invited, partly due to his aggressive, Ginger Baker–like style—Allman wanted something jazzier and more flexible—but mainly because the undisputed boss of the proceedings already had the drum bases covered. Keyboardist Reese Wynans had also been deemed expendable because Allman wanted his brother in the band.

Allman, Oakley, and Betts started off trading vocal chores, but not one of them was in the same league as Gregg Allman, who was still in Los Angeles but was disgruntled and depressed about the way his so-called career was going—or, rather, not going. After the Jacksonville Jam, Duane put in a call to Gregg and told him he had a new band and a new record deal that would afford them full creative control—basically, this was the moment they'd been waiting for all their lives. Gregg was in. Gregg Allman wrote in his autobiography that he "bummed a ride" to Jacksonville, but his friend Kim Payne, who became a roadie for the band, insists he dropped Allman off at Los Angeles International.[87]

In any event, Gregg reportedly arrived in Jacksonville on March 26. According to Gregg's autobiography, his first official rehearsal for the new lineup took place at Butch Trucks's house in the Arlington district, on the other side of the river from the Gray House.[88] Gregg wrote "Whipping Post" while staying at the Gray House with Duane and Ellen Hopkins.[89]

The band had managed to get Gregg a Hammond B-3 organ and a Leslie amplifier, both of which were extremely expensive. Most likely they were able to put these items on a charge account at Lipham Music in Gainesville (where Don Felder was a guitar teacher and Tom Petty one of his students).[90] In addition to already having written "Whipping Post" earlier that week, Gregg wrote several more songs on that Hammond while in Jacksonville, including "Black-Hearted Woman," "Every Hungry Woman," "It's Not My Cross to Bear," and "Demons."

On March 29 the unnamed band gave its first public performance at a previously scheduled Second Coming show at the Jacksonville Beach Auditorium (often erroneously referred to as the Beach Coliseum). This show featured the Load, the Second Coming, and the "fantastic group."[91] Some group names had been tossed around, including Beelzebub, which Gregg Allman said was his favorite.[92] All three groups performed again the next night at the Cedar Hills National Guard Armory on Normandy Boulevard—not far from the Normandy Lounge where Betts's Jesters had played in 1966—and once again held an all-star jam to close the show. Richard Price, bassist for the Load, has recordings of these performances.[93] The new group absorbed a good deal of the Second Coming's repertoire (and fan base), including such songs as "Don't Want You No More," "Trouble No More," "Hoochie Coochie Man," "Stormy Monday Blues," "Sweet Home, Chicago," "Rock Me, Baby," "Crossroads," and several others, most of which were blues standards and easy to throw together.

The day after the armory show, they all packed up and split for Macon. There were rumors that the police had been after the band for its flagrant drug use or had run them out of town—so said Betts—but it's more likely Phil Walden simply wanted them in Macon, where he could keep an eye on his charges.[94] One of the first projects the Allman Brothers Band undertook was making regular eighty-eight-mile trips to Atlanta's Piedmont Park to continue the be-ins Oakley had organized in Jacksonville.

Since the Capricorn studio in Macon wasn't ready, in August 1969 the group went to New York to record its debut album at Atlantic with engineer Adrian Barber, who had worked with Betts's idol, Eric Clapton, in Cream. This was the big-time. The ABB's self-titled debut album, released in November on Atco bearing the legend "Capricorn Records Series," sold fewer than thirty-five thousand copies.[95] The next ABB album, *Idlewild South*, was recorded at Capricorn and several other studios from February to July 1970. The album was named after the cabin in Macon where the band had stayed. It didn't do much better salewise than the debut. *Idlewild South* did, however, contain a song written by Gregg Allman while he was in Los Angeles, "Midnight Rider." Thirty-Eight Special guitarist Danny Chauncey told author Marley Brant, "'Midnight Rider' is the epitome of a southern-rock anthem."[96] This song featured an unusual guitar solo by Betts that sounded very much like an imitation of a pedal steel and set the stage for Betts's more countrified developments on later albums like *Eat a Peach* and *Brothers and Sisters*.

One thing that can be said for certain about the Allman Brothers Band as well as most of the Jacksonville bands who followed in its wake is that they evinced an incredible work ethic. All these Jacksonville musicians put in at least sixty hours a week, including rehearsing, performing, maintaining equipment and vehicles, traveling to and from gigs, etc. A forty-hour-a-week day job would have seemed like a vacation to them compared to what it took to compete in the music biz. Thanks largely to Oakley's example, nearly all the musicians in

Poster from 1970 concert at Jacksonville Beach Auditorium (colloquially known as the Beach Coliseum) promoted by Richard Panken.

Jacksonville got totally serious or got out of the business—no slackers allowed. This sense of determination set a precedent that would persist among Jacksonville bands for decades.

The ABB was in its element in a live-performance setting, probably better onstage than in the studio. It took a couple years of touring to "break" the band and build a significant following. This was reflected in the group's third album, recorded "live" at New York's Fillmore East and released March 1971.

In October, just as the group was poised to hit the big leagues, Duane Allman died in a motorcycle crash. The band soldiered on and released the very uncharacteristic country-rock number "Blue Sky," written and sung by Betts. Oakley, too, was killed not long after its release. Betts assumed leadership of the group, who carried on with the addition of Tuscaloosa keyboardist Chuck Leavell (Hornsby is also from that city). In 1973, the ABB released the album *Brothers and Sisters*, the single from which, another country-rocker by Betts, "Ramblin' Man," gave the ABB its only top-ten hit.

Many observers credit the ABB as the first southern-rock group. However, a couple of its members, Gregg Allman in particular, often complained about being saddled with the label.[97] If one substitutes the term "redneck rock" for "southern rock," the nature of Allman's complaint becomes clear: He didn't appreciate being lumped with rebel-flag-wavers and redneck yobbos.

The ABB members were anything but rednecks—with the notable exception of Dickey Betts. Betts, like Ronnie Van Zant, was a long-haired redneck who would stoop to bullying and violence to get his way.[98] Also like Van Zant, Betts loved country music. The other ABB members didn't want much to do with it. In fact, the ABB was even reluctant to release Betts's "Ramblin' Man" because, in Butch Trucks's words, it was "much too country" and didn't fit the band's blues-based formula.[99] Yet the song would catapult the group into the top of the charts.

The Allman Brothers Band was really *two groups*—depending on who was singing lead: the Gregg Allman–led ABB and the Dickey Betts–led ABB. Dickey Betts's ABB was indeed a southern-rock band, despite Allman's protestations.

Epilogue

The Second Coming had already signed a contract with Steady Records, and the label had an option to release an album, which Allen Facemire, the group's manager, hoped it would exercise. However, two of the group's key members, Betts and Oakley, were gone, and singer Dale Betts, for whom the label had high hopes, quit the business. Reese Wynans and John Meeks were the only remaining members.

Facemire wanted to deliver something. He added Larry Reinhardt, Richard Price, and Monty Young from the Load (Reinhardt had been an original member) and dubbed the group the New Second Coming. They went into a Jacksonville studio, Sound Lab, on Edgewood Avenue, where the Classics IV and many other groups had done demos, and recorded an album's worth of material.[100] Richard Price has possession of these tapes. The owners of Steady, however, rejected the results. Their interest in the group hinged on the participation of Dale Betts, who was living in Macon with Dickey.[101] Facemire said it never occurred to anyone that she might stay with the group.[102]

After the New Second Coming fizzled, keyboardist Reese Wynans stayed in Jacksonville for a few months, working around town with singer-bassist Gary Goddard and drummer James "Fuzzy" Land in a guitar-less trio called Ugly Jellyroll. Broke and discouraged, Wynans moved back to Bradenton and was working a day job when he got a call from Duane Allman in Macon. Wynans had made a point of keeping in touch with Allman, who hooked him up with Boz Scaggs.[103] (Former Jacksonville bassist David Brown, who had been with the Bitter Ind/31st of February, also went with Scaggs.)

Wynans went on to an illustrious career. In 1973 he was reunited with Larry Reinhardt in Captain Beyond, a Los Angeles–based space-rock outfit signed to Capricorn thanks to Reinhardt's connections with the ABB. Working with Capricorn artist Delbert McClinton brought Wynans to Texas, where he hooked up with Willie Nelson, Stevie Ray Vaughn, Joe Ely, and Lee Roy Parnell. Wynans moved to Nashville in 1992, where he has done session work with Brooks & Dunn, Trisha Yearwood, Martina McBride, and Hank Williams Jr. He has also worked with blues artists such as Buddy Guy, John Mayall, Kenny Wayne Shepard, as well as Los Lonely Boys. He currently tours with blues guitarist Joe Bonomassa and in 2019 released his own album on New York–based Provogue Records.

After giving the New Second Coming the old college try, Larry Reinhardt surmised it was a no-go and followed the ABB up to Macon. Someone from the hard-rock group Iron Butterfly in Los Angeles called Walden's office looking for a replacement guitarist. Whoever it was called the right place. Rhino volunteered, flew to LA, auditioned and got the gig. After a brief period with the Butterfly—which at this point also included Tampa guitarist Mike Pinera, formerly of Blues Image—Rhino and Butterfly bassist Lee Dorman formed Captain Beyond and signed to Capricorn. Reinhardt eventually returned to Sarasota, where he died of cirrhosis in 2012 at sixty-three.

Second Coming drummer-singer John Meeks returned to Sarasota, where he became a leather artist, sometimes making outfits for Duane

Allman along with custom guitar straps. At some point he moved to his native North Carolina. Meeks died in 2017, trapped in a house fire. He is buried in McLeansville.

Richard Price of the Load and the New Second Coming moved to Nashville, where he became a session player and worked with Vassar Clements, the Outlaws, Doug Dillard, Billy Joe Shaver, Jerry Jeff Walker, and Lucinda Williams, among others. He reunited with Reese Wynans in a short-lived project called Ultra-Fix in 2006. Price returned to Sarasota in 2009 and reunited with Reinhardt in a group called Blue Swamp.

Allen Facemire lives in Atlanta, where he operates a video-production company and equipment-rental service. He also maintains a home in St. Augustine, where he grew up.

Duane Allman is buried in Macon's Rose Hill Cemetery, the site of the ABB's earliest publicity photos, one of which comprised the back cover of the band's first album. Berry Oakley also died from injuries in a motorcycle crash only a few blocks from where Duane Allman had been mortally injured a year earlier. He too is buried at Rose Hill.

Gregg Allman, who was living in Savannah, returned to Jacksonville in 2010 to undergo a liver transplant at Mayo Clinic. He died of complications from liver cancer seven years later. He was sixty-nine. He is buried next to his brother in Rose Hill Cemetery.

The Allman Brothers Band went through several breakups and reunions, going through twenty members, including Butch Trucks's nephew, Derek Trucks, in its forty-five years of existence. The ABB performed its final show on October 28, 2014, at New York's Beacon Theater.

Drugs were a constant scourge for the band. Gregg Allman's self-destructive behavior is the stuff of legend.[104] Drugs were at the center of the ABB's first breakup in 1976, when Gregg Allman agreed to testify in a federal grand-jury hearing against one of the his roadies, John "Scooter" Herring.[105]

Swearing to never work with Allman again, Butch Trucks returned to Tallahassee but tapped into the Jacksonville talent pool to recruit players for his jazz-rock ensemble, dubbed Trucks. Players included guitarist Jim Graves, bassist and vocalist Buzzy Meekins (who had been in the Outlaws), keyboardist Ron Sciabarasi (who had worked with an early incarnation of Blackfoot), and second drummer Jimmy

Charles. That group toured extensively in 1978. While in Colorado the group added vocalist and harmonica player Pat Ramsey. The Trucks band even recorded some demos at Capricorn studios in Macon. However, Trucks abandoned the project after about eighteen months to reunite with the Allman Brothers Band.[106] In the late 1980s he built a recording studio in Tallahassee but eventually wound up in West Palm Beach. Trucks was suffering serious financial difficulties after the final breakup of the ABB when he shot himself in the head in his waterfront condo three years later. He was sixty-nine.

Dickey and Dale Betts divorced in 1971. Betts, now seventy-six, is married to his fifth wife, Donna. He lives in Osprey, Florida, only a few blocks from the Highway 41 he made famous in "Ramblin' Man." "I've had a great life," Betts said. "I don't have any complaints."[107]

4

Cowboy

IN SEPTEMBER 1968, Vanguard Records released the debut album by the 31st of February. Sales were disappointing, to say the least. Despite having recorded another album's worth of material at Criteria with producers Brad Shapiro and Steve Alaimo, and with Duane and Gregg Allman in the group, Vanguard refused to fund a follow-up.

Gregg Allman decided to return to Los Angeles in an effort to re-kindle his semi-solo career at Liberty Records. Disheartened, the other members of the 31st of February gave up. Bassist David Brown, however, found himself in demand as a session player in Hialeah, but Butch Trucks, Duane Allman, and Scott Boyer all decided to head back to Jacksonville. Trucks did stick around long enough to work with Brown on several of soul singer Betty Wright's sessions for her album *My First Time Around*, produced by Shapiro and released on Atco.

Singer-songwriter Boyer landed in Archer, Florida, a bleak little blip outside Gainesville, where he had a girlfriend. His Jacksonville cohort Bill Pillmore was living with them. Boyer and Pillmore had known each other since high school (Boyer attended Englewood High in the South-side, and Pillmore attended nearby Terry Parker in Arlington). They both matriculated to Florida State University in Tallahassee. After the 31st of February dissolved, Boyer and Pillmore reconnected in Gaines-ville, formed a folk duo that worked all over Florida, including Miami's Coconut Grove—and made good money doing so. They were doing a Gainesville gig when they ran into guitarist Pete Kowalke, another former FSU student, who had worked with Pillmore in a Tallahassee band called Matchbox.

Boyer was hankering to expand the duo into a full band.[1] Kowalke suggested to Boyer that they meet a friend of his, guitarist/singer/songwriter Tommy Talton, whom Kowalke had known since high school in Winter Park. Talton was working as a solo folksinger in local coffeehouses when Boyer and Pillmore reached out to him.

Talton had been a big man on the Orlando scene. He played with teen groups the Keyes, the Chessmen, and the Trademarks. The Trademarks, which included drummer Tom Wynn, morphed into the psychedelic garage-rock outfit We the People, who in 1966 garnered a regional hit for a local label, Hotline Records. The single "My Brother the Man" did well enough to get the group signed with Los Angeles–based Challenge Records (owned by cowboy singer/movie star Gene Autry). From there they graduated to RCA, where We the People recorded three singles supervised by Elvis Presley's producer, Felton Jarvis. However, the RCA signing did not generate any hits, so in 1968, Talton bolted for Los Angeles, where he spent a frustrating, fruitless year before returning to Orlando.[2]

Boyer, Pillmore, and Talton hit it off and immediately decided to join forces. "We sat down and pulled our guitars out, and Scott played me [his composition] 'Livin' in the Country,'" Talton recalls. "It was so neat to find someone else who wrote his own music, and the music was good. I forget what I played for him, but after I showed him a song we just sat down and asked each other who could we get in the band."[3]

Talton brought in drummer Tom Wynn from We the People, along with Orlando bassist George Clark. Kowalke was part of the package at first but suddenly split for New York. Since the original lineup included so many guitarists, Pillmore switched to keyboards but continued to play acoustic guitar occasionally. The group had several songwriters—Boyer, Talton, Pillmore, and Kowalke (who would return)—so there was no shortage of original material. The members all decided to move to Jacksonville because, in Pillmore's assessment, "there was so much going on." They rented a house near the Riverside district, where they began rehearsing all day while delivering newspapers in the wee hours to pay the rent.

One thing about bands from this area (and from this era): most knew that it took a lot of hard work and a lot of long hours to get to the top tier of the business. If a band wasn't tight and polished, it would get outclassed pretty quickly by groups who were—especially in Jacksonville, where there were *so many* bands. This is most likely the answer to the oft-asked question as to why there were so many successful musicians from the area: there was so much competition that they all realized they had to work like maniacs just to get noticed. The standard had been set by the Second Coming, who worked six nights a week at the Scene nightclub and on their day off played for free in Riverside's Willowbranch Park (see chapter 3 on the Allman Brothers Band).

The Allman Brothers Band (ABB) had already been signed and was in the process of putting together songs for its first album. Boyer, who had worked with Duane and Gregg Allman and Butch Trucks in the 31st of February, had kept in touch (see chapter 2 on the Bitter Ind). One day Duane Allman came through Jacksonville in his camper van en route to Macon from his mother's house in Daytona. Allman stopped in to see Boyer at the Euclid Avenue house where the members of the as-yet-unnamed band lived and rehearsed.[4] He pulled in early one morning and roused Boyer, saying, "I hear you got a band. . . . [P]lay something for me."[5] Boyer woke his compatriots, who filed bleary-eyed down to the music room and played a short set for Allman, who was favorably impressed.

Cowboy house, where the band lived and rehearsed near Riverside. Photo by the author.

Original members of Cowboy en route to a gig on Martha's Vineyard, ca. 1970. *Left to right*: Bill Pillmore, Pete Kowalke, Scott Boyer, George Clark, Tom Wynn, Tommy Talton, ca. 1970. Photo by Chris Thibaut; used by permission.

Returning to Macon, Allman recommended the group, soon to be christened Cowboy, to Phil Walden, owner of Capricorn Records. Walden sent staff producer Johnny Sandlin, a former member of Duane and Gregg's group Hour Glass, to Jacksonville for a closer examination. "A week later we had management, publishing and booking contracts in the mail," Boyer told biographer Scott B. Bomar.[6]

It would be years before the members would grasp the implications of signing these contracts simultaneously—and with the same entity. Walden not only got a hefty management commission on every cent the group made from each and every source, he also assigned their song copyrights to his own publishing company, No Exit Music, and assigned their worldwide recording rights to his own production company, which he then leased to Atlantic. Then he put them in his own studio and charged them hourly rates. Not only was he getting commissions from every conceivable angle, as the group's personal representative he sat on both sides of the negotiating table dealing with himself. In California these sorts of conflicts were illegal—but not in

Georgia. Talton later explained: "Phil Walden was of the school of 'You get out there and you play 250 nights a year, and we'll give you a station wagon to travel in [which he charged back to the band], and you just work and make sure I have money in my pocket from my percentage of your gigs. Then maybe I'll let you go in my studio, and I'll charge you $30,000 that you'll all of a sudden owe me.'"[7]

The members of Cowboy repaired to a farmhouse outside Cochran, Georgia, about thirty miles southeast of Walden's headquarters in Macon.[8] They recorded their first album, *Reach for the Sky*, at Capricorn Studios. Kowalke, displeased with his situation in New York, returned in time to participate briefly in the recording.[9] "The songs were fun, light hippie music," producer Sandlin told author Scott Bomar.[10]

Cowboy sounded nothing at all like the Allman Brothers Band but rather more like the California country-rock of Gram Parsons or Poco. Indeed, Boyer had been following Parsons's career since Parsons was a member of the Shilos (see chapter 1 on Gram Parsons). Talton, too, was a fan of Parsons. "Gram Parsons was and is one of my favorites through the years," Talton said.[11] Cowboy spotlighted the treacly three-part harmonies that dominated the California country-rock style, prefiguring the Eagles.[12] Cowboy's sound was clearly the Southeast's version of California country-rock and constitutes the missing link between that style and so-called southern rock. "I never thought Cowboy was a part of what was being called 'southern rock,'" Talton told interviewer Luc Brunot. "We were more California rock, country-rock or maybe folk-rock."[13] Most likely the only reason Cowboy got categorized as "southern rock" is because the group was signed to Capricorn. Capricorn was known as the home of southern rock, but it actually produced many different styles of music.

Reach for the Sky, with its amateurish cover drawn by Capricorn co-owner Frank Fenter, was released on Atco in the fall of 1970 (Walden's early records were released by Atco with the legend "Capricorn Series" on the labels). Cowboy's debut album didn't set any sales records and clearly wasn't expected to: Boyer reckons Atlantic only pressed up about five thousand copies.[14] The group's first tour was as openers for the ABB; Cowboy was in fact the opening act at the ABB's legendary show at New York's Fillmore East auditorium, where the ABB recorded its breakthrough album, *Live at Fillmore East*, in March 1971.

Cowboy's follow-up, *Five'll Getcha Ten*, which was recorded at Muscle Shoals Sound in October 1971 and produced by Johnny Sandlin, didn't fare much better sales-wise despite guest appearances by Duane Allman on a couple of songs. Allman played Dobro on Boyer's "Please Be with Me," which would be covered in 1974 by Eric Clapton on his top-selling album *461 Ocean Boulevard*. Boyer wrote or cowrote seven of the album's twelve songs. *Five'll Getcha Ten* included Boyer's "All My Friends," which Gregg Allman covered on his solo album *Laid Back*, recorded in March 1973 with an all-star cast of musicians, including Boyer and Talton.

Immediately after wrapping up *Five'll Getcha Ten*, there was a shakeup. Pillmore said Talton was unhappy with the overall level of musicianship and talked Boyer into getting new members because he felt they could "do better." Boyer and Talton recruited some new sidemen and went off on a West Coast tour. Pillmore was stunned, he said.[15]

The new Cowboy lineup didn't seem to work out, or perhaps it was simply a stopgap solution. In any case, the group was in tatters. Boyer and Talton took up the slack by working as session players and writers at Capricorn. The pair worked with soul singers Arthur Conley and Clarence Carter, country singer Kitty Wells, folk-rock artist Alex Taylor (James Taylor's brother), R&B singer Bonnie Bramlett (formerly of Delaney and Bonnie), and ABB guitarist-singer Dickey Betts. To fill the gap they cobbled together an album of previously recorded Cowboy material, 1974's *Why Quit When You're Losing?*

All was not well in the ABB camp either. With the deaths of Duane Allman and Berry Oakley, Dickey Betts had taken control of the band and steered it—at least partially—in a country-rock direction, which did not sit entirely well with the other members despite the fact that his song "Ramblin' Man" had given the group its only top-ten hit and had put lots of money in their bank accounts. Betts and Gregg Allman had both recorded solo albums, Allman in 1973 with *Laid Back*, and Betts in 1974 with *Highway Call*.

In 1974 Gregg Allman decided to assemble a large band to support his solo album and needed musicians. He relied heavily on Boyer and Talton, augmented by Tuscaloosa keyboardist Chuck Leavell, Capricorn studio drummer Bill Stewart, saxophonists Randall Bramblett

Revamped Cowboy lineup, ca. 1973. *Left to right*: David Brown, Scott Boyer, Bill Stewart, Randall Bramblett, Tommy Talton. Capricorn Records publicity photo.

and David Brown (the same David Brown who had played bass with Boyer and Trucks in the Bitter Ind/31st of February), and many others. Allman even had Boyer and Talton fronting a segment of his show.

In 1974 Cowboy released a fourth album, titled *Boyer & Talton*, which featured only the pair on the cover, although the album was credited to Cowboy. This was essentially a duo record with a bunch of studio sidemen, mostly the same all-star lineup who backed Gregg

Allman on his solo tour. Musicians included Jimmy Nalls on lead guitar, Capricorn staff producer and former Hour Glass keyboardist Paul Hornsby, Chuck Leavell on piano, Charlie Hayward from the Charlie Daniels Band on bass, Randall Bramblett on saxophone and background vocals, David Brown on saxophone and background vocals, Toy Caldwell from the Marshall Tucker Band on pedal steel, Johnny Sandlin on bass and congas, Bill Stewart on drums, and special guest Jaimoe from the ABB on drums and congas. Cowboy hit the road again with a refurbished lineup that included bassist Brown, Bramblett on sax, keys, and vocals, and Stewart on drums.

It would be yet another three years before a new Cowboy album would arrive. This one, titled simply *Cowboy*, featured a new lineup. Author Bomar characterized it as "a fairly lightweight pop affair." Gone were Brown and Stewart. The new group consisted of Chip Condon on keyboards, Arch Pearson on bass, and drummer Chip Miller; only multi-instrumentalist and vocalist Bramblett, from Jesup, Georgia, remained from the group's previous incarnation. Miller, from Jacksonville's Westside, had worked in local bands with Dru Lombar (who was at this time a member of Capricorn act Grinderswitch) and Don Barnes of 38 Special. The group's 1977 album, *Cowboy*, would be its swan song for Capricorn; the label itself would fold two years later. Miller returned to Jacksonville, where he worked with an early version of the Derek Trucks Band as well as with Kingsnake artist Ace Moreland.

Boyer lit out for Los Angeles, where he spent a year writing songs with former Wet Willie guitarist Ricky Hirsch. He also produced an album for the Seattle country-rockers the Sky Boys. He returned to Alabama to join a Tuscaloosa group called the Locust Fork Band. He later formed the Convertibles, which briefly included Talton. In 1988 he moved to Muscle Shoals, where he joined Johnny Sandlin's group the Decoys, based in nearby Decatur. He played with that group for more than twenty-five years. Boyer also recorded a solo album, *All My Friends*, in 1991. Bill Pillmore visited Boyer in Muscle Shoals around 2000 and was shocked to discover Boyer was playing four sets a night for a measly one hundred dollars. "We were making that back in 1969 with our folk duo," he said. Pillmore also said Boyer told him that in hindsight he felt getting rid of the original Cowboy members in 1971 had been a mistake.[16]

Boyer and Talton continued to work together off and on. In 1990 Boyer formed the Convertibles in Muscle Shoals, which briefly included Talton. In 2006, they worked with the Capricorn Rhythm Section, which included Johnny Sandlin on bass, Bill Stewart on drums, Paul Hornsby on keyboards, and Wet Willie singer Jimmy Hall. Boyer and Talton reformed Cowboy in 2007 and recorded tracks produced by Sandlin for a new album, which was never released. However, in 2010 they followed with a Cowboy "reunion" album, recorded live in Macon and released on Macon-based Hittin' the Note Records. Musicians on this album included Stan Robertson on bass, Bill Stewart on drums, and Randall Bramblett on sax and background vocals. The only original member besides Boyer and Talton to appear at this putative reunion was Bill Pillmore, who played pedal steel on two songs.

After the 1971 purge, Pillmore went back to Jacksonville, where he ran a hardware store and worked as a piano tuner. He later moved to St. Augustine and now lives in Asheville, North Carolina, where he runs his own studio, the Wormhole, and continues to write songs. Pete Kowalke is an occasional client. Pillmore released a solo album, *Look In, Look Out*, on his own RoadWorm label in 2005.

Tommy Talton went to Alabama and Texas, where he produced recordings for emerging songwriters. He went back to Winter Park for a while to regroup and to look after his aging mother. Talton traveled to Luxembourg in 1995 to do a six-week tour with singer-songwriter Matt Dawson, which led to nine years in Europe.[17] While there he formed a group called the Rebelizers with members of Albert Lee's band; the resulting album was released in 2008 by Hittin' the Note Records as *Tommy Talton in Europe*. In 2006 he moved to Atlanta, where he formed the Tommy Talton Band, and in 2012 he recorded an R&B-infused solo effort, *Let's Get Outta Here*, for Hittin' the Note, which included Boyer on several tracks. In his early seventies, he continues to tour with his band.

In 2012, Boyer made a duo album, *Okay, How about This*, with Shoals singer/songwriter/keyboardist N. C. Thurman, another member of the Decoys. Boyer died in 2018 of complications from peripheral artery disease. He was seventy.

Lynyrd Skynyrd

Bad-Boy Chic

PERHAPS THE MOST FASCINATING ASPECT of the Lynyrd Skynyrd story is the way the group rose from underdogs on the Jacksonville scene to such astounding success.

Few people in Jacksonville during the group's early days expected to see the kind of success Ronnie Van Zant envisioned for himself and his band. For in 1968, when the group was known as One Percent, the band was, according many accounts, not very good. The members also labored in the unenviable shadow of more formidable acts such as the Second Coming and the Load, both of which were newcomers from the Sarasota/Bradenton area.

Bassist Richard Price of the Load said One Percent had opened for his group at a local show and were "the worst band I'd ever heard in my life." He did add, however, that the group eventually developed into a formidable act.[1]

Wayne Smith was a seventeen-year-old, classically trained pianist and music fan from nearby Orange Park who recalls seeing One Percent at the Forest Inn in Jacksonville's Lake Shore district in 1969. "They weren't tight or polished," Smith said. "They sounded like they just came out of the garage."[2] The group had actually been together several years by this point.

Agent/manager Don Dana, who had managed the local groups the Illusions and the Bitter Ind as well as Ocala's Royal Guardsmen, booked One Percent on a 1970 tour opening for Strawberry Alarm Clock (SAC), a group that had had a number-one single two years previous. Dana had been involved with tours by imposter acts such as a fake version of the Zombies. When SAC members in Los Angeles heard about a group masquerading as them, the real members, who included guitarist/bassist Ed King, decided to go ahead and work the tour themselves.[3] Dana put Lynyrd Skynyrd on the tour as opening act. Eighteen years later Dana recounted: "Ronnie asked me to manage his band [One Percent]. I told him I wasn't interested, and he asked me why not. I said, 'Do you really wanna know?' He said, 'Yeah.' So I told him straight to his face, 'Ronnie, you can't sing to save your life; in fact, you really should just give up.' I thought it was good advice."[4]

Apparently Van Zant took this advice to heart, at least for a little while. He called Jimmy Dougherty, former drummer/singer of Black Bear Angel, a rival band, and asked him to step in as the band's singer. Dougherty wasn't impressed with Skynyrd at this point—he laughed and hung up.[5]

Yet, much like Limp Bizkit, another underdog band who would emerge from Jacksonville two decades years later, the Skynyrd boys got the last laugh. Most of the credit goes to Van Zant, whose steely determination in the face of all odds would finally pay off. Nothing, not even a want of talent, was going to stop this man. Van Zant knew he wasn't a world-class singer—certainly enough people had told him—and he also knew his band members weren't the greatest musicians. But he figured there was nothing hard work couldn't rectify. He knew he and his bandmates were going to have to step up their game in order to compete in the big leagues with the likes of the Allman Brothers Band. So he pushed his charges like a slave driver, rehearsing from fifty to sometimes sixty or more hours a week in a cabin with no air-conditioning in the backwoods north of Green Cove Springs. The Allmans were hard workers, but Lynyrd Skynyrd might qualify as the hardest-working band who ever lived. "We worked our asses off," bassist Leon Wilkeson told an interviewer "and it paid off."[6] Skynyrd was the virtual embodiment of the Protestant work ethic *and* the American Dream rolled into one: if one works hard enough and long enough, there's a chance you will achieve your dream. Van Zant truly believed this.

Upward mobility was a big part of the dream. David Meyer in his Gram Parsons biography referred to the members of Lynyrd Skynyrd as "teenage redneck musicians of genuine ambition who were looking to use music to escape the class they were born to."[7] What most young musicians of Jacksonville's Westside wanted more than anything was to flee the seemingly inevitable blue-collar drudgery that awaited them. Without a good college education—and that would have been difficult for most of these fellows to achieve—the few realistic prospects were in construction, warehouse work, or the navy. The idea of working forty hours a week, day in, day out, at a tedious job you hated was tantamount to a life sentence in hell. They wanted a job that was fun, a job they could love doing. Playing music for a living—even if it meant working sixty or more hours a week—was the answer.

Van Zant developed a songwriting style that contained slices of southern life, almost mini-novellas, with characters such as Linda Lou, Billy Joe, and the rest. Bruce Springsteen, who emerged on the national scene in January 1973, seven months before Skynyrd's August debut, had already been using the technique of telling stories through the eyes of his songs' characters. Van Zant's story-songs, his "songs about the Southland," resonated with young southerners who were tired of being stereotyped as ignorant rednecks and racist bigots and also reflected their working-class concerns.[8] They also came along during a period when the South was being heavily romanticized in national culture. Movie star Burt Reynolds, for one, had made it hip to be a southerner. The time was ripe for a southern Springsteen.[9]

Ironically, the lack of polish on the vocal front may have been an advantage. For one thing, Van Zant's squonky, mid-rangy voice practically leapt out of small, car-radio speakers. There was also a psychological dimension: fans could sing along to Skynyrd songs and not be intimidated or thrown off as they might be with more gifted singers such as Wet Willie's Jimmy Hall or the Elvin Bishop Group's Mickey Thomas, two of the more impressive singers of their generation. Yet, ironically, their success pales in comparison to Van Zant's.

Scott Sisson, a well-known Jacksonville drummer and session player, thinks this lack of polish gives a singer more "street-cred": "All that effort kinda makes me root for the singer, because he is working his ass off and seems to really *mean* it. I would rather hear a ragged singer like, say, Joe Cocker struggle with a song than watch Steve Perry up there *tap-dancing* his way through it like it was nothing. It's just too easy for him." The point here is that fabulously talented singers like Hall and Thomas are probably *too good* for southern rock. As Bob Dylan, Mick Jagger, Neil Young, Bruce Springsteen, and many others had already demonstrated, one doesn't need to be a good singer to be a rock star. Rock music is not about vocal talent—it's the artist's body of *songs* that counts along with his or her overall image and philosophy.

The group of local boys who eventually became known as Lynyrd Skynyrd had been working together in Jacksonville for at least three years when the Bradenton bunch—members of the Second Coming and later the Load—who were a little older and a lot more polished, hit town and shook up the scene. Local bands suddenly found they had some catching up to do.

The Skynyrd founders were a pair of Westside teens, Bob Burns (born in Gainesville) and Gary Rossington. Both started out as drummers, but Rossington quickly decided to switch to guitar. The pair began jamming in Burns's parents' carport in the Hillcrest subdivision.[10] Rossington lived in a nicer area east of Cassatt Avenue (inside the old city limits) called Pinewood. None of these areas were considered bad neighborhoods.

Jimmy Parker, who later went with Rick Doeschler's band the Squires (the name was changed to Us when Ronnie Van Zant joined), was supposed to be the new group's bassist, but he was casual about showing up for rehearsals, so Larry Steele or Billy Skaggs occasionally filled in. The boys called this outfit My Back Yard. Another neighborhood kid, Larry Junstrom, who had come from Pittsburgh at ten and had been playing with a teen group called After Five, joined as fulltime bassist, and the trio renamed itself Me, You and Him.[11] All three members lived within a one-mile radius, as did future member Ronnie Van Zant. Future member Allen Collins lived across the Cedar River and was in a rival group called the Mods.

Nearly all these boys attended Lake Shore Middle School, as did Molly Hatchet founder Dave Hlubek and future 38 Special founding member (later stage manager) Larry Steele.[12] A couple of miles southwest, Cedar Hills residents and future Skynyrd members Leon

Gary Rossington's childhood home on Stimson Street in the Pinewood subdivision, a pleasant, quiet area of Murray Hill. Photo by the author.

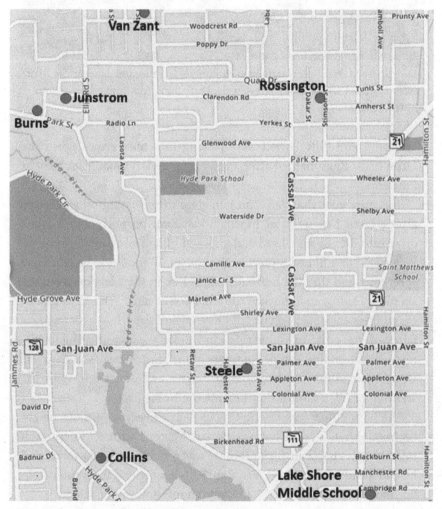

Map of Lake Shore and surrounding areas. Leon Wilkeson, Billy Powell, and Jeff Carlisi lived nearby in the Cedar Hills subdivision.

Lake Shore Middle School, attended by Ronnie, Donnie, and Johnny Van Zant, Allen Collins, Dave Hlubek, Larry Steele, Larry Junstrom, and others. Photo by the author.

Wilkeson and Billy Powell were playing in a teen group called the Little Black Eggs, named after a 1965 song by Daytona Beach's Night Crawlers.

The story goes that Van Zant joined up with Rossington and Burns after a Little League game in which Van Zant purportedly hit a line drive into Bob Burns's head and knocked him unconscious. However, Burns said in a filmed interview that he and Rossington were merely spectators and that the foul ball had hit him in the back, between the shoulder blades, and knocked the wind out of him.[13] This discrepancy exemplifies the collection of tall tales, legends, myths—and outright fabrications—that surround this band and make investigating its history a never-ending exercise in frustration.[14] In any case, Van Zant left Us and joined up with Rossington, Burns, and Junstrom. With the addition of Allen Collins they became the Noble Five.

The boys didn't dare say no to Van Zant. "Everyone [in our neighborhood] knew Ronnie because he was Mister Bad-Ass," Rossington told an interviewer in 1976. "Ronnie was a redneck, kinda-sorta, and he had a bad reputation."[15] Van Zant's lifelong friend from the neighborhood, Gene Odom, said Van Zant "simply enjoyed fighting."[16]

Aside from his unwavering determination, Van Zant brought with him a work ethic that would serve him and the other members well. They would likely not have gotten where they were going without his obsessive drive, perseverance—and discipline. "This son of a truck driver," Odom explains, "overcame his shortcomings by combining his greatest personal resources: a hidden talent for songwriting, the fury of his fists, and the sheer strength of his will."[17]

The group worked wherever it could, starting out in teen clubs (commonly referred to as "youth centers"), then on to high-school dances, proms, outdoor concerts in the city's parks, bars, "bottle clubs," what have you. Somewhere along this stage the group changed its name to One Percent, which they had likely gotten, directly or indirectly, from a 1957 biker movie, *Motorcycle Gang*.[18] Taking a page from the Rolling Stones' book, they were already developing a bad-boy image. Van Zant continued to work days while rehearsing nights with the group. Collins kept his paper route.

Two very popular teen clubs were the Comic Book Club downtown, where One Percent served a residency in 1968, and Westside's Forest Inn, where it played frequently in 1969. Both of these were teens-only clubs that served soft drinks until a specified time—usually midnight—when management ran the kids out and allowed adults to bring in their own bottles. Rossington recalls: "We used to play one joint until midnight for [teenagers]; then it turned into a bottle club, and we'd go till six a.m. . . . . When you're from the South you learn to work hard."[19] These "bottle clubs" could stay open as long as they liked because they did not require liquor licenses and were not regulated by the rules that controlled licensed establishments. After-hours patrons paid an admission fee at the door and sat down to sip their soft-drinks in plastic or Styrofoam cups, called "set-ups," which they could purchase onsite and fill with their own booze purchased elsewhere (the bottles still had to be sealed upon entry, however; it was illegal to carry around an opened bottle of liquor). These types of clubs offered a ton of work for local musicians—and a place for musicians and bar employees to gather after the 2:00 a.m. closing time—until the 1980s, when Duval County began moving to close them all down.

Many prominent regional bands had played downtown's Comic Book Club as well as Lake Shore's Forest Inn. The Allman Joys had played the Beachcomber a number of times and later performed there as the Hour Glass after it became the Comic Book Club. On the latter engagement Van Zant and his crew served as opening act.[20]

David Griffin, manager at a downtown musical-instrument store,

Marvin Kay's Music Center, began booking local groups. Among these was Van Zant's One Percent and Larry Steele's Black Bear Angel (BBA), which featured drummer-singer Jimmy Dougherty (who would go on to front the Allen Collins Band in 1983). BBA was One Percent's biggest competitor, but the members of both groups, mostly from the same neighborhood, were on friendly terms, having known each other since their days at Lake Shore Middle School or even earlier (Steele had known Allen Collins since elementary school).

In mid-1969, Griffin scheduled sessions at Norm Vincent Studio for both groups to do some recording.[21] Black Bear, deciding their original material was not ready for prime-time, chose to record cover versions of already-popular material, while One Percent recorded two of their own. In his book *As I Recall*, Larry Steele explains the primary differences between the two groups and their approach: for starters, Black Bear was run as a committee without a true leader or a clear vision: "One Percent was pretty much a dictatorship [run by Ronnie Van Zant], while BBA was a majority-rules democracy." Second, the members of Black Bear were either too stoned or too jaded to recognize the possibilities for career advancement, whereas One Percent did exactly that: "We were arrogant enough to believe that opportunities such as this would continue to come around for us. . . . One Percent, on the other hand, had no such issue. They would use the opportunity to their full advantage, getting a single out of the deal, which they were able to parlay into [a] ridiculous [amount of] exposure over the next year, including local TV."[22]

Retired recording engineer and former studio and record-label owner Tom Markham, however, recalls these events quite differently. "I don't know who David Griffin is," he said. "We never spoke with him." Jim Sutton, staff engineer at Norm Vincent Recording, spotted the group downtown at Art Eisen's Comic Book Club, Markham said.[23]

Markham was working as a broadcast engineer at WJKS Television (Channel 17). He had had some success with own label, Magnum Records, in the early 1960s.[24] By 1969, he was ready to have another go at it. Markham and Sutton decided to form a new label, Shade Tree Records. Sutton had seen One Percent and liked what he heard, so the pair signed the group to a five-year recording-and-publishing deal. Markham and Sutton didn't like the name One Percent, however.

One Percent, Shade Tree Records publicity photo, early 1969. Photo by Olan Mills Portrait Studios. Courtesy of Tom Markham.

Before starting work on the group's first recordings under the Shade Tree logo, Van Zant informed the label owners that One Percent was now "Leonard Skinner." Markham and Sutton weren't enthused about this new name either.[25]

Shade Tree Records' flagship release was a 45-rpm single comprising "Need All My Friends" and "Michelle." Released under the name "Lynard Skynard"—the spelling would be fiddled with a bit more—the single did get some regional airplay, notably on 50,000-watt WAPE-AM, and boosted the band's career, at least on a local level. Four other songs, including "Free Bird," were recorded at Norm Vincent Studio with Sutton at the board, one of which, "He's Alive," is a gospel-rock number that has rarely been heard. Markham said this was Van Zant's response to the God-is-dead cliché that was going around at the time.[26]

It was clear from the outset who the leader of the group was, Markham added. Having spent an entire week or longer meticulously working on an arrangement, most of the band members were reluctant to change anything from the way they had rehearsed it. Nonetheless, Markham, as producer, made a suggestion drummer Bob Burns didn't like but Van Zant thought might improve the song. Burns stood

LEONARD SKINNER

Physical-education coach Leonard Skinner, from the Lee High School 1967 yearbook.

HARLEY CONCERT

Forest Inn · Sun. Apr. 26 · 12·6 P.M.

Coconut Harley Needs $6,500 Bond

SWEET ROOSTER
KING JAMES VERSION
LYNYRD SKYNYRD
BLACK BEAR ANGEL

Plus John Meeks & Many Others

Please Care!!

1436 Lakeshore Blvd. - 389-9336
Turn Left on Normandy Blvd.

Forest Inn poster, 1969. One Percent had already changed its name by this point.

up to object. There was no discussion: Van Zant clobbered him upside his head, sending him sprawling into his drums. "On second thought," Burns told Van Zant, "I like your idea better."[27]

The origin of the name Leonard Skinner (and its later variants) was based on a running joke among band members about a Lee High School physical-education coach who had sent Rossington to the principal's office for having longer hair than the school's dress code allowed (Van Zant had quit Lee High in 1966, and Collins was attending Forrest High).

Coach Skinner was seen by his long-haired students as a reactionary crusader and became the bane of Rossington's existence (Rossington quit Lee High that year, 1969). Bob Burns taunted Rossington relentlessly, joking that Skinner was hounding him at all hours, even at home or at rehearsals. If the phone rang and no one was on the line, Burns would tease, "It's Leonard—he's comin' ta git ya." The other members found this hilarious. Van Zant asked the teenaged crowd at the Forest Inn what it thought of naming the group after Coach Skinner, and the crowd, which comprised many current and former Lee High students who understood the joke—many were longhairs having had a similar experience—hooted and hollered with approval.[28]

That same year, the boys in Skynyrd met and got to hang out with their idols in the Hour Glass, when Duane and Gregg Allman were crashing at the Gray House in Riverside, only a block or so away from where Van Zant's new girlfriend, Judy Seymour, a Waycross, Georgia, native, was living in the Green House with Mary Hayworth and Dean Kilpatrick. Kilpatrick later became a personal assistant for Skynyrd.[29]

Hustlers, Inc.

Pat Armstrong, an Atlanta native who had come to Jacksonville with his parents as an infant, had been a student at Jacksonville's Bishop Kenny and later Englewood High Schools. He matriculated to Mercer University in Macon in 1969. It also happened that Mercer had been talent manager Phil Walden's alma mater. Armstrong didn't meet the Waldens in Macon, however. He had a friend from Jacksonville who worked at the Waldens' booking-and-management agency, Walden Artists and Promotions. The friend introduced Pat to Phil's younger

Lynyrd Skynyrd signs with Hustlers, Inc., Macon, Georgia, 1970. *Back row, left to right*: Pat Armstrong, Gary Donehoo, Allen Collins, Alan Walden, Bob Burns. *Front row, left to right*: Gary Rossington, Hustlers president Eddie Floyd (*seated*), Ronnie Van Zant, Larry Junstrom. Photo by Bob Johnson; used by permission.

brother, Alan, in Jacksonville when Alan had come down to check on his client, R&B singer Eddie Floyd, while Floyd was appearing at the Jacksonville Coliseum with Freda Payne in mid-1970.

The Walden brothers had a falling out after Phil returned from army duty in Germany. According to Alan Walden, Phil also left him with ten thousand dollars in debt to manage. Walden client Otis Redding, at Alan's behest, came through with some money to bail out the operation and became a partner in the business. Alan felt that Phil had failed to appreciate all he'd done.[30] In April 1970, he and R&B singer Eddie Floyd left to form their own company, Hustlers, Inc., of which Floyd was the putative president.[31] Although steeped in R&B, both Waldens decided to broaden the scope of their operations to include white rock bands (Phil's big breakthrough had been the Allman Brothers Band, formed in Jacksonville in 1969, whose members he quickly relocated to Macon).

Back in Jacksonville, Armstrong, then twenty-three (a year older than Van Zant), had taken a year off between university and law school and was teaching biology at Southside Junior High. During this period he got interested in the music business and started booking local bands, one of which was Lynyrd Skynyrd. Armstrong had an office in an old warehouse building on Old St. Augustine Road that included rehearsal and storage space for his stable of bands. Knowing Walden was looking for new talent, Armstrong arranged to showcase several of his acts at the warehouse; these included Skynyrd, Black Bear Angel, and R&B band Anthony Speight and the Soul Revival, among others.[32] Walden came down from Macon and took a listen. He reckons he had heard 187 acts by this point.[33] The only act he felt strongly about was Skynyrd.

Walden had clearly taken a page from his brother's book: He signed the band to management *and* publishing contracts, which was a clear conflict of interest. However, this was par for the course in those days. What is more, he demanded and got a 30 percent commission of *gross* earnings—meaning he got a huge commission on every cent the band brought in, *before* expenses were deducted.[34] The band at the time consisted of five members; if they took in five hundred dollars on a gig and spent one hundred dollars on gas, motels, vehicle and equipment maintenance, then paid Walden his $150 commission "off the top," there might be $250 left over for the five of them to split. So he was making three times as much as the individual members.

The group's first order of business was to get out of its contract with Tom Markham and Jim Sutton of Jacksonville's Shade Tree Records. Van Zant approached them and asked for a release from the five-year recording contract, which Markham and Sutton graciously granted.[35] Shade Tree's publishing affiliate, Double T Music, retained the publishing rights to the songs the label actually released but due to a standard "reversion clause" had to relinquish the rights to "Free Bird" because it had gone unreleased during the term of the contract.[36]

The most important thing Walden did was to bring the boys to Muscle Shoals to record new demos. During Alan Walden's tenure with Phil Walden Artists and Promotions, one of whose clients was Muscle Shoals R&B singer Percy Sledge, Alan had gotten close to Quin Ivy, owner of Quinvy studio, where Sledge's hits had been recorded. Walden and Ivy made a deal wherein Walden would bring all his acts to Ivy. Walden and his new partner, R&B singer Eddie Floyd, brought three rock bands to Ivy, the Male, Birnam Wood, and Lynyrd Skynyrd.[37] Studio owner/executive producer Quin Ivy explained, "I owned the first recording contract on Skynyrd[38] and subsequently sold my rights to Jimmy Johnson for about $3,500 of studio time we had on the books."[39] Producer David Johnson added: "I first produced the band for Quin and then shopped their recordings around for some months. It was only after I [was unable] to get them a deal that Alan Walden finally played the Skynyrd demos to Jimmy Johnson and only then that Muscle Shoals Sound got involved."[40]

The first Muscle Shoals sessions commenced in October 1970, but by the time of the group's second sortie, drummer Bob Burns had left the group. There are different stories floating around as to why. "I had no place to stay," Burns himself explained in a 2011 interview. "I was crashing in people's bushes . . . it just got to me."[41] Another explanation is that he had a girlfriend who wanted him to lead a more normal life.

In any case, the group urgently needed a drummer. Guitarist Allen Collins had recently spoken with former Fresh Garbage drummer Rickey Medlocke, who was now playing guitar and fronting Blackfoot, living in New Jersey, and not doing well. Collins advised Medlocke to call Van Zant. Van Zant asked Medlocke if he still played drums. Medlocke was more or less ready to do anything at this point. He practiced hard for a week, got his drum chops together, and was soon ready to roll.[42]

Bassist Larry Junstrom was unceremoniously dismissed just as the band was leaving for its second excursion to Muscle Shoals. Junstrom told Larry Steele, who ran into him at the band's house in Mandarin after the group had left him behind, "Can you believe it? They fired me!" According to Steele's account, the other members hadn't even offered Junstrom an explanation.[43] Junstrom later said he left the group because he was starving, so he went to Miami, where he landed steady work as a bassist in a lounge band.[44]

Van Zant brought Blackfoot bassist Greg T. Walker aboard and began replacing Junstrom's tracks with Walker's.[45] Skynyrd not only had Blackfoot's rhythm section but several new songs borrowed from Blackfoot as well as an alternate lead singer who could sing circles around Van Zant. Producer Jimmy Johnson of Muscle Shoals Sound

(MSS) heard the Quinvy demos and brought the band into MSS, where Medlocke wrote and sang three songs on the band's unreleased debut album. During this time Walker, who had hoped to reassemble Blackfoot, left Skynyrd and was replaced by Leon Wilkeson from Dru Lombar's Christian-rock group, King James Version.[46] (See chapter 6 on Blackfoot.)

Johnson recorded a batch of songs, from which they culled the best three or four and shopped these around to labels. The result: not one nibble. "Nine record companies had turned us down," Walden told interviewer Michael Buffalo Smith. "I don't mean, 'We like you but you need better material,' I mean, 'Not interested; no need to contact us again.'"[47] Eventually Alan Walden, hat in hand, approached his brother about a deal at Capricorn. Alan Walden said Phil turned him down after seeing the band in Macon, saying, "Your lead singer's too goddamn cocky, he can't sing, the songs are weak, and they sound too much like the Allman Brothers."[48]

*　*　*

Perseverance in the face of all obstacles, a trait Van Zant possessed in spades, was a crucial lesson he shared with his charges—and he would be proven right. The band soldiered on, working medium-sized juke joints throughout the Deep South. In 1972 Frank Joiner at the Rodgers Agency put the band into Funocchio's, an Atlanta dive known as a "knife-and-gun club."

Producer and musician Al Kooper, who was well-connected in the industry and had enjoyed many successes, happened to be in town and went into Funocchio's one night and was intrigued by the band. He didn't like the group at first, but it sort of grew on him, especially the cocky lead singer. By the end of the week he was up jamming with them and offering to produce some tracks for them and try to land them a deal.

A native New Yorker, Kooper was one of the few people, along with Phil Walden, to realize that something special was happening down South. While producing tracks for the duo Frankie and Johnny at Studio One in Doraville, where he worked with the Atlanta Rhythm Section—a group who included Jacksonville musicians J. R. Cobb and Robert Nix—Kooper fell in love with Atlanta and decided to move there. Kooper, who had briefly been an A&R rep at Columbia Records, initiated talks with executives at MCA via his manager about starting his own label, Sounds of the South Records. He showcased three acts for MCA: Lynyrd Skynyrd along with Atlanta groups Mose Jones and Elijah. Mose Jones may have been the best of the bunch but nonetheless found itself in Lynyrd Skynyrd's shadow, mostly because Skynyrd had catchier songs that wormed their way into a listener's ear instantly, whereas Mose Jones's songs were baroque, artful, even jazzy—and didn't sound one bit southern. Skynyrd, on the other hand, specialized in *jukin'* music—music for barflies and party animals.[49]

Before the MCA showcase, Skynyrd wrote and worked up "Workin' for MCA," which impressed the suits. The MCA execs offered to finance a joint venture with Kooper. Kooper moved into a house in Roswell with a rustic, 150-year-old cabin out back, which he photographed and used as his label's logo.

The point that needs to be emphasized is that "Yankee Slicker" Kooper was to a major extent the conceptual architect of southern rock, whatever that might actually mean. Even though Phil Walden's Macon-based Capricorn label nearly had the southern-rock market cornered, Walden himself never used the term "southern rock" and in fact disliked it.[50] Capricorn was actually quite diverse, with acts as wide-ranging as Martin Mull, Kitty Wells, Johnny Jenkins, Dobie Gray, and Livingston Taylor (James Taylor's brother). It was Kooper who codified the southern-rock concept.[51] The concept was memorialized in the name of his label, Sounds of the South, and its logo, a log cabin. Kooper's operation was far more focused than Walden's, essentially a one-act label with Skynyrd reigning supreme and Mose Jones and Elijah soon falling by the wayside. In this Skynyrd was extremely fortunate: Kooper took far more of a personal interest in the band than Phil Walden would have—maybe too personal.

With no other prospects, Lynyrd Skynyrd grudgingly accepted Kooper's lowball offer in 1972. The proffered contract was "the biggest piece of shit" Alan Walden had ever seen, he told an interviewer.[52] The contract called for Kooper to get 10 percentage points and the *entire band* only 5—roughly seven-tenths of a point each; Kooper was making *fourteen* times what each member got.[53]

After signing with Sounds of the South, the group expanded to seven members with the additions of keyboardist Billy Powell, who'd been serving as a roadie for nearly a year, and former Strawberry

Alarm Clock guitarist/bassist Ed King, from Southern California. Regular bassist Wilkeson abruptly returned to Jacksonville to get back to playing Christian rock, as he had done before joining Skynyrd. Wilkeson, who was very religious, became anxious about playing what the Christian-music community dubbed the devil's music.[54] He also took a day job in the freezer warehouse at Farmbest Dairy Products. King was brought in to replace Wilkeson on bass and played on the first album. However, Wilkeson reconsidered and returned to the fold during the last stages of recording. Instead of letting King go, however, the group moved him from bass to guitar, creating the classic "three-guitar army." King, a phenomenal guitarist, would turn out to be the group's proverbial secret weapon: it was his quirky guitar solos on "Sweet Home, Alabama"—along with the catchy intro riff he created—that put the band over the top a year later.

Bad-Boy Shtick

Florida Times-Union writer Matt Soergel said when he was growing up in California and first encountering southern-rock groups like Skynyrd and Molly Hatchet, the sense of danger emanating from them was palpable. It's one of the defining aspects of southern rock, he said.[55]

Bassist Leon Wilkeson told an interviewer, "It was Al Kooper who actually started the whole rowdy image for us."[56] After signing the group, Kooper immediately went to work on ideas for marketing the band: "I decided to paint a rough-house image for them." He designed a skull-and-crossbones logo for the group, to which someone in MCA's art department later affixed a rebel-flag bandanna.[57] Kooper successfully invoked a sense of menace for the group, shooting their album cover in a rough-looking section of Jonesboro, Georgia, making them look like an urban street gang. At this point the only truly hard-drinking, brawling redneck in the group was Van Zant, who had been arrested many times in Jacksonville for fighting and disorderly conduct. The others were mostly regular suburban kids who went along with the gag. But after Kooper more or less codified the bad-boy shtick, the members all knew how they were expected to behave—and even went a bit overboard at times.

Perhaps some savvy operator explained to Van Zant that Americans love an old-fashioned rags-to-riches story. Thus he duly declared that

"Lynyrd Skynyrd are nothin' but street people, right straight off the streets, skid row" and that his neighborhood was like a ghetto.[58] He might as well have said he'd been born in a log cabin. In actuality, Van Zant's family was not wealthy, but neither was it poor: his father, a truck driver, had bought him a brand-new Ford Mustang for his sixteenth birthday. Allen Collins's mother, Eva, had indulged her son with three or four extremely expensive guitars.[59] Wilkeson and Powell were navy brats who generally managed to stay out of trouble. Rossington, whose father had died when he was young, may have grown up struggling, but he came from a quiet, clean area near Murray Hill inside the old city limits.

Manager Walden agreed that Lynyrd Skynyrd's redneck-hippie image set the band apart from other long-haired groups in the early 1970s. He played it to the hilt, describing his charges as "wild, crazy, drinking, fighting rednecks with a capital 'R' and proud of it!"[60] But by 1977 the band was looking to tone down its rowdy image. Wilkeson admitted that the image "sorta scares me" because it brought out the worst kind of behavior in some of the group's fans—sooner or later someone was going to get hurt by an overzealous fan who took the bad-boy shtick too seriously.[61] Van Zant, too, got sick of it and felt it was getting out of hand: "We've had enough of it, you know? It's been carried a little bit too far."[62] But it had served its purpose—it got them noticed.

"Sweet Home, Alabama" Controversy

After the group finished its first album at Studio One, the members went back to Jacksonville and started writing more songs. After Wilkeson was coaxed into coming back, King moved from bass to guitar. It was Ed King who came up with the opening riff—not to mention the bizarre guitar solos—for "Sweet Home, Alabama."

Willing to risk censure in order to get noticed, the Skynyrd boys had an inkling they were playing with fire when they wrote the song. Certainly Van Zant did: "It's either gonna break us wide open or piss everybody off so bad that we won't get a second chance."[63] He rolled the dice with "Sweet Home." Besides being a catchy little ditty, most likely it was a way to push some hot-buttons and garner more press-generating controversy, controversy that rages to this day, with observers still trying to figure out if the song is pro- or anti-racist. The arguments seem to go both ways. Van Zant knew it would be a hit, "There's our 'Ramblin' Man,'" he said after it was recorded.[64] The song soared to number eight in *Billboard*'s Hot 100 on October 26, 1974, Skynyrd's only top-ten single.

One person who apparently loved the song was Alabama governor George Wallace, king of the segregationists (although he did later recant and apologized for his racist stance and policies). In 1975 the members accepted plaques onstage from Wallace, inducting them as honorary colonels in the Alabama state militia, the same organization that had terrorized civil-rights protestors a decade earlier. Van Zant brushed it off as "a bullshit gimmick" designed to drum up some quick publicity—which it no doubt was, mostly for Wallace—but the band members graciously accepted the plaques nonetheless.[65] Charlie Daniels, a close friend and confidant of Van Zant's, later said Van Zant indeed "had a great respect for Wallace. [When] they got the plaques from the governor . . . they were just tickled to death about it."[66] Ed King, cowriter of "Alabama," said the group supported Wallace. He told author Mark Kemp: "Ronnie was a big fan of George Wallace's. He totally supported him. We all did. . . . Anybody who tells you any different is lying."[67] However, bassist Leon Wilkeson, who was actually a peace-loving hippie in real life, demurred, saying, "I support Wallace about as much as your average American supported Hitler." Backpedaling, however, Wilkeson added, "I respect him [Wallace], not as a politician but as a man who hasn't given up what he was after—that's how we all feel."[68] Apparently it was Wallace's defiance and intransigence they admired most. Van Zant, exemplifying the Jacksonian tradition, said as much: "He's a tough motherfucker, and we respect him for that."[69]

Many music fans have responded to Skynyrd's various brouhahas—mostly designed, at least in the band's early days, to garner publicity—by saying musicians, largely uneducated in such matters, should stay out of politics. But politics wasn't the point—it was leadership. Van Zant was not only the leader of his band; he also became the leader of a massive following, a veritable cult of personality.[70] In their displays of decisiveness and defiance, both Wallace and Van Zant were modeling Jacksonian leadership qualities.

The Recurring Rebel-Flag Issue

Ronnie Van Zant claimed the rebel flag was the record company's idea, and it is true that someone in MCA's art department stuck a rebel-flag bandanna on the death's-head logo Al Kooper had designed for the band. But it was the group members' own idea to fly it onstage. Fans had already begun waving tiny Confederate battle flags at Skynyrd shows. Rossington said the group thought it might expand on that idea, creating a giant rebel-flag backdrop, which it dramatically unveiled on British television.[71]

What is more, the use of the flag as a backdrop was not original. Gram Parsons had used it onstage a year before—and was castigated for it.[72] Black Oak Arkansas had used it in 1970, and Hank Williams Jr. had used it onstage back as far back as 1960.[73] At first the Skynyrd boys approached the flag issue as a bit of a lark, part of their bad-boy image. They knew controversy was good for publicity. However, it may have generated more controversy than they wanted—controversy that would reappear decades later. It would come back to haunt them in 2015, when renewed debate emerged surrounding the South Carolina legislature's decision to remove the flag from the state capitol.[74]

Rossington insists that it meant nothing more to the boys in the band than an homage to their southern origins, a symbol of regional pride.[75] Historian Cecil Kirk Hutson explains this as a kind of identity politics that appeals to the narcissistic instincts of people who feel a need to feel be distinct and somehow special:

> To these white southerners the confederate flag was not only a "container of the past," it was the living manifestation of their history. The Civil War had defined them as southerners. . . . Through the use of confederate memorabilia, performers reassured white southerners that they were still a unique group of people. . . . [M]any southerners still hate the thought of being seen as normal Americans. . . . [T]hey do not want to be seen as typical.[76]

The flag trope itself is quite complex, conveying multiple meanings that are worth examining. To some it means regional pride; to others it's "dog-whistle" code for "blacks not welcome." In fact, some observers, including Dr. Raphael Warnock, pastor of Dr. Martin Luther King's home church, the Ebenezer Baptist Church in Atlanta, interpret the flag as the American equivalent of a swastika—a symbol of hatred toward an entire ethnic group.[77] Rossington later said the band was simply naïve and had no idea it would be taken this way.[78]

For many the flag is a great, big middle finger pointed at the Establishment.[79] This last aspect is somewhat logical if one considers that the so-called Establishment is perceived to be based in New York City (primarily on Wall Street) and that the working-class, young males who adopt the flag as a totem are perhaps evincing their reluctance to bow to bourgeois norms. Some argue that, in this sense, the flag has become a free-floating symbol of defiance and rebellion, although this rebellion is often unfocused and misplaced—much like Marlon Brando's puerile character in *The Wild One*, who, when asked what he was rebelling against, replied, "Whattaya got?"

Some of the mainstays of Lynyrd Skynyrd's success came undone around 1975. The group borrowed $250,000 from MCA to buy out the remainder of Walden's contract, but he continued to own the rights to their publishing income, which he later sold to MCA. It was not a clean break. Walden's management contract had a stipulation that if he were to cease being involved for whatever reason, Pat Armstrong would get first option on the right to manage the group. Armstrong waived the option as a favor to Van Zant.[80] It didn't take long to recoup the money, however, as record sales continued to be brisk.

The group then borrowed a million dollars from MCA to buy out Al Kooper, primarily in order to get back some of the percentage points they should have gotten from the get-go. The raise in their royalty rate helped pay off the million-dollar advance. However, even after buying Kooper out, they hired him—as a free agent this time—to produce their third album, *Nuthin' Fancy*, which shot to number nine. It was the first to feature the new drummer Artimus Pyle. Bob Burns had gone haywire in England, experiencing delusions due to an undiagnosed case of bipolar disorder exacerbated by LSD use.[81] It would be their last album with Kooper.

During a tour, guitarist Ed King left abruptly, later citing physical abuse from Van Zant—who perhaps took his paternal role a bit too seriously—as the last straw. "One night in Lake Charles, Louisiana, he broke a lamp in a hotel room, slammed me up against a wall, and held the broken-jagged-glass lamp to my neck," King wrote in his blog. "He said he could cut my throat if he wanted to!"[82] That was the night King walked out, leaving his guitars behind. According to King's blog, Van Zant was a nice guy when sober but a mean-as-hell drunk, and he was drinking every night at this point.[83] "The Jekyll-Hyde thing [got] real old real quick and, for me, it wasn't worth the trip."[84]

As a replacement for King, the members considered hiring Barry Lee Harwood, who was born in North Carolina but raised in Jacksonville's Southside. Harwood, who also sang well and wrote good songs, was living in Atlanta at the time, working as a session musician, playing on songs by Jim Stafford, Lobo, and Melanie (Safka). He had already played Dobro and mandolin on Skynyrd's albums *Nuthin' Fancy* and *Gimme Back My Bullets*. He got the call to replace King but was already booked on a tour with Melanie. They also considered Jeff Carlisi, a fellow Westsider who would go on to massive success with 38 Special.

Skynyrd's next album would be 1976's *Gimme Back My Bullets*, helmed by famed producer Tom Dowd, who had worked with dozens of highly successful acts including the Allman Brothers Band. However, Skynyrd members were not entirely happy with Dowd's results, with Leon Wilkeson calling it "sterile."[85] Van Zant told interviewer Cameron Crowe in 1976, "We were going for a completely different sound . . . and it didn't work."[86] There were two crucial elements missing from the mix: Ed King and Al Kooper. Still, the album reached number twenty, not as high as the previous but a very respectable showing nonetheless. They followed it later in the year with a live, in-concert album, *One More from the Road* with Dowd again at the helm.

The group's golden boy appeared in the form of Missouri-born, Oklahoma-bred guitarist-singer Steve Gaines, brother of backup singer Cassie Gaines. Gaines not only played guitar in the same league as Ed King but was an incredible singer, easily in a league with Wet Willie's Jimmy Hall. Not only did he bring a load of talent and material to Lynyrd Skynyrd, he lit a fire under the band's collective ass. A new album, *Street Survivors,* was recorded in 1977, which included four Gaines numbers (two written solo and two cowritten with Van Zant). Though there was an internal revolt over Dowd's production and mixes—much of it was rerecorded at Studio One in Doraville, where the group had recorded its 1973 debut—it was getting a strong reception at radio thanks to three singles, "That Smell," "What's Your Name," and "You Got That Right," the last of which featured a duet between Van Zant and Gaines with blistering vocals by Gaines and his astounding lead work on "I Know a Little." It was the group's best album in years—maybe its best ever—and the band was back on track.

Crash Landing

On October 20, 1977, three days after the album's release, the band members boarded a fateful flight in Greenville, South Carolina, for Baton Rouge in which Van Zant, both Steve and Cassie Gaines, personal assistant Dean Kilpatrick, and both pilots were killed in a crash landing in a swamp near Gillsburg, Mississippi. The cause of the crash was put down to fuel insufficiency due to an engine malfunction that caused it to run too rich.[87] The pilots had agreed that the engine needed work but decided to put it off until arriving in Baton Rouge. This was a fatal miscalculation that all the members, including Van Zant, seemed to passively accept. They had been warned that the thirty-year-old Convair CV-240 they had leased was unsafe and that that the pilots were lacking in terms of professionalism; nonetheless they climbed aboard for the final flight of the "free bird."[88]

Drummer Artimus Pyle, a trained pilot himself, said he should have known better than to step on that plane with those pilots at that particular time: "We didn't ask questions. That's where *we* made *our* mistake," he told interviewers in 1983. "We should've been more aware of our transportation situation."[89] Six people died on that flight; twenty survived. Many of the surviving members sustained life-threatening injuries, and it took years for them to heal.

All This Self-Destruction

Van Zant had not only led his group to success beyond their wildest dreams but also down a primrose path of self-destruction. He was not the first to do so and would not be the last. By the time he decided to slow down, it may already have been too late—the course was set and could not be diverted. Drinking, drugging, and bad judgment took its toll and would continue to do so, in one way or another, for too many southern rockers.

Excess was in fact a principal element of the southern-rock mystique. It was a macho thing to out-do your cronies when it came to abusing oneself, as if it were some kind of contest. In the 1970s the drug of choice for most rock stars was cocaine. There was also a status element: if you were making enough money to afford this so-called designer drug, then you had arrived. Even their injuries didn't deter some members from doing all the cocaine they could afford.

In December, two months after the crash, Leon Wilkeson and Billy Powell barely escaped a police dragnet targeting George Edwin "Eddie" Mangum via telephone wiretaps. Wilkeson had been purchasing drugs from Mangum and distributing them to other members of the band. Mangum testified: "I can't tell you how many times Leon called me at three a.m., and said, 'We need you over here, man.' He came to my house once at three a.m. wearing a buffalo headdress with one horn up and one horn down and said, 'Let's party.' We'd just snort all night. Leon loved to snort."[90] Movie star Linda Blair, who had been hanging out with members of the band, was also caught in the dragnet along with Jacksonville musician Phil Driscoll, concert promoter Sidney Drashin, and two offspring of a state senator, Lynn and John Scarborough.[91]

Alias

After recuperating somewhat, the surviving Skynyrd members joined with guitarist-songwriter Dorman Cogburn along with former Black Bear Angel drummer-vocalist Jimmy Dougherty, this time out front, and former Skynyrd backup singer JoJo Billingsley to play on an album by a short-lived trio dubbed Alias. The trio's only album, *Contraband*, recorded in Orlando and Atlanta, was released by Mercury Records in 1979. All of the surviving Skynyrd members plus friend Barry Lee Harwood performed on it. Some fans assumed it might be a new incarnation of Lynyrd Skynyrd, but that hope proved misplaced. Even though the former Skynyrd members were looking for a new project, this wasn't it. With little support from Mercury, the album tanked.

Rossington Collins Band

According to an interview with Judy Van Zant Jenness conducted by Jaan Uhelszki, Gregg Allman approached Rossington and Collins a year after the crash about forming a new group to be called Free Bird. Allman presumably would have been lead singer and keyboardist.

However, Jenness, who was representing Rossington and Collins, decided the two weren't ready, and plans were scrapped.[92]

By late 1979, however, Rossington and Collins were ready to get back to work. Fortunately they still had a good relationship with MCA. They still had Leon Wilkeson and Billy Powell on board. Collins had nearly lost an arm in the plane crash, and his playing was still affected, so Harwood was brought in as third guitarist and singer. Drummer Artimus Pyle had broken a leg in a motorcycle accident, so he was replaced with former Running Easy drummer Derek Hess, a cohort of Harwood's from Jacksonville. The only question was who was going to front the new band. They considered using Dougherty, with whom they had worked in Alias. However, they felt any male singer would likely invite unfavorable comparisons to Van Zant, so they hit on the idea of using a female instead. The woman they chose was twenty-seven-year-old Dale Krantz from Indiana, who had been singing backup in 38 Special alongside Jacksonville native Carol Bristow.

The Rossington Collins Band (RCB) recorded its debut at El Adobe Studio in El Paso, Texas, the idea being to go someplace where there were few distractions and little to do but work.[93] The album, *Anytime, Anyplace, Anywhere,* was released on MCA in 1980 and shot to number thirteen on *Billboard*'s Top 200 Albums, propelled by the single "Don't Misunderstand Me," written and sung as a duet by Harwood and Krantz.

While on tour to support the album, Allen Collins received some devastating news: his wife, Kathy, had had a miscarriage and died of a hemorrhage. Collins was dazed by the news. He and the group somehow managed a follow-up album, 1981's *This Is the Way,* also recorded in El Paso, but it didn't perform nearly as well. Gary Rossington and Dale Krantz became a couple by 1982 and left the group. Rossington and Collins had a falling out, mostly over Krantz. Rossington felt Krantz had been spending too much time consoling Collins. Collins insisted there had been no hanky-panky.[94] Whatever the case, Rossington and Krantz departed.

Allen Collins Band

Somehow Collins managed to keep going—at least for a while. He and the remaining members of the RCB soldiered on, changing their name

The author (*left*) onstage with Allen Collins in Vidalia, Georgia, 1984.

to Horse Power. However, this name was already in use, so the group went with the Allen Collins Band. Jacksonville guitarist Randall Hall, who had been working with Jimmy Dougherty in the Younger Brothers Band at Hyde Park Liquors, was brought aboard, as was Dougherty himself. The Allen Collins Band recorded its debut album *Here, There and Back* at Studio One in Doraville, released on MCA in 1983.

Collins, however, finally came unglued, which didn't come as a surprise to anyone paying attention. To make matters worse, the group had been dropped by MCA, which had undergone a change of management; the executives who had been loyal to the Skynyrd crew were gone. During a show in Poughkeepsie, Collins threw his guitar into the audience and stalked offstage. Later that night, without telling anyone, Collins somehow got himself to the nearest airport and bought a ticket back to Jacksonville. He had two motherless daughters to tend to.

The Rossington Band

After marrying, Rossington and Krantz bought a place in Jackson Hole, Wyoming, and started a family. In 1986 they formed the Rossington Band, which included Jacksonville musicians Derek Hess (former drummer of the Rossington Collins Band as well as the Allen Collins Band), bassist Tim Lindsey (currently with Molly Hatchet), and keyboardist Gary Ross. The group recorded an album for Atlantic, *Returned to the Scene of the Crime*, which met with critical indifference. Atlantic soon dropped the act. Two years later, the band released another dud called *Love Your Man* on MCA. Things were not going well for the surviving Skynyrd members.

Johnny Van Zant

The third and youngest Van Zant brother, Johnny Roy, was fourteen when Skynyrd hit the big-time. He started off in music as a drummer. In the late 1970s he led his own band, the Austin Nickels Band (the name was a nod to the manufacturer of Wild Turkey whisky). With guidance from older brother Donnie, the group recorded demos at Phil Driscoll's Jacksonville Beach studio. Stu Fine at Polydor Records signed the group in 1979. The group, whose members included guitarists Robbie Gay and Erik Lundgren, bassist Danny Clausman, and drummer Robbie Morris, signed with manager Joe Boyland and changed its name to the Johnny Van Zant Band upon release of its 1980 album, *No More Dirty Deals*. The album was supervised by former Skynyrd producer Al Kooper and recorded in Doraville at Studio One. The Johnny Van Zant Band released two more albums with Polydor and then switched to Vancouver-based Nettwerk Records (distributed by Geffen) in 1985, whereupon the name was changed to simply Van Zant (not the same Van Zant that would consist of brothers Johnny and Donnie in the early 2000s).

Tribute Tour

By 1985, Allen Collins was trying, unsuccessfully, to re-form the Allen Collins Band, but he was in no condition. After his wife died in 1983, Collins dived into to a bottle for solace and never came out, Billy

Powell said.[95] He stayed drunk or high most of the time on whatever he could get his hands on.

Collins had accumulated a long record of driving offenses. His license had been revoked. He was always doing crazy things behind the wheel, endangering himself and others, but in 1986 he went too far, skidding his new Ford Thunderbird sideways into a culvert near his home, killing his girlfriend, Debra Jean Watts, and injuring his spine, leaving him a paraplegic. He swore he had no memory of the incident and pleaded no contest to charges of driving while intoxicated. His attorney argued that imprisoning Collins would serve no purpose since Collins's injuries had been punishment enough. Collins was sentenced to probation and community service, and ordered to use his fame to educate young people on the dangers of drinking and driving.

Even though he could no longer perform, Collins decided to put Lynyrd Skynyrd back together for a tenth-anniversary commemoration of the plane crash. Wilkeson and Powell, who had been working with Rocco Marshall's Christian-rock group, Vision, returned. Ed King would return as well, as would Artimus Pyle, who had been leading his own band, APB, which had released two low-selling albums on MCA. Rossington had some initial misgivings but decided to come on board as well; his group, Rossington, would also serve as opening act, and he would play with both. Collins chose Randall Hall, formerly of the Allen Collins Band, to fill his own spot in Skynyrd. Ronnie Van Zant's youngest brother, Johnny—easily the best singer of the Van Zant siblings—was persuaded to put his own band on hold while the tour hit the road for a string of dates that kept growing. The group even hired a horn section led by Jacksonville saxophonist Rick "Hurricane" Johnson. Backup singer Carol Bristow joined Dale Krantz Rossington onstage as the New Honkettes. However, neither Johnny Van Zant nor Gary Rossington intended to give up their own groups at this stage.

Carrying the Torch

The tribute tour went so well—and there was so much money to be made—that the group decided to reunite permanently. However, there was one big problem: not long after the crash, the members had decided to retire the name Lynyrd Skynyrd; all of them had signed an agreement saying none of them could ever use the name. That decision, however well-intentioned, later turned out to be highly inconvenient.

The 1975 corporation, Lynyrd Skynyrd Productions, was reinstated, with principals listed as Collins, Rossington, Wilkeson, and Powell. Ronnie Van Zant's widow, Judy, who was not included, would have none of it. After some legal wrangling, she agreed to waive the 1977 agreement on the provisos that she be assigned control of Ronnie's rights and share of royalties and that there would be at least three members of the "classic" lineup in the group at all times (although eventually she would waive this too). Having little choice, the band members signed the consent decree in 1988.

In 1990, Johnny Van Zant landed a solo deal with Atlantic Records and released *Brickyard Road,* which was featured on MTV and reached number 108 on *Billboard*'s Top 200 Albums. Having disbanded his group, he continued to tour as Skynyrd's front man. Van Zant's manager, Joe Boyland, and Rossington's manager, Charlie Brusco, took over as Skynyrd's comanagers, and Lynyrd Skynyrd also signed with Atlantic (both Rossington and Johnny Van Zant had already signed with the label).

The owners of the trademark "Lynyrd Skynyrd" at this time were Rossington, Collins, Judy Van Zant, Leon Wilkeson, and Billy Powell. Ed King, Artimus Pyle, Randall Hall, Johnny Van Zant, and the rest were hired guns. Collins died that year at thirty-seven from respiratory problems, and his father, Larkin Collins Sr., became executor of his estate.

The group soldiered on—basically a nostalgia act—for more than three decades, never managing a hit record other than reissues and compilations of vintage recordings. One by one members dropped out of the picture. Drummer Pyle left in a fit of pique in 1991 because, he said, the band members were doing too many drugs and not playing well. However, group members felt his playing and his behavior were becoming erratic, and they unanimously voted him out of the group.[96] Pyle re-formed APB and has been working steadily since. Guitarist Hall left in 1994 when the principals decided to convert his share of receipts to a straight salary. King, who served as the group's musical director, left in 1996 due to heart trouble that required a transplant. He moved to Nashville and got involved with a couple of unsuccessful southern-rock-revival groups before retiring from music. King died in his Nashville home in 2018. Wilkeson died in 2001 after mixing Oxy-Contin with Valium.[97] Billy Powell died in 2009 of cardiac arrest.

In 2015, original drummer Bob Burns ran his car off the road near his home in Cartersville, Georgia, hitting a tree, dying instantly. Original bassist Larry Junstrom went on to work with 38 Special for nearly four decades. Junstrom died in 2019. All in all, Lynyrd Skynyrd has had something like thirty-eight members, with Rossington remaining the sole original member still performing with the group.

Coda

It appears many of the band members bought into the bad-boy hype, fantasizing that they were indestructible. Author Mark Ribowsky explains: "Their image was intertwined with their success. . . . To be sure, the bandmates were threats to themselves and anyone around them, particularly when one of them turned the key in a car." Like rubberneckers ogling an auto accident, part of the public's fascination might have been in watching band members destroy themselves or seeing just how far they could push their luck. They even turned a near-fatal auto accident—caused by guitarist Gary Rossington's own negligence—into a hit song ("That Smell").

Anyone who really knew these guys could predict that this drama wasn't going to end well; Ronnie Van Zant himself began having premonitions of an early demise. He'd created a Frankenstein monster, or rather several of them, and he knew it: "I wrote ['That Smell'] when Gary had his car accident," Van Zant told journalist Jim Farber in 1977, months before the band's fateful plane crash. "Allen and Billy were also in car accidents, all in the space of six months. I had a creepy feeling things were going against us," he lamented.[98] Jacksonville rockers Molly Hatchet took that same reckless, bad-boy shtick a step further. It's no wonder so many southern rockers died at relatively young ages.

Thirty-one years after the reunion, Lynyrd Skynyrd announced its final tour in 2018. Although Rossington has said the group will continue recording new material, it's not difficult to foresee how this plan will play out, as the public has demonstrated—justifiably or not—its indifference to Skynyrd's post–Ronnie Van Zant recordings.[99]

The band could not get out from under Van Zant's shadow even if it wanted to. Even if its albums had proven to be excellent, which some may be, few fans seem to care enough to even listen to the new songs. Much like the Beach Boys—another group with only one member left—the group continues to crank out blasts from the past, and the public keeps paying to join in on the nostalgia. And that's all it really wants. Head honcho Gary Rossington has had plenty of time to reflect on and confront this issue and seems to have made his peace with it. After all, the money is still rolling in, and everyone has families to support.

Rossington admits that his health is not good and his days with the band are numbered. If he had to drop out, would the band continue without him? Front man Johnny Van Zant told interviewer Dave Everley, "I don't think any of us would want to do that." Rickey Medlocke echoed Van Zant's protestations: "We wouldn't do that, and I wouldn't want to do that," he told Everley. However, Rossington himself said he wouldn't mind if they did. He told Everley it would be fine with him as long as "they wanted to do it and the management thought it would be a good idea. It would be weird, though, because none of the original guys would be in it."[100] There is a possibility the group will do a residency in Las Vegas.[101]

Blackfoot

Southern Metal

BLACKFOOT'S HISTORY IS SO COMPLEX and convoluted one almost needs a worksheet to follow it. It is also so intertwined with Lynyrd Skynyrd's that the group at times could have almost been considered a Skynyrd adjunct. Yet Blackfoot has made powerful music of its own, and its lead singer, Rickey Medlocke, a native of Jacksonville, is one of the most talented singers to emerge from the city. He is also an accomplished guitarist and drummer.

Medlocke was born (without the final "e") in Jacksonville in 1950 and raised in the city's working-class Westside area of Woodstock. He claims Native ancestry on his father's side. His mother was barely sixteen and could not raise him alone, so he was adopted by his maternal grandparents, Ruby and Paul Medlock. Paul, known as "Shorty," was a bluegrass musician from Buford, Georgia, who moved to Florida in the 1940s, later landing a gig in the house band on Toby Dowdy's *Country Frolics*, a Saturday-evening television show on WMBR (Channel 4). The elder Medlock played blues-inflected country on guitar and banjo and taught his grandson to play several instruments at an early age including banjo, guitar, mandolin, and drums. Shorty brought the young boy to the television show, where Rickey became a semi-regular. One of his babysitters, a musical friend of Shorty's who lived a few blocks away, was promoter Mae Axton, putative cowriter of "Heartbreak Hotel"

Blackfoot with Shorty Medlock, ca. 1979. *Left to right*: Greg T. Walker, Charlie Hargrett, Paul "Shorty" Medlock, Rickey Medlocke, Jakson Spires. Photo by Bo Radar. Courtesy of *Florida Times-Union*.

and mother of singer-songwriter Hoyt Axton. In August 1956 she gave Shorty and his family tickets to see Elvis Presley at the Florida Theatre, where Rickey decided he wanted to be singer (echoing the experience Gram Parsons had had at a Presley concert in Waycross the night before). By eight Rickey was playing drums with Shorty's band. Medlocke had severe lung problems and at about ten underwent an operation that removed part of his left lung.[1]

Medlocke played in a series of teen bands such as the Candy Apples, the Sunday Funnies, and the Miracle Sounds. He had known aspiring musicians Greg T. Walker and Jack "Jakson" Spires since elementary school; they had even formed a short-lived group, the Rocking Aces. After graduating from Paxon High (where J. R. Cobb and Robert Nix of the Classics and the Atlanta Rhythm Section had graduated), Medlocke and Walker began forming a rock band called Fresh Garbage, named after a 1968 hit by California psychedelic-rockers Spirit. Medlocke played drums and sang lead; Walker played bass. Spires was playing drums with a group called Tangerine.

Not long after arriving in Jacksonville with his family from Scranton, keyboardist Ron Sciabarasi took to hanging out at downtown Jacksonville's Comic Book Club, where he sat in with One Percent, the group who became Lynyrd Skynyrd. One Percent already had a keyboard player at this point, David Knight, so singer Ronnie Van Zant recommended Sciabarasi to Medlocke and Walker. Sciabarasi recommended guitarist Charlie Hargrett, who had moved to Jacksonville in 1963 with his family from New York. Fresh Garbage snagged a gig as house band at the Comic Book Club, where the Bitter Ind, the Allman Joys, and One Percent had all served residencies. Sciabarasi, who had a demanding day job, was coming in late and leaving early, so the other members began looking for a keyboardist of a similar caliber.[2] They decided on Jacksonville native DeWitt Gibbs, another former Paxon High student who happened to be working in Gainesville at Dub's Steer Room, at this point a topless bar, with Tangerine. That group included Spires, along with Jacksonville guitarist Jerry Zambito and, briefly, Gainesville bassist Mark Pinske.[3] After contacting Gibbs, the two groups decided to merge. Pinske and Zambito were out, Spires assumed drum duties, and Medlocke was put out front as lead singer. In September 1969 the revamped, five-piece lineup, dubbed Hammer, took over Tangerine's gig at Dub's.[4]

A Gainesville woman, Nancy O'Connor, who was then living in New York and working in the music industry, happened to be home for the holidays and saw Hammer at Dub's on New Year's Eve. After returning to New York, she raved about the band to her bosses at Hollybrook Records in the Brill Building, who sent the group a letter in care of Dub's, encouraging the band to submit some demos. Hammer went into Jacksonville's Sound Lab Studio, cut five songs, and sent the tapes up. The label's response seemed encouraging enough to convince the guys to drive up to Manhattan. In March 1970 they lit out for the Big Apple, where five musicians and a roadie crashed on the floor of O'Connor's East Village apartment.[5]

One thing that can be noted about this group, aside from its obsessive work ethic—shared by many Jacksonville groups—is the fact that its members were willing to relocate anywhere opportunity presented itself, a trait they shared with members of the Second Coming and the Allman Brothers Band. Additionally, these fellows weren't afraid of roughing it—they would sleep on floors, in vans, six to a motel room. Discovering that there was already a group called Hammer, they changed their name to Blackfoot, based on the fact that three members, Medlocke, Walker, and Spires, claimed Native—though not specifically Blackfoot—descent.

O'Connor had a friend in the Brill Building, Ira Sokoloff, who ran an ad agency across the hall. He took a liking to the group and tried to help them, serving as a sort of unofficial manager. The band's van had been broken into, and the members had lost about half their equipment, so Sokoloff lent them money to buy replacement gear. After O'Connor lost her lease, Sokoloff put them up in his parents' basement in New Jersey, but things got tense after two members of the group were arrested for carrying firearms in their van on a trip to the shore with Sokoloff's fifteen-year-old sister in tow (it's legal to carry firearms in your vehicle in Florida but not in New Jersey). Later they served a residency at the Royal Hotel in Randolph, then moving to a house near Princeton shared with a band called Yiege. There was not a lot of decent-paying club work to be had, and the situation was getting dire. By the summer of 1971, the members, frustrated with the group's lack of progress—as well as with each other—decided to call it quits. This was only the first of many breakups.

Fishing for something to do, Medlocke called his Westside pal Allen Collins of Lynyrd Skynyrd. Having once served briefly as the group's light man, he thought Skynyrd might put him to work as a roadie or something—anything. He got lucky. Skynyrd had signed with Macon-based manager Alan Walden, who arranged for the group to cut some demos at Muscle Shoals. Original Skynyrd drummer Bob Burns, who had already played on an early set of sessions recorded in Muscle Shoals in June, had abruptly left the group to move in with his parents near Orlando. Collins advised Medlocke that the group needed a drummer ASAP since it was getting ready to go to Muscle Shoals to record again. Medlocke made a quick follow-up call to Skynyrd leader Ronnie Van Zant, who sent him money for a plane ticket.[6] Medlocke spent a few days brushing up on his drum technique and joined the band in its rehearsal house in the Mandarin section of Jacksonville. Walker returned to Jacksonville as well.

For the second set of Skynyrd sessions, Medlocke contributed five Blackfoot songs, four of which had already been cowritten with Spires, and a fifth, "Wino," that been cowritten with former Blackfoot bassist

Greg Walker with later contributions from Van Zant and Allen Collins. Bassist Larry Junstrom played on several songs on these first sessions, but by the second trip in October found himself left behind in Jacksonville, replaced by Walker. Hence by this point Skynyrd had incorporated half of Blackfoot, including its front man and some of its material.[7]

Walker only stayed with Skynyrd for seven months. Walker told interviewer Michael Buffalo Smith, "I was really missing Blackfoot and told Medlocke I wanted to get [Spires] and [Hargrett] back together and resume where we left off."[8] Medlocke decided to go with Walker to re-form the group. "I thought Blackfoot had more talent," Walker said.[9] Skynyrd replaced Walker with Westsider Leon Wilkeson on bass, and drummer Bob Burns returned from his self-imposed exile.

Spires soon joined up with Walker and Medlocke, keyboardist De-Witt Gibbs from Hammer was readded, but Charlie Hargrett, who had decided to stay in New Jersey, was replaced by guitarist Bobby McDowell. However, this effort to revive Blackfoot did not last long, as Medlocke had second thoughts and decided to return to Skynyrd. Since Bob Burns, too, had returned, Skynyrd used both drummers for a while.[10]

The 1972 reunion of Blackfoot, sans Medlocke, was renamed Raintree. The group spent a few months in Atlanta recording demos, trying to land a recording contract. Gibbs and McDowell gave up and went back to Florida. Walker and Spires went back to Gainesville for few weeks, whereupon Walker bolted for New York, where he landed a gig with a group called Cross Country, which included three former members of the Tokens, whom he had met in the Brill Building two years earlier.[11]

Hargrett moved to North Carolina, where he worked with a bar band called Blackberry Hill. That group found itself in need of a drummer, so Hargrett put in a call to Spires. Later Medlocke, having left Skynyrd again, joined the group. When Blackberry Hill's bassist got sick in the summer of 1973, Walker left Cross Country to rejoin his former cohorts, recompleting the classic Blackfoot lineup.[12] The members decided to return to New Jersey, where they signed with booking agent/manager Lou Manganiello.

After a false start in Muscle Shoals, Lynyrd Skynyrd landed a deal with MCA and started breaking big. Back in Muscle Shoals, producer

Jimmy Johnson realized that the fact that Medlocke and Walker had played in Skynyrd might be worth something. Johnson sent word through Ed King, who was doing some overdubbing on Skynyrd's early recordings, for Medlocke to give him a ring. He did. Johnson and production partner David Hood decided it might be worthwhile to work with these guys during the studio's "down time" (that is, between paying sessions) and then shop the results around to labels.[13] By this point Medlocke and Spires had become the group's chief songwriters. Blackfoot spent a month in Muscle Shoals recording an album that was picked up by Island Records (the Muscle Shoals crew knew Island owner Chris Blackwell because three of them had worked with British group Traffic, who was signed to Island). The first Blackfoot album, *No Reservations,* was released in 1975 to no great acclaim. The group returned to Gainesville. Johnson and Hood were able to get Epic Records interested in a follow-up album, also recorded at Muscle Shoals. *Flyin' High* was released in 1976, also to no great acclaim. Epic declined to exercise its option for another album in 1977.

The group decided new management might be in order. Blackfoot had opened shows for Black Oak Arkansas (BOA), so they decided to get in touch with BOA's manager, Butch Stone, who was not taking on any new clients. However, Ruby Starr, who had been a background singer with BOA, was striking out on her own and needed musicians. She hired Blackfoot as her band, an arrangement that lasted only three or four months.

Blackfoot again struck out on its own in 1978, opening for Brownsville Station, who was signed to Atlantic subsidiary Big Tree Records. One of Brownsville's roadies alerted manager Al Nalli, owner of Nalli's Music store in Ann Arbor, Michigan, of Blackfoot's potential. Coincidentally or not, Nalli's sister, Reen Nalli, had gone to work at Big Tree as a receptionist in 1971 and worked her way up to vice president.

With Lynyrd Skynyrd's tragic demise in October 1977, suddenly there was a hole in the market that Jacksonville groups like Molly Hatchet, 38 Special, and Blackfoot were uniquely positioned to fill. Al Nalli figured—correctly—that Blackfoot had hit potential and signed the group to management and production deals. Blackfoot cut its breakthrough album, *Blackfoot Strikes,* in the basement studio of Nalli's music store with Brownsville drummer Henry Weck engineering. Released in 1979 on Atco, which had subsumed Big Tree, *Strikes*

RICK MEDLOCKE   JAKSON SPIRES   CHARLIE HARGRETT   GREG T. WALKER

BLACKFOOT

ATCO

DMA
DIVERSIFIED MANAGEMENT AGENCY

Blackfoot publicity photo, Atco Records.

did well, thanks to FM-radio-friendly songs like "Train, Train" (written by Shorty Medlock, who also played harmonica on the intro) and "Highway Song," which sounded like a cross between Marshall Tucker and Lynyrd Skynyrd with its "Free Bird"–style out-choruses. The latter charted at number thirty-four on *Billboard*'s Hot 100 singles chart. It seemed Blackfoot had finally struck the right formula, the album eventually achieving coveted "platinum" status (sales of one million units). The group snagged a tour opening for the Who and found new and receptive audiences.

Blackfoot's next record, 1980's *Tomcattin'*, which like its predecessor was recorded in Nalli's basement studio, didn't do as well, possibly due to a dearth of radio-friendly singles. The dreaded "sophomore slump" reared its ugly head. The band lost momentum at a crucial moment. It seems likely that Blackfoot had made a decision to forsake radio in favor of a heavier, more metal-ish sound that appealed largely to young males. Although Skynyrd, too, evinced a good deal of heaviness, that group was very careful to keep radio—and female listeners—in the loop: despite its macho pose, Skynyrd made a point of whipping up a half dozen or so lighter, hookier numbers that could command general audience acceptance. This capability seemed to elude Blackfoot—or perhaps its members didn't care enough about it at this point.

After releasing *Marauder* in 1981 and a live album in 1982, Atco started demanding more hit singles. What is more, the southern-rock genre was starting to fade with the introduction of Warner-Amex's twenty-four-hour cable-TV music channel, Music Television. The entire music landscape had abruptly shifted: suddenly, thanks to music video, how a band looked became as much if not more important than its sound. The sound of pop also changed, with keyboards and synthesizers taking a more prominent role. Changes were in order if the band wanted to remain relevant. An effort was made to update Blackfoot's sound and look to appeal to the new MTV audience. Former Uriah Heep keyboardist Ken Hensley was brought aboard along with some synthesizers, despite objections from some band members, who felt the band was in danger of losing its identity.[14] The band's look, too, was deemed lacking, especially that of guitarist Hargrett, whose hair was disappearing as fast as the group's hits.

In 1983, the group recorded the album *Siogo*, which it told label execs was a Native word for "togetherness." Actually it stood for "suck it or get out," a misogynist message directed at groupies. The album was deemed unacceptable by the label and sent back for retooling. *Siogo* was by many accounts neither fish nor fowl, deemed too soft by some die-hard fans but not pop-oriented enough to attract many new ones. Reviewer Brian Rickman writes: "Gone were the southern-rock throwbacks. Instead, listeners were met with stuff that sounded as if it might be more comfortable on a Bon Jovi record."[15] Sales were disappointing.

Atco was owned by Warner Communications, a public corporation with hungry investors wanting quick returns. It seems the unrelenting pressure from label executives—one of whom was manager Al Nalli's sister—for instant hits created two factions in the group and drove a wedge between them: Medlocke and Nalli on one hand and the remaining members on the other. Medlocke appeared determined to stay with a major label and do its bidding while the others wanted to stay true to their no-frills, hard-rock roots. The most likely way of accomplishing this latter objective would have been to find a smaller, independent, or European label, where they would be allowed more creative control and to continue to develop a hard-core cult following through relentless touring. Obviously Nalli and Medlocke deemed it more desirable to stay the course at Atco. This turned out to be a desperate, last-ditch effort that the others predicted would inevitably fail. "That was the kiss of death," Walker said.[16]

Hargrett, sick of the constant carping about his look, bowed out. Hensley filled in, doubling on guitar as well as his usual keyboards. Blackfoot's next album, *Vertical Smiles*, was recorded in Atlanta with British producer Eddie Offord, who had worked with Atlantic act Yes. Despite the sometimes embarrassing concessions to commerciality, the album failed to take off. Hensley left in late 1984 in the midst of a tour, citing exhaustion; with little time to prepare, guitarist-vocalist Bobby Barth of Axe, another of Nalli's acts, stepped in. Barth, who later married Spires's first wife, Nancy, injected some new blood into Blackfoot, but it was too little too late. The hits weren't happening, despite the group's halfhearted efforts at revamping its sound. In the process of trying to gain new, younger fans, Blackfoot was losing many of its older fans, who were disappointed with the new sound and style. Gigs started drying up.

In February 1986, the band threw in the towel, dissolving its Michigan-based corporation Blackfoot Enterprises. Medlocke later stated to an interviewer that he purchased the exclusive rights from the other members to use the name at that time.[17] Walker, however, remembers the occasion differently: "We went our separate ways and agreed that none of us would ever use the name unless it was all of the original members [together]. We shook hands on it," he said.[18]

With one more album remaining on the Atco contract, Medlocke assembled a new group with former members of Epic Records' funk-rockers Mother's Finest to release an album under the name Rick Medlocke & Blackfoot. This was one of the few so-called southern-rock groups to incorporate black musicians. Medlocke at this stage was apparently serious enough about scoring a hit that he was willing to bring in outside hit-writers like Russ Ballard—still to no avail. With one of the greatest voices in rock, Medlocke could not seem to get his hands on the right material. Possibly the label had given up on the act and cut back on promotion, or perhaps the band's time in the limelight had expired, or perhaps it was simply a case of bad luck. Atco declined to offer a new contract.

Medlocke carried on recording for a series of smaller labels with a succession of new bands he called Blackfoot. Nothing seemed to click. Al Nalli released the album *Medicine Man* on his own Nalli Records in 1990. *After the Reign*, with yet another new lineup, was released on Wildcat Records in 1994, produced by Medlocke himself with only his face featured on the cover. It was greeted by fans as a return to form, but unfortunately there weren't enough of them to keep the band going. Rhino Records released a best-of compilation that year also. By 1996 there was another new lineup, but it was pretty much all over for Rickey Medlocke & Blackfoot.

About this time Gary Rossington of Lynyrd Skynyrd called. That group was looking to replace departing guitarist Mike Estes, who had worked with Skynyrd from 1993 to 1996 (coincidentally, Estes would later replace Bobby Barth in Blackfoot). Medlocke also had the distinct advantage of being an early alumnus of Skynyrd (1971 through 1972), which may have counted for something with regard to Judy Van Zant's putative "rule of three." She demanded that the group have at least three recognizable members from Skynyrd's classic lineup, whatever that meant. In any case, Medlocke got busy learning the deceased Allen Collins's guitar parts and promised Rossington he'd stay with the group to the end. True to his word, he's been with Skynyrd more than twenty-three year as of this writing.

In 2000, Medlocke tried his hand at an acting career. His *IMDb* biography states, "In 2000 Rickey saw the new millennium as time for some new challenges and decided that he wanted to pursue the acting career he's always dreamed of." According to the bio, Medlocke had done some acting in high-school musical productions. He was offered a role in the 2001 CBS police series *Nash Bridges*. In 2002 director William Shatner cast him in a feature film, *Groom Lake,* and he also appeared in two feature films in 2006.[19]

Three years after Blackfoot's dissolution, Spires and Hargrett formed the Dixie All-Stars with former Molly Hatchet guitarist Dave Hlubek. Hargrett, however, left to form Black Molly with former Hatchet bassist Banner Thomas. He was replaced by Jay Johnson, a former member of the Rossington Band and son of Muscle Shoals Sound founder Jimmy Johnson. This lasted until Walker, Spires, and Hargrett decided to try resurrecting Blackfoot. In 2004, the three contacted Medlocke to see what he thought of the idea. Medlocke declined the offer to rejoin but told Hargrett he didn't have any objections to the others pursuing the project without him.[20]

Walker discovered that the trademark "Blackfoot" had never been registered with the U.S. Patent Office, so he hired a lawyer to take care of it. This set off a legal battle between Walker and Medlocke over who owned the rights to the name. Medlocke, too, registered the name, and the case went to federal court, where a judge ruled in Medlocke's favor. Despite this, Medlocke agreed to license the use of the name to Walker and the others for a period of seven years.

The three original members needed a singer and rhythm guitarist to replace Medlocke, who by any criteria would be difficult to replace. They contacted former Axe guitarist-vocalist Bobby Barth, who had come into the band for a couple of years in the mid-1980s, to take the spot. However, before the new edition really got off the ground, disaster struck: Spires suffered a sudden brain aneurysm and died in 2005. His replacement was Christoph Ullmann from Austria. Barth was then sidelined by neck surgery and replaced by Jay Johnson, who had been in the Dixie All-Stars alongside Walker and Spires. Barth returned in 2007, and Johnson was phased out. This was a strong lineup even though Barth was not in Medlocke's league as a singer. With original members Walker and Hargrett, Blackfoot undertook extensive touring in Europe, where they were welcomed with open arms by the heavy-metal crowd. Even without hits there was still money to be made, and it beat sitting around the house, Walker said.[21] Barth left again in 2010 and was replaced by former Lynyrd Skynyrd guitarist-vocalist Mike Estes, whom Medlocke had replaced in Skynyrd in 1996. Hargrett left shortly after Barth did. By 2011, Walker was the only remaining original member.

Medlocke opted not to renew the license. In 2015, Walker, Hargrett, Barth, and Ullman regrouped as Warrior's Pride and played a couple of cruise tours. By 2017, Barth and Hargrett were gone. Walker continued with a new lineup, playing local bars in and around Gainesville.

Even though he was making good money touring with Skynyrd, Medlocke and partner Al Nalli had plans to use the name for a *new* version of Blackfoot, which Medlocke would assemble, mentor, and produce. "I hand-picked four guys over a period of three or four years," Medlocke told an interviewer. "I took them in the studio and produced a new record on them . . . co-wrote half the songs and did some guitar work on it."[22] The "new Blackfoot," unveiled in 2015, signed with Loud and Proud Records, an independent label run by Tom Lipsky, former owner of Raleigh-based CMC International Records (Loud and Proud happens to be the same label Skynyrd appears on). "There is a brand-new generation of younger guys under the name 'Blackfoot,'" Medlocke adds.[23] This is not necessarily a good thing, one reviewer said: "It might be forgivable if the band were any good. They're awful. . . . For me, this is a shame. The original Blackfoot really has a legacy that should be celebrated. . . . Blackfoot gave us some good stuff. The band has long-since been dead—but this is Rickey Medlocke putting the headstone on the grave."[24]

Altogether there have been approximately forty musicians associated with the name Blackfoot. Hargrett lives in Hawthorne, outside Gainesville, where he performs occasionally with local bands. Bobby Barth spent some time in New Orleans, where he operated a recording studio and record label and led his own blues-rock band, the Louisiana Hoodoo Krewe. He now lives near Branford, Florida, and has recently released a new Axe album on UK label Escape Music. Walker, too, lives near Branford, on land that has belonged to his family for generations. He is recording an album with his new project, Two-Wolf, which performs on the Rock Legends Cruise. Medlocke is working with Skynyrd on the last leg of the band's two-year-long farewell tour.

7

38 Special

Holding on Loosely

DISCUSSIONS ABOUT JACKSONVILLE and southern rock usually center on Lynyrd Skynyrd or the Allman Brothers Band, as these groups have acquired an almost-legendary cachet. But 38 Special has had more hit singles than both acts combined. From 1980 to 1991, 38 scored fifteen hits in *Billboard*'s Hot 100 singles chart, including two in the top ten.

Singer Donnie Van Zant, younger brother of Lynyrd Skynyrd singer Ronnie Van Zant, had been involved in music-making nearly as long as his elder sibling. Sons of a truck-driving man, they and their three siblings lived in a modest home at the corner of Woodcrest Avenue and Mull Street. The house is now a designated historical site in a blue-collar Westside neighborhood that was nowhere near as rough as Ronnie Van Zant liked to paint it—he called it "Shantytown," but there are no shanties (perhaps he was being metaphorical).

In 1965 Donnie, then thirteen, started his first band, the Other Side. He later formed Sons of Satan with Steve Brookins on drums and guitarists Del Sumner and Ronnie Lee. All the members lived in the Hillcrest subdivision west of Cassatt Avenue, in what was then an unincorporated area between the city and the outlying Cecil Field naval air base. Van Zant's mother, Marion, nicknamed "Sister," objected to the band's name, so it was changed to Sons of Satin, later to Standard Productions.

The group's equipment trailer was parked outside Brookins's house one night. A fourteen-year-old Forrest High student named Don Barnes happened by. Barnes recollects: "I rode my bike over to where they had a trailer with their gear in it. I broke into the thing, and I got caught with my hand in the trailer trying to get a guitar out of it. They came running out and called the police. . . . Donnie told me years later he kind of felt sorry for me."[1]

Richard Donald Barnes came from a musical background; his father was music director at a local Baptist church, so Barnes had heard and sang all the old hymns. He'd even had piano lessons as a child. Barnes went to Forrest High with Allen Collins and Leon Wilkeson and would pedal over to Collins's house nearby and trade guitar licks (the Van Zants and most of the members of Skynyrd, however, lived on the northeast side of the Cedar River, which was in the Lee High School district). Like most of the Westside players, Barnes and Collins were acolytes of Eric Clapton, especially his work with Cream. "We all wanted to be Clapton," Barnes told an interviewer.[2]

Barnes sometimes opines in interviews why so many successful groups emerged from Jacksonville. A theme he often returns to is the fierce competition, borne from the sheer number of local groups vying for attention. Barnes told an interviewer, "If you don't make your thing [that is, career] number one, somebody's gonna come along . . . and walk right over you."[3] Although many Florida cities had thriving teen-band scenes, Jacksonville's was huge, most likely because of the large number of venues in which they could perform, but obviously there was also a big demand. To give an example of how many bands there were in the late 1960s, David Griffin, manager of Marvin Kay's Music Center, organized a Jaycees-sponsored "Battle of the Bands" that featured no fewer than twenty-one groups performing in the parking lot of Regency Square Mall from 10:30 a.m. to 3:45 p.m.[4]

No fewer than six of these groups contained members who would go on to score major-label deals. These included Rickey Medlocke's group the Miracle Sounds, Donnie Van Zant's Sons of Satan, Jeff Carlisi's Doomsday Refreshment Committee, and Don Barnes's Camelots (Medlocke would go on to success with Blackfoot; Barnes, Van Zant, and Carlisi with 38 Special). From Gainesville came Tom Petty's group,

10:30	CELLOPHANE FLOWER	REX CREEKMUR
10:45	THE MIRGLE SOUNDS	RICKEY MEDLOCK
11:00	MULTIPLE SOUNDS INC.	PHILLIP CHAPSE
11:15	SUNS OF SATAN	DONNIE VAN ZANT
11:30	SOUND MUTATION	STEVE MOODY
11:45	THE NATURAL'S	WAYNE LOSCA
12:00	DOOMSDAY REFRESHMENT COMM.	ROBERT CORCORAN
12:15	THE INVICTAS	RONNIE EDENFIELD
12:30	UNKNOWN	WILLIAM GILSDORF
12:45	THE DISTORTIONS	MICHAEL KNEBEL
1:00	THE AGENTS	NORMAN PAGANO
1:15	INVASIONS OF PSYCHEDELIC SOUNDS	RICK EVELT
1:30	THE CAMELOTS	JOHN ROBBINS
1:45	THE EPICS	DON BAKER
2:00	THE MONARCHS	GLENN JACKSON
2:15	THE CRYPTS	JERRY HAMPTON
2:45	OUR GANG	RUSSELL GILBERT
3:00	WE THE PEOPLE	DENNIS CONLIN
3:15	THE BARONS	RICK POLAND
3:30	THE CRESCENDOS	DENNIS OTT
3:45	BLU-VISIONS IN-TYME	SPIKE LOUDERMILK
8:30	THE TEN FINALISTS BEGIN	

Jacksonville Jaycees–sponsored "Battle of the Bands," date unknown.

the Epics, and from Orlando, Tommy Talton's We the People. Lynyrd Skynyrd was scheduled to perform but opted for a paying gig instead.[5] Barnes's band, the Camelots, won the prize, a four-hundred-dollar recording session at Charles Fuller Productions in Tampa.[6]

Jeff Carlisi, a navy brat from Boston, was living in the nearby Cedar Hills subdivision, the same area where navy brats Leon Wilkeson, Billy Powell, and Kevin Elson also lived. Carlisi, however, did not attend Forrest High; he went to St. Johns Country Day School in nearby Orange Park (Clay County). Carlisi's parents bought him his first guitar, a Gibson Melody Maker, at thirteen; he soon joined his first group, the Summer Sons, playing rhythm. He would, like Barnes, pedal his bike to Allen Collins's house to trade licks.

Inspired by the success of the Allman Brothers Band, Carlisi and Van Zant joined forces in 1969 to form Sweet Rooster, which included Kevin Elson on rhythm guitar and keyboards, former Standard Productions bassist Ken Lyons, and drummer Bill Pelkey. Three members of this group—Van Zant, Carlisi, and Lyons—would wind up in 38 Special five years later.

Elson played keyboards with Donnie Van Zant's next group, Alice Marr, and with another local group called Running Easy alongside guitarist Randall Hall (who would later join the Allen Collins Band and take Collins's place in Lynyrd Skynyrd). Elson played keyboards on some of Lynyrd Skynyrd's early recordings in Muscle Shoals. In 1973 he went to work for Skynyrd as a roadie and soon became the group's sound mixer. He stayed with the band and unofficially coproduced its last album, *Street Survivors*, but didn't get a credit. Elson was in the plane with the members of Lynyrd Skynyrd when it went down. After recuperating he went with 38 Special as front-of-house mixer. From 38 he jumped to Journey and became the band's studio producer as well. Elson produced or coproduced five albums for Journey. This led to a career producing albums for Europe, Mr. Big, Night Ranger, Loud and Clear, Strangeways, Shooting Star, and others. He also produced Johnny Van Zant's second album, *Round Two*, in 1981.[7] Elson has also engineered and mixed studio tracks for the Beach Boys and Aerosmith. He returned to doing mostly live sound and helmed the boards for Aerosmith, Michael Jackson, Don Henley, Van Morrison, Carole King,

Sweet Rooster, ca. 1970. *Left to right*: Jeff Carlisi, Ken Lyons, Bill Pelkey, Donnie Van Zant, Kevin Elson. Courtesy of Jeff Carlisi.

Foreigner, Bush, Jewel, Madonna, and Kelly Clarkson. Elson recently produced a reunion album for the original members of the rock band Mr. Big. He lives in St. Augustine.

Carlisi, having graduated from high school in 1970, left Sweet Rooster to attend Georgia Tech in Atlanta, where he studied architectural engineering. Sweet Rooster broke up, so Van Zant formed Alice Marr, adding Don Barnes on guitar and vocals; he and Barnes traded vocal duties. Alice Marr also included bassist Larry Steele (author of *As I Recall, 1964–1987: Jacksonville's Place in American Rock History*; now deceased), and drummer Bill Pelkey, formerly of Sweet Rooster. Rounding out the roster was keyboardist Billy Powell, who would only stay briefly, preferring to work as a roadie for Skynyrd. Van Zant had actually been considering leaving the music business to get a more secure career at a Jacksonville-based railroad but was encouraged to stay the course by his elder brother, Ronnie, whose band had recently signed with Al Kooper's MCA-distributed Sounds of the South label in Atlanta.

Carlisi returned to Jacksonville in 1974 and within weeks found himself rejoining Donnie Van Zant in the newly formed 38 Special, which at that point included Van Zant, Barnes, Steele, and Brookins, the latter having been with Donnie Van Zant since the Sons of Satan. A second drummer, Jack Grondin, a Jacksonville University student from New Jersey, was added. Steele, thinking Carlisi was a spoiled preppie, decided he did not want to be in the band with him and pulled out.[8] He was replaced by Ken Lyons, who had been in Sweet Rooster. The group's debut was in fall 1974 at a large club in Gainesville called the Granfalloon.

In June, Lynyrd Skynyrd scored a huge hit with "Sweet Home, Alabama." Skynyrd singer Ronnie Van Zant promised to share his newfound connections with his younger brother's band. As Don Barnes told Larry Steele, "Ronnie's behind us a hundred percent and he's going to do everything he can to help us out, once he thinks we're ready." True to his word, Ronnie Van Zant would do a lot for the guys in 38, starting with hooking them up with his agency, Paragon, co-owned by Phil Walden and Alex Hodges, in Macon. Van Zant also hooked them up with Alan Walden's former partner, Pat Armstrong, who had brought Skynyrd to Walden. However, by this point Armstrong had been pushed out of the group's management by Walden. Armstrong passed on 38 because he felt the group wasn't ready. He decided 38 lacked the hit songs that would break an artist's career—and he was proved correct.

Paragon put 38 through the wringer, playing every honky-tonk and dive from Miami to St. Louis and beyond. Barnes told interviewer Brian Rademacher:

> Ronnie asked [Paragon agent] Terry [Rhodes] to book our band, but he told him, "I don't want them to have the easy road; they have to do it the way we did it. They have to starve. Put them in the worst places, the farthest-away places, so they pay their dues." We slept in the back of a dirty van and took the hard road; we always thought, "Why did he do this to us?" But he knew struggling and starving will create more of a bond; if you have it too easy, you can walk away.

The selection of the name *38 Special* has much to do with typical southern, working-class males' fascination with firearms. The Smith & Wesson .38 Special pistol was mostly used by police departments. Historian Cecil Kirk Hutson writes: "Southern groups such as Black Oak Arkansas, Lynyrd Skynyrd, the Outlaws, the Marshall Tucker Band, 38 Special and Molly Hatchet routinely displayed firearms because they and their record companies understood working-class southern males identified with these items. . . . Two of [38 Special's] most popular albums, *Special Forces* and *Wild-Eyed Southern Boys* stressed guns. In the latter the rough- and cocky-looking band members are standing underneath a neon light shaped like a pistol." These bands recognized that this pistol-wielding, tough-guy posturing, forged largely by Lynyrd Skynyrd, was an important part of the southern-rock mystique and a fantasy their fans would likely gobble up.[9]

Sometime during 1976, after Ed King bolted Lynyrd Skynyrd, Jeff Carlisi had an opportunity to work with Ronnie Van Zant. Skynyrd had bought an old cinderblock building in a run-down (now gentrified) area on Riverside Avenue. When the sandwich shop next door went out of business, Skynyrd bought that too and turned it into a small recording studio. The guys from 38 used the building as well. One night after a rehearsal, Ronnie Van Zant asked Carlisi to stay and help him with a song he was working on, "Four Walls of Raiford," a gospel-tinged number unlike anything Skynyrd had ever done, with

Hell House, ca. 1975. *Back row, left to right*: Billy Powell, Ronnie Van Zant, Gary Rossington, Jeff Carlisi. *Front row, left to right*: Allen Collins, Leon Wilkeson, Artimus Pyle. Courtesy of Jeff Carlisi.

just Van Zant on vocals and Carlisi on Dobro. However, "Four Walls" wasn't released until 1987. Carlisi had also begun spending some time at Hell House with Skynyrd; it's possible the band had been considering adding him to the lineup to replace Ed King. Carlisi would have been a logical choice. The group had already considered adding him back in 1970. Former Skynyrd guitarist Ed King wrote that "[Carlisi] might have been in Skynyrd had he not decided to [go to Atlanta to] get his degree in architecture."[10]

Carlisi stayed with 38 Special, however. During a gig in Memphis, the group recorded its first demo at Sun Studio with Knox Phillips, son of owner Sam Phillips. The recordings were, by Barnes's account, not very impressive.[11]

Skynyrd's success would help 38 Special immensely. Not long after striking it big with "Sweet Home," Skynyrd ditched Alan Walden and replaced him with the Who's manager, Peter Rudge (Skynyrd had done a tour opening for the Who). In 1975, at Ronnie Van Zant's behest, Rudge took 38 Special under his wing. Rudge got 38 onto tours opening for big-name acts such as Peter Frampton, Foghat, and Kiss. Thirty-Eight even opened for Skynyrd a couple of times. Rudge took 38's demos to executives at A&M and Arista Records, who, echoing Armstrong, didn't think the songs were strong enough. "They said, 'When you have something better, come back,'" Barnes told Rademacher.[12] Rudge, perhaps on the strength of his clout alone, managed to snag 38 a two-album deal with A&M, an artist-friendly label co-owned by trumpeter Herb Alpert.

A&M assigned the group to producer/songwriter Dan Hartman. Hartman had been the front man for the Edgar Winter Group and was responsible for its 1973 hit "Free Ride." He had a studio in an old schoolhouse in Westport, Connecticut, and 38 parked itself there for a couple of months in early 1977, emerging with its self-titled debut album. All songs were written by group members with the exception of a Chuck Berry remake. Bassist Ken Lyons played on most of the tracks but was having domestic troubles and abruptly left the group during the recording process. Lyons was replaced by Lynyrd Skynyrd's original bassist, Larry Junstrom, who played on two songs. Junstrom was working for 38 as a roadie at the time and already knew most of the group's material. Not long after the album was released, Donnie Van Zant married Barnes's sister Brenda.

Reviews for *38 Special* were not generally enthusiastic. The band was perceived by some critics as a lame imitation of Skynyrd. Barnes later admitted that the group was tilling ground that had already been plowed: "We were trying to be Skynyrd, the Charlie Daniels Band, Marshall Tucker," Barnes told an interviewer, "but it had already been done."[13] At this point the members also opted to add two female backup singers to the lineup, Indiana singer Dale Krantz (who is now with Lynyrd Skynyrd and is married to Gary Rossington) and Carol Bristow. When Krantz went on to front the Rossington Collins Band in 1979, she was replaced by Jacksonville vocalist Nancy Henderson.

Only months after 38's debut, while the band members were busy touring to support the album, their mentor, Ronnie Van Zant, was killed in the infamous plane that went down outside Gillsburg, Mississippi. This was a tragic blow for both bands. Not only had the members of 38 lost their patron saint, adviser, and friend, Donnie Van Zant had lost a brother. To make matters worse, 38 now needed a new manager. Their mutual manager, Peter Rudge, went into a tailspin after Skynyrd's crash and more or less withdrew from the business for a time.

Producer Dan Hartman supervised the group's sophomore effort, *Special Delivery*, in 1978. It's a shame the members didn't cowrite with Hartman, because he was an excellent songwriter and could have helped them immensely in this department. *Special Delivery* didn't do any better than the group's eponymous debut, and by 1979 A&M was about to drop the group. "Our first couple of albums failed miserably," Barnes said. "It really didn't work out for us."[14] Career prospects were bleak. "We actually went back to Jacksonville and were standing in the unemployment line for a while," Barnes told journalist John Wirt. "That was embarrassing."[15] Yet the label gave the group one more chance—with the proviso that it come up with some *hits*—that is, songs that could attract radio play.

Mark Spector, an executive at A&M Records, felt the group still had great potential if only they had the right kind of direction. He quit his job at A&M to start his own management operation, and 38 became his first client. He set about refurbishing the band's sound and image. Who could possibly know better what the label wanted than one of its former executives?

Thanks largely to MTV, southern rock had become passé, so Spector and the group decided to pursue a new direction, turning toward a more mainstream-rock style. The main requirement was *hits*. Donnie Van Zant explained, "We started writing with outside songwriters," namely Jim Peterik of the Chicago-based pop-rock group Survivor (Peterik had previously made the charts with the Ides of March).[16] It was Spector who suggested the group work with Peterik, giving 38 its first real hit. A&R man John Kalodner, then working for Atlantic, Survivor's label, slipped a song Peterik had cowritten for Survivor, "Rockin' into the Night," to Spector. Survivor had intended to include it on its debut, but producer Ron Nevison didn't think it fit, so it was axed. Peterik told interviewer Matt Wardlaw that the guys in Survivor were displeased with this unexpected development.[17]

A third, as-yet-untitled 38 Special album was in the can, but Spector felt it lacked a potential single. As Spector had quickly recognized, "Rockin' into the Night" was clearly radio-friendly. It promised a

38 SPECIAL

38 Special, A&M Records publicity photo, ca. 1980.

solution to many of 38's problems at A&M, so it was included as a last-minute addition to the album. Don Barnes explained, "You're about to lose the record deal, and the record company sends you a song, you figure, 'Look, We'll try anything at this point.'"[18] However, Donnie Van Zant didn't like it and didn't want to—or couldn't—sing it.[19] So Barnes—who had better vocal technique and range anyway—stepped up.

Another change the group implemented was hiring a new producer along with a new studio. They went to Doraville, Georgia, where Skynyrd had recorded its early hits. Staff engineer Rodney Mills was hired as 38's producer, and the combination of new songwriting, a new lead singer—at least on the singles—and a new producer apparently turned the trick. Released in early 1980, the album *Rockin' into the Night* achieved moderate success, charting at number 57 on *Billboard*'s Hot 100 albums chart, and gave the band a new lease on life. Mills would go on to supervise eight albums for 38.

Also in 1980, the year of the band's big breakthrough, drummer Jack Grondin married Ronnie Van Zant's widow, Judy. The group would also cowrite more hits with Peterik. When it came time to make the next album, manager Spector told Barnes he and Carlisi should get together with Peterik and see what they could come up with. They visited Peterik at his home in Chicago.[20] Carlisi had a muted, staccato chord progression that sounded like something by the Cars.[21] The three quickly fashioned it into "Hold on Loosely," which became a hit in 1981.

Since the group's southern-rock leanings—personified by Donnie Van Zant—had become a liability, an entirely new sound and image had to be created. Van Zant still sang some of his southern-rock songs in the live shows and on albums, but Barnes sang all the singles, most of which made the charts in the 1980s, including:

YEAR	TITLE	CHART POS.
1980	"Rockin' into the Night"	43
1981	"Hold on Loosely"	27
1981	"Fantasy Girl"	52
1982	"Caught up in You"	10
1982	"You Keep Runnin' Away"	38
1984	"If I'd Been the One"	19
1984	"Back Where You Belong"	20
1984	"Teacher, Teacher"	25
1986	"Like No Other Night"	14
1986	"Somebody Like You"	48
1987	"Back to Paradise"	41

In 1984 the group began looking further afield for material, incorporating "Teacher, Teacher" (which appeared in the 1984 movie *Teachers*) by Canadian songwriter, producer, and multi-instrumentalist Jim Vallance and singer Bryan Adams (also an A&M artist). Vallance and Adams, along with singer Pat Benatar, also wrote the song "Back to Paradise" (from the movie *Revenge of the Nerds*). "Paradise" was essentially a Don Barnes solo single. Vallance played most of the instruments, recorded in his home studio in Vancouver. No one from 38 appeared on the recording with exception of Barnes.[22]

Released in 1987, "Back to Paradise," would be Barnes's last hit with 38. Barnes has said in interviews that he simply needed a break.[23]

The fact is that tensions had been running high between band members for quite some time. Larry Steele, who by this point had become the group's stage manager, recalls: "Don had carried this band on his shoulders for thirteen years. He had grown tired of it." What is more, Barnes and Carlisi could barely tolerate each other, and Barnes's relations with some of the other members weren't going smoothly either thanks to his backstage blowups.[24]

Barnes left the group to record a solo album, *Ride the Storm*, for A&M. The album was shelved. A&M had just been sold to international conglomerate PolyGram, and his album, he reckons, got lost in the shuffle.[25] Barnes had gambled and lost. The group replaced him with former Jack Mack & the Heart Attack vocalist/multi-instrumentalist Max Carl. The group also brought in San Francisco guitarist Danny Chauncey. Brookins, too, made his exit around this time and was not replaced, the group having deemed at this point that having two drummers was no longer necessary.

Still, 38's biggest hit was in front of them. It would come when Max Carl reworked a song Carlisi had cowritten back in 1983, a soft ballad that Barnes had rejected.[26] That song became "Second Chance," and in May 1989 it would go to number six on *Billboard*'s Hot 100 singles chart. *Billboard* also named it Adult Contemporary Song of the Year. "[Carl] really brought it home," Carlisi told author Marley Brant. "[He] had such a marvelous voice. I mean, the guy could sing 'Mary Had a Little Lamb' and you'd go buy it, he was so good."[27] Thirty-eight was beginning to find new audiences for its new sound, which was *nothing* like its older sound. This was the second time the group had reinvented itself. However, finding new audiences with a new style and image would also risk losing older, more loyal fans, who had kept the group going for ten years or more—and who *still* keep it going.

The album that contained "Second Chance," *Rock and Roll Strategy*, its eighth for A&M, went gold (sales of 500,000 or more) and charted at number sixty-one. Despite 38's garnering its biggest hit ever, A&M dropped the act. The group's next album, 1991's *Bone against Steel*, also featuring Carl on lead vocals, was issued on the British label Charisma Records. This one barely cracked the lower reaches of the charts. Jack Grondin left in 1991 to became a missionary and was replaced by drummer Scott Meeder, who was replaced a year later by Scott Hoffman.

The band's new formula was apparently not working as hoped. It was time to revert to the tried-and-true. Max Carl departed in 1992, and Barnes—who had been out in the cold for five years—returned. Arkansas native Bobby Capps, who had been with the Jacksonville-based Johnny Van Zant Band, came in on keyboards and vocals. With no record deal, the group survived by continuing to do what it did best: play for live audiences and tour like crazy.

After five years of this, the group landed a deal with New York–based indie Razor & Tie and began recording a new album, *Resolution*, with stalwarts Jim Peterik cowriting and Rodney Mills producing, back at Studio One. Despite some friction, Carlisi worked with the group during this period and even cowrote some songs for the album—but didn't perform on it. By the time it was released, the album's cover featured only four members: Barnes, Van Zant, Junstrom, and Chauncey. The band would not record again until 2001, a Christmas album for North Carolina–based CMC International, the same label for which Skynyrd had recorded. Thirty-Eight released a twelfth album, *Drivetrain*, in 2004 for the British label Sanctuary Records (which is now owned by Universal Music, the same conglomerate that acquired A&M from PolyGram). Its most recent album was 2011's *38 Special Live from Texas*, which contains all the hits and is basically a commercial for the band's live show.

Donnie Van Zant and younger brother Johnny formed a side project back in 1998 called Van Zant. The duo's first album, *Brother to Brother*, was released on CMC. It was followed in 2001 by *Van Zant II* on Sanctuary. Following a switch to a country format in 2005, the duo signed with Columbia Records' Nashville division and enjoyed a number-eight country hit with the single "Help Somebody." The accompanying album, *Get Right with the Man*, went to number two on *Billboard*'s country chart. They followed with *My Kind of Country*, also on Columbia, in 2007. That album went to number ten on the country chart. This easy crossover illustrates how much country music itself had morphed into southern rock, to the point where the two styles became interchangeable. In fact it could be said that a new generation of southern rockers had taken over Nashville.

Despite the success of the duo—which parted ways with Columbia for some unknown reason—Donnie Van Zant continued to tour with

38 Special until retiring in 2013. He lives in Clay County near Middleburg, Florida.

One by one the original 38 members dropped out and were replaced, except for Barnes. Larry Junstrom retired in 2014 due to health issues. He died in 2019. In 1998, Jeff Carlisi, who left in 1996, and Atlanta drummer Michael Cortellone, who would later work with Skynyrd, put together an all-star band called Big People, which included guitarist/vocalist Pat Travers, bassist/vocalist Benjamin Orr (from the Cars), drummer Liberty DeVitto (formerly of Billy Joel's band) replacing Cortellone, and singer Derek St. Holmes (formerly with Ted Nugent). Big People didn't get signed and disbanded not long after Orr died in 2000. Carlisi later worked with Bad Company singer Brian Howe. Carlisi and former Atlanta Rhythm Section members Robert Nix and Dean Daughtry later formed the short-lived group Deep South, featuring singer Jimmy Hall of Wet Willie and former Lynyrd Skynyrd guitarist Ed King. Carlisi also ran a band camp for kids. He is the coauthor of *Jam! Amp Your Team, Rock Your Business,* published by Wiley. He lives in Destin, Florida.

Barnes, who lives in Atlanta, is the only original member. The group, which now features perhaps the strongest lineup it has ever had, performs about one hundred dates per year and still rakes in respectable fees. There is a nostalgia boom for the 1980s—kids who were in their teens in 1987 are now in their forties—and 38 is in a perfect position to capitalize on this. Like many classic-rock acts, 38 Special has discovered that it doesn't *need* hit records anymore—or any records at all, for that matter—to continue to draw fans to its concerts. An act can run on fumes literally for decades after having enjoyed a few major hits on the radio.

8

Molly Hatchet
Southern Spinal Tap

ONE OF THE OFT-OVERLOOKED ASPECTS of southern rock is the contribution of the "navy brats." Since Jacksonville was at one time home to four naval stations with a significant segment of the populace being U.S. Navy personnel, it was inevitable that these kids would join the explosion of musicians and bands in the area. Among these were folk/country singer Hoyt Axton, Leon Wilkeson, and Billy Powell of Lynyrd Skynyrd, Jeff Carlisi of 38 Special, and Dave Hlubek of Molly Hatchet.

Hlubek was actually born in Jacksonville at the naval hospital in 1951. His mother was a local girl who married a sailor. The family got transferred to Hawaii in 1956 and later to Moffett Field near San Jose. Hlubek's parents split up when he was fourteen, and his mother returned to her hometown to live with her mother until she reestablished herself.[1] By the time Hlubek rearrived in Jacksonville, he was a solid West Coast dude. Like nearly all Jacksonville rock guitarists of the day, his idol was Eric Clapton.[2]

Hlubek attended Lake Shore Middle School and told his new schoolmates he had played with the Doors.[3] He later attended Lee High School alongside Gary Rossington and Bob Burns. Hlubek founded Mynd Garden in 1968, which included bassist Tim Lindsey, who would later join the Rossington Band and is a current member of Molly

Hatchet. Mynd Garden was one of the groups Pat Armstrong scheduled to audition for Alan Walden, who selected Lynyrd Skynyrd as management clients in 1970. There was a multitude of bands to choose from. As Hlubek explained to a reporter in 2017: "The talent pool in Jacksonville alone was just amazing. I'm proud to be from Jacksonville. I know all the bands that came out of there at that time. We were all intertwined. . . . There's like a dozen major bands [who] came out of Duval County."[4] Hlubek attributes these bands' success to their work ethic as well as to friendly but fierce competition: "It doesn't surprise me at all that the bands [who] stuck it out made it as big as they did. . . . We worked our asses off. Molly Hatchet, Lynyrd Skynyrd, .38 Special, Grinderswitch, all of us. It was so competitive, but it made us strong."[5]

Hlubek graduated in 1971 and decided to form another band. The Allman Brothers Band had broken big that year with *Live at the Fillmore East*, and many Jacksonville groups were hoping to follow in its footsteps. Hlubek was looking at guitars at downtown's Paulus Music when he ran into guitarist Steve Holland, who had recently arrived from Virginia Beach, another navy town. In 2001, Hlubek told biographer Michael Buffalo Smith: "I heard this voice behind me saying, 'That guitar really sucks.' I turned around and asked who he was, and he said, 'I'm Steve Holland. Wanna start a band?' . . . We started rehearsing that very afternoon, and that band went on to become Molly Hatchet."[6]

An early incarnation of Hatchet consisted of Hlubek, who sang most of the songs, guitarist Holland, drummer Fred Bianco from New Jersey, and bassist Banner Thomas from Savannah. Hatchet's third guitarist, Duane Roland, had moved from Indiana at seven with his family and lived in the Arlington area near Jacksonville University. According to an interview conducted by Michael Buffalo Smith, Roland had been trying to put together a band with Thomas and drummer Bruce Crump, both from the Southside, but that didn't work out, so Roland went with a group called the Ball Brothers.[7] Roland came aboard Hatchet early on but left after about a month and was replaced by Kenny Niblick.

Hatchet was working at Dino's Disco on the Northside when a big, beefy guy approached Hlubek during break. He complimented Hlubek on his guitar playing but insisted Hlubek couldn't sing to save his life.

"You need me," he said. Danny Joe Brown, who had graduated from Arlington's Terry Parker High, had started as a roadie for guitarist Bobby Ingram's band Rum Creek and had graduated to the group's singer. Hlubek invited Brown to sit in with the group at its next gig at La Vida Lounge in Neptune Beach. Brown did three Skynyrd numbers and was hired on the spot.[8]

Molly Hatchet started touring regionally, but Bianco and Niblick left the group in mid-1975. Drummer Bruce Crump, whose family was from Memphis, joined not long after. He had attended the prestigious Bolles School, the same school Gram Parsons attended. Duane Roland came back that same year, and the classic Molly Hatchet lineup was set.

Talent manager Pat Armstrong recalls someone from 38 Special recommending Hatchet to him. Armstrong, a former Jacksonville resident, was then based in Macon, where he had attended law school. He brought Hatchet to the Red Lamp Lounge in 1976, liked what he heard, and began working with the group. The group signed management, production, and publishing deals with Armstrong in the parking lot of a McDonald's restaurant in Valdosta, Georgia. "They didn't want to drive to Macon [to sign the papers], and I didn't want to drive to Jacksonville, so we met halfway," Armstrong said. "Then they demanded I buy them dinner, so I bought them all Quarter-Pounders and milkshakes. They wouldn't settle for Happy Meals," he joked.[9] Armstrong thought the group needed another guitarist, so Duane Roland was added.

About a year later, Armstrong introduced the band to Skynyrd singer Ronnie Van Zant. Hlubek had known Van Zant from the old neighborhood. Armstrong took Van Zant and audio engineer Kevin Elson to see his new charges in Daytona Beach. The group played "Gator Country," a smart-alecky answer-song to Skynyrd's "Sweet Home." This initially irked Van Zant, Armstrong said, but he warmed up to the idea.[10] Van Zant offered to produce some demos and shop them around to record labels.[11] Hatchet went into Skynyrd's studio on Riverside Avenue, where Van Zant and Elson helped the group tighten up its arrangements. "Ronnie made the songs on our first album make sense," Hlubek told an interviewer.[12] Van Zant was ready to go bat for Molly Hatchet at Skynyrd's label, MCA Records.[13] Unfortunately he would not live to do so.

Despite this setback, the boys in the band soldiered on. They recorded another set of demos in Jacksonville at the Warehouse studio, owned by Tom Markham, who had coproduced Skynyrd's first (local) singles for his Shade Tree label.

Armstrong had been booking Molly Hatchet all over the South. The group had already done quite a bit of work in Atlanta, where it attracted the attention of studio owner (and peep-show operator) Mike Thevis, who offered Molly Hatchet a contract with his GRC label. Armstrong demurred, largely due to Thevis's reputation as a dangerous character.[14]

Thevis also owned Atlanta's Sound Pit recording studio, where Epic Records' A&R man and staff producer Tom Werman liked to work, because he enjoyed working with engineer Tony Reale. After meeting Thevis, Armstrong had gotten to know Reale, who went to bat for Hatchet. Reale recommended the group to Werman and set up a live audition in the studio so he could hear them.[15] Werman was duly impressed and took the act to his boss, Lenny Petze, head of A&R at Epic.[16] Epic signed Molly Hatchet in December 1977. The group recorded its Epic debut at the Sound Pit.[17] It was mixed by Werman at the Record Plant in Los Angeles.

Molly Hatchet's self-titled debut—with a Frank Frazetta painting on the cover augmented by a banner-style logo designed by Armstrong—was released September 1978. On the back cover is a picture of the group with singer Brown wearing a T-shirt emblazoned with the slogan "redneck power." Journalist Derek Kinner wrote in *Folio Weekly*: "That eponymous record . . . was quintessentially Southern rock, quintessentially Jacksonville rock—obviously spawned from the same primordial soup as Lynyrd Skynyrd and .38 Special. But at the same time it was harder, rougher, grittier, unapologetically blue-collar, [as] if Skynyrd were taken over by hardcore bikers."[18]

The Allman Brothers Band was in disarray, and Lynyrd Skynyrd had been devastated by its plane crash a year earlier. The circumstances required passing the southern-rock baton, such as it was, to Hatchet and 38, though of course there were other competitors, such as the Marshall Tucker Band, the Atlanta Rhythm Section (which included two members from Jacksonville, J. R. Cobb and Robert Nix), and the Outlaws. Being from the same town where the ABB and Skynyrd had emerged gave the Jacksonville boys a slight edge on the competition.[19]

Hatchet had taken more than just musical cues from Lynyrd Skynyrd; it also borrowed Skynyrd's image-building modus operandi. This meant garnering publicity for being hard-drinking, brawling, macho-male renegades, which almost became a trademark for southern rockers in general. Hlubek told an interviewer Armstrong had advised Hatchet members to go out and get into bar fights, which would help them get their names in the papers and create controversy.[20] Armstrong denies having made any such recommendation. "I wouldn't say something like that," he said. "In the first place I wouldn't want to see my guys get hurt. In the second place, if one of them did get injured and couldn't perform, we'd all lose money."[21]

Hatchet's first single released to radio was a remake of a remake, a third-hand version of the Allman Brothers Band's 1969 "Dreams." In 1970 R&B-rock singer Buddy Miles had recorded a version of the jazz waltz with a whole new groove—the same rhythm Hatchet would use in 1978. Hatchet had gotten the idea for the arrangement from Jacksonville band Jules Verne, which included former Outlaws bassist Buzzy Meekins. Hatchet expanded the title to "Dreams I'll Never See," and its rendition performed well on FM radio and got the group noticed. The next single, "Gator Country," which name-checked most of the southern-rock groups at the time, also got some play. The album didn't sell especially well but showed enough promise—it reached number sixty-four on *Billboard*'s album chart—to get Epic executives stoked.

The group's follow-up, *Flirtin' with Disaster*, however, broke through. This one had been recorded in Orlando at Bee Jay Studio, again with Werman at the helm. Hatchet's second single, "It's All Over Now," was, like "Dreams," a remake of a remake. This one mimicked the Rolling Stones' 1964 version of a Valentinos song written by Bobby Womack. Armstrong's strategy of launching the band with remakes worked. *Flirtin' with Disaster* sold well, with the title track as well as a third single, "Jukin' City," getting extensive radio play. In December 1979 the album peaked at number nineteen and quickly went "gold" (sales of 500,000). Over the course of a decade it would reach two million. It was Hatchets' biggest seller.

Molly Hatchet, Epic Records publicity photo, 1976. *Left to right*: Bruce Crump, Banner Thomas, Duane Roland, Dave Hlubek, Danny Joe Brown, Steve Holland. Courtesy of Pat Armstrong.

Success Takes Its Toll

The members of Molly Hatchet soon found themselves performing more than two hundred dates per year, many to packed stadiums. Despite this success—or perhaps because of it—the group began falling apart. The rigors—and diversions—of the road took their toll. Cocaine and booze were consumed in massive quantities, and this began warping people's perspectives. These guys weren't kidding when they said they were "flirtin' with disaster." One by one, the original members started dropping out.

The first to go was singer Danny Joe Brown, citing health issues including exhaustion. However, journalist Derek Kinner writes unidentified former band members told him "they fired [Brown] because he was out of control."[22] Brown himself told an interviewer that a major reason he left was because of a dispute with Armstrong: he, and the rest of the group, he said, felt Armstrong's ownership of the publishing rights to the group's songs was a conflict of interest. Armstrong responded that this was a standard music-industry practice.[23]

Armstrong said Brown's departure was a mutual decision; the others wanted him gone because he was "a complete bully" and "was combative with all the members."[24] A power struggle emerged between Hlubek and Brown over control of the band, with outsiders egging Brown on, telling him he was the key man in the operation, although much later Brown would concede that "Dave Hlubek is Molly Hatchet."[25] Brown threw a wastebasket full of ice water on Hlubek while he was sleeping, resulting in Hlubek giving "bad-ass" Brown a beating.[26] Brown and Crump also had fistfights.[27]

Brown formed his own band and landed his own deal with Epic, signing with a new manager, Atlanta-based Charlie Brusco, who also comanaged the Tampa southern rockers the Outlaws with former Skynyrd manager Alan Walden. The Danny Joe Brown Band, modeled on Skynyrd's seven-man lineup, included former Rum Creek cohort Bobby Ingram on guitar and vocals, guitarist-vocalist Steve Wheeler, guitarist Kenny McVay, Detroit keyboardist John Galvin, former Outlaws bassist-vocalist Buzzy Meekins, and drummer Jimmy Glenn. The Danny Joe Brown Band recorded its sole album at Compass Point Studio in Nassau, Bahamas, with famed producer Glyn Johns at the helm. Its 1981 debut single, "No One Walks on Me," written by Wheeler, became a staple on MTV. Despite this exposure, the album, *Danny Joe Brown and the Danny Joe Brown Band*, reached only number 120 on *Billboard*'s album chart. Sales were not impressive. During the band's first tour, with some dates opening for fellow Jacksonville rockers Blackfoot, the entire band walked out on Brown, re-forming as Vigil Annie. Brown had become a multiple-substance abuser, displaying all of the unwholesome behavior of an addict and alcoholic. Brown had to scramble to find a pickup band in order to complete the tour.

* * *

Hatchet quickly—perhaps too quickly—had replaced Brown with singer Jimmy Farrar from LaGrange, Georgia. Farrar had great pipes but lacked the look, stage presence, and charisma Brown displayed. The group made no mention in the press of Brown's leaving, hoping fans might not notice.[28] The plan appeared to have worked: Molly Hatchet's 1980 album, *Beatin' the Odds*, recorded with producer Werman at Bee Jay in Orlando, actually sold rather well, reaching number twenty-five on *Billboard*'s album chart and scoring the group another platinum disc.

The group continued its relentless touring madness. Molly Hatchet's next album, 1981's *Take No Prisoners*, was recorded at Compass Point (and mixed at LA's Record Plant), once again produced by Tom Werman. Although the album charted at number thirty-six, this was the first time the group had failed to attain at least gold-record status. Sales were trending downhill. In the middle of a tour to support *Take No Prisoners*, bassist Banner Thomas would leave the group, replaced by Ralph "Riff" West of Sanford, former bassist with White Witch. To make matters worse, southern rock was losing its market share, and the label demanded Molly Hatchet update its sound and look. "I picked a good time to get out," Thomas later told interviewer Philippe Archambeau. "Not long after, under pressure from management and the record company to produce more hit singles, the band started to lose its identity and started to look like [Canadian pop-rock group] Loverboy. I'm glad I wasn't there for that."[29] Hlubek explained: "We were going into 17,000-to-20,000-seat coliseums and filling about a quarter of them. . . . We managed to pull the wool over the public's eyes for one album, but after that they wouldn't buy it anymore."[30]

By the end of the 1982 tour, Brown wanted to come back. Things had not gone well for the band without Brown, nor had they gone well for Brown without the band. Cocaine and bad judgment had been a major factor in the group's downfall, Armstrong said. He told the band members, "You guys scratched and clawed your way to the top—now you've snorted your way to the bottom."[31]

Farrar made his exit along with drummer Crump. Crump was replaced by former Mother's Finest drummer Barry "B.B." Borden. Hatchet's next album, with Brown back in front, was 1983's *No Guts, No Glory*, recorded at Bee Jay once again with Werman at the helm. Brown had brought in his former keyboardist from the Danny Joe Brown Band, John Galvin, to play on a couple of tracks. Jacksonville guitarist Dru Lombar (from Capricorn act Grinderswitch) appears on a couple of tracks. The cover featured the band members in full desperado regalia replete with pistols, rifles, shotguns, and ammo belts. This gun-totin' image, designed to appeal to a super-macho, white-male demographic, signified a return to the group's redneck roots. Critic Michael B. Smith praised the group's "return to the powerful sound that was so prevalent on its debut effort."[32]

By the next album, 1984's *The Deed Is Done*, recorded at Bee Jay with ZZ Top producer Terry Manning, Crump had returned to the drum seat, but guitarist Steve Holland flew the coop, replaced by keyboardist John Galvin. Author Scott B. Bomar calls this album "a calculated and slickly overproduced grab for commercial success."[33] Hatchet did a live album in 1985, its last for Epic.

The drinking and drugging had gotten out of hand. Galvin said Brown and Hlubek were "the hardcore party men, the ones who would take the most risk and hang out with the riskiest people."[34] Hlubek later told an interviewer, "I had a horrendous, horrendous cocaine problem."[35] The man who founded the group and whose vision drove the band himself dropped out in 1987 and was replaced by former Danny Joe Brown Band guitarist Bobby Ingram. Ingram's entry would prove portentous.

Brown, Crump, and Roland were the remaining original members at this point; however, Brown and Crump had left the band earlier and as a result had relinquished their rights as principals. Hence ownership of the group's assets, especially its trademark, fell into Duane Roland's lap.

Hatchet's deal with Epic came to a close after an eight-year run that included three platinum albums. Its next album, 1989's *Lightning Strikes Twice*, appeared on Capitol and would be recorded at Bee Jay and produced by Armstrong along with engineer Andy DeGanahl and guitarist Duane Roland. In an attempt to court commercial success and appease label executives, the group brought in outside writers such as Ron Perry, a singer friend of Galvin's from Detroit.[36] Despite these commercial concessions, however, *Lighting Strikes Twice* failed to chart, and Capitol quickly dropped the act. Epic released a greatest-hits compilation in 1990 that eventually went gold.

It would be six years before Molly Hatchet—with an entirely new lineup—would release another album. Later that year, the members of Molly Hatchet decided they needed a break and agreed to take a one-year hiatus. Bassist Riff West explained, "We just wanted a break [from the road]."[37]

How the Band Members Lost the Rights to the Name

Molly Hatchet never had a formal business structure set in writing. Pat Armstrong said he tried three times, unsuccessfully, to get the members to form a corporation with appropriate by-laws that would regulate their responsibilities and provide for continuity of ownership and other crucial contingencies. They preferred a loose structure that would allow them to get rid of any member by simply pushing him out without having to make any settlements or recompense. One by one the members walked away—with the sole exception of Duane Roland—forgoing any share of the group's assets. In other words, when a member quit, it was understood that he would have no rights nor title to further use of the name Molly Hatchet or any other collective assets.

Any of the original owners who left could have challenged this understanding and insisted on some sort of settlement, which might have consisted of a cash buyout or perhaps a share of future revenues; amazingly, not one did. When Danny Joe Brown came back in 1983, Armstrong insisted it would be as a contract employee and not an owner—in other words, a salaried sideman. This also happened with Bruce Crump, who quit and came back. He, too, lost his share of future profits and all rights to the name. By 1987 all but one of the original members had dropped out, including Dave Hlubek, the driving force behind the band from day one. The last man standing was Duane Roland. Molly Hatchet became Roland's band by default.

The nonstop partying had taken its toll. In 1990, Roland, like Brown, had become a severe alcoholic. He felt he had to get off the merry-go-round in order to survive. Roland also had a bad hip that required replacement and was using pain pills on top of the booze. His liver was shot. After a year off, Roland—fearing life on the road might truly kill him—still did not want to go back out.[38]

However, there was money to be made, and Danny Joe Brown and Bobby Ingram wanted to make it. Brown and Ingram got a new agency, Artists International Management (AIM) in Boca Raton, and hired keyboardist John Galvin and some new guys to go on a new tour with them. In 1993, Ingram rerecruited original bassist Banner Thomas, who returned briefly, as well as guitarist Erik Lundgren of the Johnny Van Zant Band. A year later Bryan Bassett, formerly of Wild Cherry, replaced Lundgren, and Buzzy Meekins replaced Thomas. One could say the lineup experienced a high turnover rate.

Armstrong said Brown and Ingram took it upon themselves to use the name Molly Hatchet without obtaining authorization from Roland. This infringement was quickly rectified, however, when Brown and Ingram agreed to pay Roland 10 percent of gross revenues as a licensing fee.[39]

In 1995, Brown started developing serious health issues and became unable to perform, so with Brown's endorsement, Ingram replaced him with singer Phil McCormack and carried on.[40] By now Molly Hatchet appeared without a single original member. Ingram tried to recruit original drummer Bruce Crump as a salaried sideman but was brusque with him on the phone, and both refused to negotiate. Crump said he was humiliated by the very thought of working for Ingram and felt he at least deserved some special consideration for having helped put the band "on the worldwide stage" in the first place. However, Ingram's initial offer stood; take it or leave it. Crump hung up on him.[41]

Another problem arose when Armstrong and Roland found out Ingram had been shorting them by not reporting all the band's concert dates. Roland declared them in breach and intended to rescind the license.[42] Steve Green at AIM proposed a solution: Roland should just *sell* the name to Ingram. Roland of course had every right to sell, plus he needed money for a hip operation. The figure settled upon was $250,000. Ingram borrowed some money, Green put up part, and by 2000 the deal was done.[43] Bobby Ingram was now the proud owner of Molly Hatchet. There was nothing illegal, unethical, or immoral in any of this. It was all just business.

In 1995 Hatchet, which included Brown at this point, was signed by the German label SPV and began work on its first album in seven years. Brown had begun working on these recordings in Germany but could not finish the job. McCormack was brought in. Molly Hatchet did three more albums for the German label, which were licensed for release in the United States by North Carolina–based CMC International Records, the label that released Lynyrd Skynyrd's albums during this period. Molly Hatchet developed a large and loyal following in Germany and still tours there often. A 2008 album, consisting entirely of remakes of classic songs, was recorded at Vision Sound in Orange Park, Florida (near Ingram's Clay County home), released by Los Angeles–based Cleopatra Records, followed by another on SPV in 2010.

Things did not go as planned for Dave Hlubek after he left Hatchet. Back in Jacksonville, he and former Rossington Collins Band singer/guitarist Barry Lee Harwood formed the short-lived Hlubek-Harwood Band. Nothing happened with this project, said drummer Scott Sisson, mainly because Hlubek wouldn't show up for rehearsals.[44] By 1988 or so Hlubek was working a day job at a custom auto shop painting racing stripes on Corvettes.[45] In 1989 Hlubek hooked up with former Blackfoot drummer Jakson Spires to form the Dixie Allstars (later changed to Southern Rock Allstars). He stayed with that group until 2003, when he was briefly replaced by Duane Roland.

In 2004, former Molly Hatchet bassist Riff West decided to get as many of the original members of Molly Hatchet back together as he could. He brought in Dave Hlubek, Steve Holland, Duane Roland, and Bruce Crump. Banner Thomas was not needed because West himself had the bass position covered. Danny Joe Brown was ill and unable to perform, so his earlier replacement in Hatchet, Jimmy Farrar, was brought back. They called this new lineup Gator Country after a song from Hatchet's first album.

This posed a very odd situation: Gator Country had four of the six original members of Molly Hatchet while Bobby Ingram's version had zero. However, this dilemma was somewhat ameliorated for Ingram when Hlubek suddenly deserted his cohorts in Gator Country and went over to Ingram's Hatchet as a salaried sideman. In an ironic twist, Hlubek was now working for his former employee—the very situation Crump had felt humiliated even considering. Hlubek's son Aaron said it was just business, that Hlubek was chasing the money and intended to go with whomever was writing the biggest paycheck.[46]

With the formation of Gator Country, Hatchet fans split into two camps, the classic and the new, and the debate between the two has gotten heated, especially on Facebook, where Ingram and Crump had a very public feud (Crump died in 2015).[47] Ingram, who insists that keeping the name and legacy of Molly Hatchet is a labor of love, has his supporters. "I have always felt a need and strong desire to keep the Molly Hatchet tradition, legacy, and spirit alive," he told interviewer Lisa Morgan.[48]

Singer Phil McCormack died in 2019 and was replaced by Jimmy Elkins from Bounty Hunter, a Molly Hatchet tribute band. The current lineup consists of Elkins, Ingram, bassist Tim Lindsey (who had worked with Hlubek in Mynd Garden), keyboardist John Galvin, and drummer Shawn Beamer. The group still sounds strong, but the band once famous for its "three-guitar army" now has only one guitarist.

Molly's Curse

Not only are there no original members in the current edition of the band, there are no original members either. Danny Joe Brown died in 2005, Duane Roland in 2006, Bruce Crump in 2015, and Dave Hlubek and Banner Thomas in 2017. Steve Holland, the last remaining founding member, died in Brunswick, Georgia, in 2020.

Not only have five of the six original members died, but several replacements have perished as well: singers Jimmy Farrar in 2018 and Phil McCormack in 2019 along with bassists Buzzy Meekins in 2013 and Riff West in 2014. Hatchet has gone through approximately eighteen members over the course of four decades, half of whom are deceased.

9

Derek Trucks

Channeling Duane

There's a towheaded ten-year-old in a ball cap on the bandstand with the Greg Baril Band at Iggy Wanna's, a patio bar on the Intracoastal Waterway near Jacksonville Beach. His guitar, a Gibson SG Standard, is almost as big as he is. As one of the best blues groups in the area rips into "Statesboro Blues," the kid's guitar lets out a banshee wail. The crowd is amazed by this young marvel and applauds wildly. The shy kid looks surprised but can't help but respond with a toothy grin.

The year was 1989; the kid was Derek Trucks, son of Chris Trucks, a Jacksonville roofer, whose brother, Butch, was drummer for the All-man Brothers Band. Derek Trucks was born in Jacksonville in 1979 and named after Eric Clapton's pseudonym from the album *Derek and the Dominos*. You could say he was born to play. His younger brother, Duane Trucks, is also a guitarist, a member of the jam band Widespread Panic.

Derek Trucks discovered the guitar at age nine. He started taking lessons from his father's friend, Jacksonville guitarist Jim Graves, who had worked with Butch Trucks in a jazz-rock ensemble called Trucks. Interested in the slide guitar popularized by his uncle's musical partner, Duane Allman, Derek took a couple of lessons in that style from guitarist Steve Wheeler, a well-respected Jacksonville player who had worked with the Danny Joe Brown Band, among others. "We talked

Young Derek Trucks (*right*) onstage with Ace Moreland
looking on, ca. 1989. Courtesy of Marc Wysocki.

about Duane Allman's style, and I showed him some tunings," Wheeler
said. "He got it real quick." Trucks found it was actually easier for him
to play slide than regular guitar because of his small hands. He adopted Allman's slide of choice, a glass Coricidin bottle.[1]

The kid was so ridiculously good it was obvious he would become
successful. Soon his father began taking him around to sit in with
local bands to get him some stage experience. Young Trucks began
sitting in regularly with Ace Moreland's band, West Side Story (Moreland had recently relocated to Jacksonville from Oklahoma), a group

that also included Westside drummer Chip Miller, a former member of Cowboy.

Thanks to support from Uncle Butch, who was living in Tallahassee at this time, young Trucks began sitting in with the Allman Brothers Band. Audiences were astounded. Trucks recalls: "I was nine or ten, playing in [Miami] at this little dive bar, Tropics International [with Ace Moreland's group]. The Allmans were making that reunion record [1990's *Seven Turns*]. Butch brought Gregg [Allman], Warren [Haynes] and [bassist] Allen Woody out [to the gig]. That was the first time I played with Butch. I'm almost certain we played 'Statesboro Blues.'"[2]

Trucks decided to form his own group, Derek and the Dominators, which included Miller along with recent Connecticut transplant guitarist-vocalist Greg Baril and bassist-vocalist Buzzy Meekins. Some time later the name was shortened to the Derek Trucks Band, and Miller was replaced by former Rossington Collins Band drummer Derek Hess, who was in turn replaced by David "Plywood" Pressley. A keyboardist, Mike Hollingsworth, was added.

By fifteen he had enjoyed opportunities to sit in with Gregg Allman, Joe Walsh, Johnny Winter, Stephen Stills, Buddy Guy, and Bob Dylan.[3] Drummer Hess recalls, "We did a couple of dates [opening for Dylan], and ol' Dylan invited the young guitar wiz up onstage to play with him."[4]

Things Heat Up in Atlanta

In 1991, the group began doing many dates in Atlanta. It also began touring extensively, including a stint in Canada. Meekins remained on bass and vocals, but Baril would be replaced by former Mudcrutch guitarist/vocalist Danny Roberts. Keyboardist Larry Oakes replaced Hollingsworth. Hess remained on drums for the time being.

According to an interview with Hess, this group was signed by Capitol Records about 1995 and recorded a five-song demo produced by former ABB keyboardist (and current Rolling Stones sideman) Chuck Leavell, who also performed on the tracks, along with Wet Willie's Jimmy Hall on vocals.[5] Hess told interviewer Michael Buffalo Smith he has no idea why that project was shelved.[6] Allman Brothers Band producer Tom Dowd had also recorded some demos for the group in Miami.[7]

Things really started happening for Trucks in Hot'lanta. He needed to spend more time there. Relocating to Atlanta, however, necessitated putting a new band together since none of his Jacksonville players—most of whom lived on or near the beach—wanted to leave their hometown, where they could continue to work predictably. Moving to Atlanta would have been financially dicey, since some members had families—or drug habits—to support.[8]

Trucks's new group included Atlanta musicians Todd Smallie on bass, Yonrico Scott on drums, and Bill McKay on keyboards, all of whom were closer to his own age. Bunky Odom, who had worked for Phil Walden and Associates, the Allman Brothers' former management company, came aboard as the group's manager. Odom in turn landed the group a booking agency, New York–based Entourage Talent, who still books Trucks's band.

Atlanta-based blues artist Tinsley Ellis brought Trucks into the studio to play on Ellis's 1994 album *Storm Warning*, released by Atlanta's Landslide Records, which happened to be operated by a Jacksonville native, former Bolles School student Michael Rothschild. "The first time I saw Derek was in Jacksonville," Rothschild said, "He had his own group. It was at a festival near the stadium. I [also saw] him sitting in with the Allmans at Lakewood Amphitheater in Atlanta not long after."[9]

In an astute business move—likely designed to give Trucks full creative control in order to make the album *he* wanted to make—the group and its backers formed a production company, put together its first album, 1997's *The Derek Trucks Band*, and in turn licensed it to Landslide. It was recorded in Maurice, Louisiana, at Dockside Studios and produced by John Snyder, who is the department chair of the Loyola University College of Music in New Orleans. Trucks stretched the boundaries of what could be done on the slide, incorporating some heavy jazz into the set, which includes two Coltrane numbers and one each by Miles Davis and Wayne Shorter. This was a largely experimental affair, yet the album sold well by indie standards, Rothschild said.[10]

Trucks's association with Landslide was brief. The Derek Trucks Band's second album, *Out of the Madness*, was released in 1998 on House of Blues Records, a joint venture with BMG. This album contained more traditional material appropriate to the blues-based foundations of the slide guitar. In the midst of all this activity, Trucks somehow managed to graduate from Watauga High School in Boone, North Carolina. Counselors at the school designed a special program that let him study while on the road.

* * *

Several ABB members had created side projects to fill in between tours or during breaks. One such project was Frogwings, formed in 1997 by drummer Butch Trucks, a group that included nephew Derek along with members of the Aquarium Rescue Unit, including Oteil Burbridge, who would later join the ABB itself, and South Carolina singer-guitarist Edwin McCain, who went on to have hits of his own. Derek Trucks learned he had to juggle projects in order to stay busy. He was invited to join the ABB in 1999. "When I joined, Dickey [Betts] was the in-charge leader," Trucks told David Fricke of *Rolling Stone*. "Everybody deferred to him, whether they wanted to or not. Then after a year or so, Dickey was out."[11]

Trucks was playing with the ABB in New Orleans, where R&B singer Susan Tedeschi was opening act for the group. Tedeschi, who is from Boston and a graduate of the Berklee School of Music, had already recorded two highly acclaimed albums on Tone-Cool Records. She and Trucks discovered a shared love of blues, gospel, and jazz. Trucks was twenty, Tedeschi twenty-eight. "I told him he was too young for me, but everybody knows he's an older soul."[12] The two married in 2001, whereupon Tedeschi relocated to Jacksonville (she also recorded an album there with producer Tom Dowd at Judy Van Zant's Made in the Shade recording studio). The pair own a home in the Mandarin area, where they have raised two children. For ten years Tedeschi ran her own band while Trucks toured with the ABB, his own band, and Eric Clapton.

In between tours with the ABB, Trucks worked with his uncle in Frogwings and somehow managed to keep his own thing going. The Derek Trucks Band signed with Columbia Records in 2002, where it recorded three albums, with two others appearing on associated Sony-owned labels, Masterworks and Legacy. None of these albums, however, made much of a mark on the industry, so Trucks held on to his steady gig with the ABB for fifteen years.

In 2006 he was invited to play on Eric Clapton's album *Road to Escondido*. "I just got a call from him randomly on a cell phone one night,"

Derek Trucks performing with the Tedeschi Trucks Band at MagnoliaFest in 2015. Photo by Frank Allen Sr.

Trucks said. "He asked me to come out and record on the album he's doing with J. J. Cale."[13] Trucks also toured with Clapton that year, reprising Duane Allman's slide parts from Clapton's 1970 album *Derek and the Dominos*, on which Allman had made a notable contribution. In another astute business move, Trucks, who was paid a considerable sum for the Clapton tour, used the funds to build a recording studio,

Swamp Raga Studio, on his property. In 2007, he and Tedeschi combined their bands to form Soul Stew Revival, a large band with a horn section that also included Trucks's younger brother, Duane.

Trucks recorded the 2009 album *Already Free*, released on Columbia/Legacy, with his band at his home studio. However, a year later the Derek Trucks Band went on hiatus and subsequently dissolved. Yet Derek Trucks's most successful venture still lay before him.

In 2010, he and Tedeschi formed a new, twelve-piece group, the aptly named Tedeschi Trucks Band, six of whose members are African American. They recorded their album titled *Revelator* in Trucks's studio; it was released in 2011 by Sony Masterworks. *Revelator* performed well, reaching number twelve on *Billboard*'s Top 200 albums. It also won a Grammy for Best Blues Album. The Tedeschi Trucks Band's second album, *Everybody's Talkin'*, was recorded live and released in May 2012, followed by 2013's *Made-Up Mind*. Both were released on Sony Masterworks and both charted, reaching number eleven and fifteen respectively on the Top 200. All the while Trucks continued to play dates with the ABB.

After the ABB dissolved in 2014, Trucks returned to work full-time with the Tedeschi Trucks Band, who by 2016 had switched to Fantasy Records. The new band encompasses a far more R&B-oriented southern style, not unlike that of Delaney and Bonnie. Is it southern rock? Arguably yes, but like JJ Grey's Mofro, the sound leans toward the bluesier side of the spectrum.

Trucks also found time to record another album with Clapton, *Live in San Diego*. The Tedeschi Trucks Band continues to tour heavily, averaging two hundred dates per year. Trucks's mother takes care of the kids while the folks are on the road. Trucks has appeared twice in *Rolling Stone*'s list of "100 Greatest Guitarists of All Time." He may be the future of southern rock—or he may be the last of a dying breed.

10

Conclusion

SOUTHERN ROCK IS A HYBRID of many musical styles, not all of them from the South. It is also a dialectic of two opposing philosophies: the nonviolent, long-haired, drug-using hippie and the hard-drinking, brawling, fiercely independent redneck. This would have been a very unlikely amalgamation in 1969, but somehow it took hold in the 1970s.

Southern rock might also have been a reaction against what was seen by certain young, southern males as the feminization of rock music during the gender-bending "glam" era. This was a period when Alice Cooper performed in fishnet hose, David Bowie was prancing around in a pink jockstrap, T. Rex and Kiss members were painting their faces and strutting onstage in ten-inch platform shoes. Even the Rolling Stones dabbled in drag. Suddenly southern rock came in like a hurricane and blew all the glitter out to sea.

Some scholars and others have noted that whenever feminism became a significant force in society, insecure males felt threatened, and a reassuring cultural backlash appeared to placate them.[1] Music historian Barbara Ching addresses this issue, writing, "Southern rockers engaged in a struggle over the role and meaning of white southern manhood."[2] Southern-rock singers wrestled with the complexities of modern masculine identity and at the same time set new examples for their peers: "Southern men occupy a contradictory place in U.S. culture as the rest of the country stereotypes them as backwards and deviant yet simultaneously celebrates Southern males as quintessential exemplars of American manhood. . . . [S]outhern rebels empower the masculine self by protesting authority figures, dominating women and signifying their independence by drinking, using drugs, and brawling."[3]

Drinking, consuming massive amounts of drugs, and brawling were all too often part and parcel of a southern-rock band's image. Unfortunately, some of these fellows failed to realize they didn't have to actually *be* the hard-drinking, hard-living characters they created. Apparently part of an attempt to prove their masculinity, this some-times degenerated into a contest to see who could consume the most drugs and/or alcohol. It would unnecessarily shorten many lives. Molly Hatchet even wrote a song about self-destruction ("Flirtin' with Disaster") and how senseless it all was. To be fair, self-destructive be-havior was not specific to southern rock. Self-destructive behavior was endemic in rock music: Jim Morrison and Janis Joplin—both from the South—are prime examples, along with Keith Richards of the Roll-ing Stones and Keith Moon of the Who. Many country as well as blues artists also sang ardently about it. It seemed to be some sort of badge of honor.

Southern historian W. J. Cash explains that cartoonish construc-tions of masculinity were particularly significant to lower-class whites (probably blacks as well) who could not compete for social status with their more prosperous neighbors. In order to prove their viril-ity, they had to compete in more primitive ways. These men seem to have hitched their identities to atavistic displays of masculinity—the stuff of cowboy movies. These ideas, Cash argues, became embodied in an archetype he identified as the "hell of a fellow": "To stand on his head in a bar, to toss down a pint of raw whisky in a gulp, to fiddle and dance all night, to bite off the nose or gouge out the eye of a favorite enemy, to fight and love harder than the next man, to be known even-tually far and wide as a hell of a fellow—such would be his focus."[4] This sounds exactly like the way the singer-narrator in Lynyrd Skynyrd's "You Got That Right" portrays himself:

I like to drink and dance all night
Comes to a fix not afraid to fight[5]

This overblown, overly dramatic sense of masculine prowess, simi-lar to the Spanish concept of *machismo*—probably comes to the South by way of the Ulster Scots. Also known as "Scots-Irish," these descendants of Scottish lowlanders ("borderers") arrived in Philadelphia in the eighteenth century, fanned out through the Appalachians, and came to be referred to as "hillbillies." Author and so-called warrior-intellectual Jim Webb, himself of Scots-Irish stock, explains that these people were practically bred to fight. In his 2004 book, notably titled *Born Fighting*, Webb valorizes the Scots-Irish and their heritage of violence.[6] These people, an oft-unacknowledged ethnic group, are referred to in political circles as "Jacksonians," after their idol, military-leader-cum-president Andrew Jackson, whose parents were from Ulster.[7] Jackson himself was a "hell of a fellow." Indeed, Jackson is often cited in such circles as the shining example of how a leader should behave: tough and unbending.[8] In fact, Jackson's nickname was Old Hickory. Can it be mere coincidence that Jacksonville, Florida, was named after this fierce, authoritarian leader? Jacksonians are often referred to simply as "rednecks." Admiration of defiance and intransigence—not to mention raw machismo—have been redneck virtues at least since Jackson won the White House in 1829. This explains why several members of Lynyrd Skynyrd supported George Wallace: he was perceived as tough and unbending, like Old Hickory himself—also like Ronnie Van Zant.

Not all southern males bought into this fiction. An entirely different problem for a perhaps more sensitive breed of young southern males was *not* wanting to be seen as ignorant, violence-loving yahoos. Until the emergence of the so-called New South, to be a "southern man" often meant to be stereotyped by outsiders as a racist, a redneck, or both.[9] Author Mark Kemp writes that southern rock reflected the newness of the New South, incorporating hippies and "freaks" like the Allman Brothers, mostly free from racial prejudice. This relieved Kemp and his cohorts of a good deal of embarrassment and allowed them to be proud of where they came from.[10] Henceforth the South would be seen not as the last bastion of racism, intolerance, and blind conformity, as it had been only a decade earlier, but as an open-minded cauldron of creativity that gave the nation some of its best-performed and perhaps most relevant music.[11] Producer and musician Al Kooper, a New Yorker, certainly saw it that way when he arrived in Atlanta in 1972: "Things had changed. It was looser than I remembered it. It wasn't so *southern*. . . . The rednecks had long hair now. People got along better. I liked this."[12]

* * *

The term "southern rock" seems to defy all attempts at a working definition. A more accurate term for the music might be "redneck rock." But what exactly is a *redneck*? Most folks assume the term "redneck" and "hillbilly" are interchangeable, but there is a difference: hillbillies, as the term implies, come from Appalachian areas and are often of Scots-Irish stock. Since the land is rocky and not conducive to farming, hillbillies traditionally garnered much of their sustenance by hunting, somewhat like the stereotypical hillbilly Jed Clampett of the CBS-TV series *The Beverly Hillbillies*, often seen holding a shotgun. Rednecks, on the other hand, were flatlanders. The term originally referred to yeoman farmers and sharecroppers, whose necks would get burned from long hours in the sun.[13]

However, when I landed in Jacksonville in the very midst of the hippie movement's arrival, the term "redneck" had a *very specific* meaning. Whereas hippies were all about peace, love, and psychic enlightenment through drugs, rednecks spent their recreational time getting drunk and looking for fights. They were considered atavistic throwbacks who resorted to violence to solve problems. This fear and loathing of rednecks was exacerbated by the final scene of the 1969 film *Easy Rider*, which was required viewing for all hippies.

"Redneck Hippie": The Key Trope of Southern Rock

Then there was a third category: the redneck hippie. This was a guy who outwardly embraced the trappings of hippie culture but not the philosophy behind them—a guy who grew his hair out to impress "hippie chicks" and maybe get some of that "free love." Philosophically, long hair was supposed to be more than a fashion statement: it was an *antiwar* statement and by extension a repudiation of violence. "Redneck hippie" was the vilest epithet a hippie could hurl at another: a fake, a fraud, a wolf in sheep's clothing—worse than a run-of-the-mill redneck because at least you could see those coming.

Ronnie Van Zant converted the term "redneck hippie" from an

insult into a badge of honor. He took control of the term and the image and by sheer force of will made it work *for* him instead of against him—and thousands if not millions of young, southern males followed suit. In doing so, he—perhaps unwittingly—molded an image that became an archetype, the "long-haired country boy." Al Kooper deserves some of the credit—or blame—for spotting this in Van Zant and egging it on. As noted in chapter 5 on Lynyrd Skynyrd, even Van Zant himself grew sick of it and wanted the music to speak for itself.

Van Zant had his pensive side, according to friends,[14] and this is reflected in some of his lyrics, yet, after all, the redneck-hippie image was where his bread was buttered. Van Zant occasionally questioned but never relinquished his propensity for violence as an expedient.[15] An experienced streetfighter, he punched and pummeled his bandmates if they angered him for any reason, with the exception of drummer Artimus Pyle, who was a former U.S. Marine but an avowed peacenik. Pyle told an interviewer he had seen Van Zant "turn into the devil right in front of me and hurt people."[16] But Van Zant wouldn't dare try to bully Pyle.[17]

Was Van Zant, then, the original redneck-hippie troubadour? Did he create this character—or caricature? It seems more likely that this dubious honor falls at the feet of Dickey Betts. Although Betts looked and acted like a hippie, he would not hesitate to resort to violence when he felt it expedient. Betts, whose music paid lip service to peace and love, revealed his redneck streak many times when he resorted to bullying and outright violence when dealing with other ABB members. But unlike Lynyrd Skynyrd, whose bad behavior was a point of pride—as well as a selling point—the Allman Brothers Band members were embarrassed by suggestions that they might be taken for rednecks.[18]

Not only were the Skynyrd mainstays proud of their reputations as drunken brawlers, they made a gimmick of it. Instead of distancing themselves from the Redneck South, they embraced it—although some of the members, specifically Leon Wilkeson, Ed King, and Artimus Pyle, sometimes seemed a bit sheepish about all this. This attitude would eventually bite the band in the ass, but in the beginning it served its purpose: it got them noticed. The rowdy, self-destructive Skynyrd boys became the most terrible of the *enfants terrible* of rock, which, in a milieu of bad-boy bands like the Who and Led Zeppelin, is saying a lot.

Perhaps the defining elements of southern rock were best expressed by Charlie Daniels in his 1975 single "Long-Haired Country Boy," which was sort of an "answer song" to Haggard's "Okie from Muskogee":

'Cause I get stoned in the mornin'
I get drunk in the afternoon . . .

And I aint askin' nobody for nuthin'
If I can't get it on my own
You don't like the way I'm living
You just leave this long-haired country boy alone[19]

Take the term "country boy" and replace it with "redneck" and you get the picture. In fact, this is more or less what David Allan Coe did a year later with his song "Longhaired Redneck," which approaches the issue from the country side of the coin. The protagonist in Coe's song is not a longhair with a redneck streak but a dyed-in-the-wool redneck who happens to have long hair and is *mistaken* for a hippie:

The loudmouth in the corner's getting' to me
Talking 'bout my earrings and my hair . . .

'Cause my long hair just can't cover up my red neck
I've won every fight I've ever fought
I don't need some turkey telling me that I ain't country
And sayin' I ain't worth the damned ol' ticket that he bought[20]

While Skynyrd was a rock band with a strong country influence, Coe was, ostensibly, a country artist with a rock sensibility. Yet they seem so much alike as to be virtually indistinguishable. Coming from what was assumed to be polar opposites, they met in the middle. It's amazing how many country singers jumped on the redneck-rock bandwagon—not a difficult transition since it was so close to country to begin with.[21] This melding of "outlaw country" with southern rock would include not only Daniels and Coe but Willie Nelson, Waylon Jennings, Hank Williams Jr., and Travis Tritt and would keep on going, right on up to Jason Aldean, Jason Isbell, and Chris Stapleton.

Lynyrd Skynyrd would ultimately become the band most referred to in connection with the term "southern rock," possibly the most famous from Jacksonville, despite the fact that 38 Special garnered many more hit singles. This is mostly due to the lasting mystique laid down by Ronnie Van Zant, upon which the band still trades.

Aside from his songs and his immense drive and ambition, perhaps Van Zant's most significant accomplishment was his image, specifically the role of redneck hippie—egged on, of course, by Al Kooper.

"Redneck rock" seems like a more precise term. For what, after all, is "rock"? The term has taken on two meanings over the years. The first connotes music with a hard-driving beat. The "big beat" of the drums emerged with rhythm and blues and was later applied to all kinds of music, hence terms like "pop-rock," which came along in the mid-1960s. However, the term "rock" later came to describe the music of the so-called counterculture, which emerged on the West Coast in 1967 about the time of the Summer of Love. At that point, rock was music for hippies. Hence "southern rock" must be music for southern hippies—some of whom evinced a redneck streak and were not ashamed of it.[22]

NOTES

Introduction: What Is Southern Rock?

1. Scott B. Bomar, *Southbound: An Illustrated History of Southern Rock* (Milwaukee: Backbeat Books, 2014), 152.

2. It is crucial to note that there is a strong Native American influence—with its straight 4/4 rhythms and tom-tom beats—that embodies the "rock" feel and was also a huge influence on early blues music (see *Rumble: The Indians Who Rocked the World*, dir. Stevie Salas [Rezolution Films, 2018]).

3. Bill C. Malone, *Country Music, U.S.A.* (Austin: University of Texas Press, 1968).

4. "Take It Easy" was recorded in February 1972, and "Ramblin' Man" in October, so the Eagles got there first.

5. Malone, *Country Music, U.S.A.*, 28, 80–81.

6. Tom Moon, *One Thousand Recordings to Hear before You Die* (New York: Workman, 2008), 157.

7. Arlene Weiss, "Gregg Allman's Thoughts on ABB Stating They're Not Southern Rock," *Hittin' the Web with the Allman Brothers Band*, n.d., https://allmanbrothersband.com/modules.php?op=modload&name=XForum&file=viewthread&tid=144753. See also Alan Paul, "Dickey Betts on the Term 'Southern Rock,'" AlanPaul.net, n.d., http://alanpaul.net/2016/10/dickey-betts-on-the-term-southern-rock/.

8. Robert Hilburn, "Tom Petty Tries His Hand at Southern Rock," *Los Angeles Times*, March 31, 1985.

9. Darianne Schramm, "Los Angeles through the Eyes of Tom Petty," *Journiest*, n.d., https://www.journiest.com/pt-tom-petty-top-spots-2497662720.html.

10. Randall Roberts, "Tom Petty and the Heartbreakers, an L.A. Band, Stare at 'Hypnotic Eye,'" *Los Angeles Times*, July 18, 2014, https://www.latimes.com/entertainment/music/la-et-ms-tom-petty-hypnotic-eye-20140720-column.html.

11. Andy Greene, "Tom Petty on Past Confederate Flag Use: 'It Was Downright Stupid,'" *Rolling Stone*, July 14, 2015, https://www.rollingstone.com/politics

/politics-news/tom-petty-on-past-confederate-flag-use-it-was-downright-stupid-177619/.

12. "Rebels" by Tom Petty. © 1985 by Gone Gator Music.

13. The presence of female voices in country music is a gnawing issue. In 2017, only a small percentage of country artists were women. Chris Jancelewicz, "Female Country Singers Have Far Less Radio Time, and It's Not Changing Any Time Soon," *Global News*, August 13, 2017, https://globalnews.ca/news/3625516/country-music-radio-women-men/. Radio research indicates the reason for this is because women listeners themselves prefer male artists (Keith Hill, radio consultant, qtd. in *Country Aircheck*, May 26, 2015, https://www.countryaircheck.com/pdfs/current052615.pdf).

14. Ted Ownby, "Freedom, Manhood and White-Male Tradition in 1970s Southern-Rock Music," in *Haunted Bodies: Gender and Southern Texts*, ed. Anne Goodwyn Jones and Susan V. Donaldson (Charlottesville: University of Virginia Press, 1997), 383.

15. Lynyrd Skynyrd, "Call Me the Breeze," Sounds of the South Records, 1974. Song lyrics © 1971 by Johnny Bienstock Music.

16. Allman Brothers Band, "Ramblin' Man," Capricorn Records, 1973. Song lyrics © 1973 by Forrest Richard Betts Music and Unichappell Music.

17. For more details, see Sarah Cohen, "Men Making a Scene: Rock Music and the Production of Gender," in *Sexing the Groove: Popular Music and Gender*, ed. Sheila Whitely, 17–36 (New York: Routledge, 1997).

18. It is quite likely that many of the workers who migrated to Jacksonville had come from farms and longed to escape such backbreaking work.

19. Billy Ray Herrin, telephone interview by the author, March 13, 2019.

20. "Welcome to the Home of the Georgia Bulldog Club of Jacksonville: America's Largest Bulldog Club," *Georgia Bulldog Club of Jacksonville*, 2019, https://jaxbulldogs.com/.

21. Tom Dowd, personal interview by the author, 2002.

22. Herrin telephone interview, March 13, 2019.

23. WMBR-TV, Channel 4, now WJXT.

24. Dorothy K. Fletcher, *Historic Jacksonville Theatre Palaces, Drive-ins and Movie Houses* (Charleston, SC: History Press, 2015), passim.

25. Blair Miller, *Almost Hollywood: The Forgotten Story of Jacksonville, Florida* (Lanham, MD.: Rowman and Littlefield, 2012), 121. See also Richard Allen Nelson, "Movie Mecca of the South: Jacksonville, Florida, as an Early Rival to Hollywood," *Journal of Popular Film and Television* 8, no. 3 (Fall 198): 38–51; and "Distinguish Jacksonville: The Silent Film Industry," February 27, 2007, https://www.metrojacksonville.com/article/2007-feb-distinguish-jacksonville-the-silent-film-industry.

26. "Winter Film Capital of the World: The Early Cinematic History of Jacksonville." *Coastal*, June 7, 2018, https://thecoastal.com/featured/jax-cinematic

-past/. See also "Jacksonville's Place in Film History," City of Jacksonville, n.d., http://www.coj.net/departments/sports-and-entertainment/film-and-television/film-history-in-jacksonville.

27. Ennis Armon Davis, *Jacksonville* (Charleston: Arcadia, 2015), 19.

28. Lynn Abbott and Doug Seroff, *The Original Blues: The Emergence of the Blues in African American Vaudeville* (Jackson: University Press of Mississippi, 2017), 10.

29. Charles lived at 752 W. Church Street, which is now the site of LaVilla School of the Arts (Ray Charles, *Brother Ray: Ray Charles' Own Story*, with David Ritz [New York: Da Capo, 1992], 66).

30. Mae Axton, *Country Singers as I Know 'Em* (Fort Worth, TX: Sweet Publishing, 1973), 253.

31. Michael Ray FitzGerald, "Boss Jocks: How Corrupt Radio Practices Made Jacksonville One of the Great Music Cities," *Southern Cultures* 17, no. 4 (Winter 2011).

32. Axton purported to have cowritten "Heartbreak Hotel," but some sources say coauthor Tommy Durden, a regular on Toby Dowdy's WMBR-TV program *Country Frolics*, had been performing the song long before he met Axton (Marshall Rowland, telephone interview by the author, 2002). In any case, she personally delivered it to Presley at a disc-jockey convention in Nashville, whereupon he recorded it for RCA Records, and it became his first million-seller (Axton, *Country Singers as I Know 'Em*, 253).

33. Michael Ray FitzGerald, "NE Florida Music Scene More than Lynyrd Skynyrd," *Jacksonville Business Journal*, July 15, 2002, https://www.bizjournals.com/jacksonville/stories/2002/07/15/story1.html.

34. For a comprehensive listing of famous musicians from the region, see Michael Ray FitzGerald, *Swamp Music* (Jacksonville: Hidden Owl, 2019).

35. Colin Escott, "Rickey Medlocke of Lynyrd Skynyrd Checks in with the Southern Rock Cruise Roundup," Southern Rock Cruise, April 5, 2017, https://southernrockcruise.com/news/ricky-medlocke-checks-in with-the-southern-rock-cruise-roundup.

36. Scott Sisson, personal interview by the author, November 29, 2018.

37. Steve Houk, "38 Special's Don Barnes: Fostering the Spirit of the Underdog," *Live for Music*, September 22, 2014, https://liveformusic.com/features/38-specials-don-barns-fostering-the-spirit-of-the-underdog/.

38. Houk, "38 Special's Don Barnes."

39. Houk, "38 Special's Don Barnes."

Chapter 1. Gram Parsons: A Walking Contradiction

1. Margaret Fisher in David N. Meyer, *Twenty-Thousand Roads: The Ballad of Gram Parsons and his Cosmic American Music* (New York: Random House, 2007), 103.

2. Pauline Wilkes qtd. in Meyer, *Twenty-Thousand Roads*, 14.

3. Meyer, *Twenty-Thousand Roads*, 87–88.

4. Meyer, *Twenty-Thousand Roads*, 38.

5. Meyer, *Twenty-Thousand Roads*, 153.

6. Billy Ray Herrin, telephone interviews by the author, March 12 and 13, 2019.

7. Larry Murray, telephone interview by author, March 25, 2019.

8. Meyer, *Twenty-Thousand Roads*, 32.

9. Mae Boren Axton, *Country Singers as I Know 'Em* (Austin: Sweet Publishing, 1973), 253. Mae Axton is the mother of Hoyt Axton, an accomplished singer-songwriter in his own right as well as an actor.

10. Meyer, *Twenty-Thousand Roads*, 159, 168.

11. Ian Dunlop qtd. in Ben Fong-Torres, *Hickory Wind: The Life and Times of Gram Parsons* (New York: Knopf, 1990), 68. See also Ian Dunlop, *Breakfast in Nudie Suits* (Huntingdon, UK: Clarksdale Books, 2011), 47.

12. Gram Parsons in Jacoba Atlas, "Gram Parsons: The Burrito Ego Man," *Melody Maker*, April 3, 1973, cited in John F. Stanislawski, "Grievous Angel: Gram Parsons and the Country-Rock Movement" (PhD diss., University of Illinois–Urbana, 2014), 268.

13. Gram Parsons qtd. in Jason Walker, *God's Own Singer* (London: Helter Skelter, 2002), 100.

14. Telephone interviews by the author, April 3 and April 5, 2019. See also David W. Johnson, "Crediting 'Hickory Wind,'" Folklinks, n.d., http://www.folklinks.com/hickory_wind.html. See also John Einarson, *Hot Burritos: The True Story of the Flying Burrito Brothers* (Minneapolis: Jawbone Books, 2008), 34.

15. Johnson telephone interview, April 5, 2019. See also Johnson, "Crediting 'Hickory Wind.'"

16. Margaret Fisher qtd. in Meyer, *Twenty-Thousand Roads*, 103–4.

17. James Mallard qtd. in J. Taylor Rushing, "Waycross' Forgotten Son," *Florida Times-Union*, July 20, 2005, retrieved March 20, 2019 from http://buffettnews.com/forum/viewtopic.php?t=38274.

18. Ryan Trevett, personal interview by the author, March 11, 2019; Hugh Simpson, email correspondence with the author, April 1, 2019.

19. Tom Williams in Rushing, "Waycross' Forgotten Son."

20. Meyer, *Twenty-Thousand Roads*, 125.

21. Regarding Parsons seeking out Neil, see Bob Kealing, *Calling Me Home: Gram Parsons and the Roots of Country Rock* (Gainesville: University Press of Florida, 2012), 97. Regarding Neil's "passion for heroin," see David Hajdu, *Positively Fourth Street: The Lives and Times of Joan Baez, Bob Dylan, Mimi Baez Farina, and Richard Farina* (London: Bloomsbury, 2002), 78; excerpts reprinted at http://www.fredneil.com/positively-4th-street/.

22. Bill Conrad, personal interview by the author, March 27, 2019.

23. Conrad interview, March 27, 2019; see also Meyer, *Twenty-Thousand Roads*, 107.

24. Simpson, email correspondence, April 1, 2019.

25. Bud Scoppa, review of *Grievous Angel*, *Rolling Stone*, March 28, 1974, http://rollingstone.com/music/albumreviews/grievous-angel-19730301.

26. Dickey Smith in Meyer, *Twenty-Thousand Roads*, 31. See Rufus McClure qtd. in Kealing, *Calling Me Home*, 88.

27. Dick Weissman, telephone interview by the author, April 3, 2019.

28. Dick Weissman in Kealing, *Calling Me Home*, 16. Weissman also said the story about his and John Phillips bringing the Shilos to Albert Grossman is probably apocryphal. Weissman did not participate in any such dealings (Weissman telephone interview, April 6, 2019).

29. Jim Stafford qtd. in Kealing, *Calling Me Home*, 117. See also Sid Griffin, *Gram Parsons: A Music Biography* (Pasadena, CA: Sierra Books, 1985), 29.

30. Jim Carlton qtd. in Walker, *God's Own Singer*, 27.

31. Parsons withdrew from Harvard in February 1966.

32. Meyer, *Twenty-Thousand Roads*, 154.

33. David W. Johnson, "His Talent Died in the Desert," *Harvard Journal*, July-August 1994. Johnson himself was a Harvard student and had met Parsons there in 1965 (Johnson telephone interview, April 5, 2019).

34. Barney Hoskyns, *Waiting for the Sun: A Rock 'n' Roll History of Los Angeles* (Milwaukee: Backbeat Books, 2009), 167. See also Einarson, *Hot Burritos*, 42–44.

35. Meyer, *Twenty-Thousand Roads*, 153.

36. Meyer, *Twenty-Thousand Roads*, 160.

37. Judy Sims, "Ex-Byrd Gram Solos: He's No Longer in a Hurry," *Rolling Stone*, March 1973, 14.

38. Jim Carlton qtd. in Meyer, *Twenty-Thousand Roads*, 73; see also John Corneal qtd. in Meyer, *Twenty-Thousand Roads*, 204.

39. Bud Scoppa, liner notes to *Return of the Grievous Angel: A Tribute to Gram Parsons* (Almo Sounds, April, 1999), reprinted at http://www.furious.com/perfect/gramparsons/budscoppa.html.

40. Olivia Carter Mather, "Cosmic American Music: Place and the Country Rock Movement, 1965–1974" (PhD diss., University of California–Los Angeles, 2006), 84.

41. Bill Conrad, *Country-Rock Journals* (New York: Knopf, 2015), 127.

42. "Richards Leads Parsons Tributes," *Billboard*, July 11, 2004, https://www.billboard.com/articles/news/67393/richards-leads-parsons-tributes.

43. Chris Jagger in Patrick Donovan, "Unsung Jagger Rolls His Own Way," *Brisbane Times*, August 12, 2009, retrieved from https://www.brisbanetimes.com.au/entertainment/unsung-jagger-rolls-his-own-way-20090812-ehlr.html.

44. Victor Bockris, *Keith Richards: The Biography* (New York: Da Capo, 2003), 148.

45. Conrad interview, March 27, 2019.

46. Margaret Fisher in Meyer, *Twenty-Thousand Roads*, 420–23.

47. Murray telephone interview, April 3, 2019.

48. Meyer, *Twenty-Thousand Roads*, 439.

49. Gram Parsons qtd. in Jay Ehler, "Gram Parsons Sweeps out the Ashes," *Crawdaddy*, October 1973, 74. See also Meyer, *Twenty-Thousand Roads*, 366.

50. Murray telephone interview, April 3, 2019.

51. James E. Perone, "Gram Parsons: Grievous Angel," in *The Golden Age of the Singer-Songwriter, 1970–1973* (Santa Barbara, CA: Praeger, 2012), 8.

52. Meyer, *Twenty-Thousand Roads*, 358.

53. Merle Haggard, "The Fightin' Side of Me." © 1970 Tree Music. See also Carol Marin, "Listening Closely to Merle Haggard," *Chicago Tribune*, July 23, 2003, https://www.chicagotribune.com/news/ct-xpm-2003-07-23-0307230214-story.html.

54. John Einarson, *Desperados: The Roots of Country Rock* (New York: Cooper Square, 2001), 213.

55. Gram Parsons qtd. in Griffin, *Gram Parsons*, 146.

56. Musicologist John Stanislawski agrees with this view (Stanislawski, "Grievous Angel: Gram Parsons and the Country-Rock Movement," 261.

57. Butch Trucks qtd. in Alan Paul, *One Way Out: The Inside History of the Allman Brothers Band* (New York: St. Martins-Griffin, 2014), 182–83.

58. As far as I can tell, Van Zant never mentions Parsons in any interviews.

59. Herrin telephone interview, April 15, 2019.

60. Artimus Pyle, telephone interview by the author, April 14, 2019.

61. Griffin, *Gram Parsons*, 13. See also Fong-Torres, *Hickory Wind*, 182.

62. Van Zant even rewrote the song as "Jacksonville Kid" (Lynyrd Skynyrd, "Jacksonville Kid," *Street Survivors*, MCA Records, 1977).

63. David W. Brown, personal message to the author, April 14, 2019.

Chapter 2. The Bitter Ind/31st of February

1. David Brown, telephone interview by the author, April 12, 2019.

2. Butch Trucks, "First Blog," *The World According to Butch Trucks*, July 13, 2011, http://thebutchtrucks.blogspot.com/2011/07/first-blog.html; J. Michael Butler, "Lord, Have Mercy on My Soul: Sin, Salvation and Southern Rock," *Southern Cultures* 9, no. 4 (December 2003): 77.

3. I do not think this was the same Echoes that featured Dennis Yost, later singer for the Classics, on drums and vocals.

4. Randy Poe, *Skydog: The Duane Allman Story* (Milwaukee: Backbeat Books, 2006), 26.

5. Kevin Spangler and Ron Currens, "Butch Trucks, the Different Drummer," *Hittin' the Note* 15, n.p., n.d., cited in Poe, *Skydog*, 25.

6. Brown telephone interview, April 12, 2019.

7. Trucks, "First Blog"; Poe, *Skydog*, 26.

8. Brown, telephone interview, April 12, 2019.

9. Brown, telephone interview, April 12, 2019.

10. Poe, *Skydog*, 27.

11. Brown, telephone interview, April 12, 2019.

12. "Let's Get Together," written by Valenti under the name Chet Powers, was originally recorded by the Kingston Trio on their 1964 Capitol album, *Back in Town*.

13. Butch Trucks in Poe, *Skydog*, 65.

14. Poe, *Skydog*, 65.

15. Brown, telephone interview, April 12, 2019.

16. Daniel Sanchez, "Hounded by Debt, Allman Brothers Butch Trucks May Have Committed Suicide," *Digital Music News*, January 27, 2017, https://www.digital-musicnews.com/2017/01/27/allman-brothers-butch-trucks-commits-suicide/.

Chapter 3. The Allman Brothers Band

1. Mack Doss, telephone interview by the author, April 19, 2015. Doss had led a Bradenton-based teen group called the Thunderbeats who included guitarist Larry Reinhardt. Reinhardt was too young to play some of the Thunderbeats' dates, so Betts filled in occasionally. Doss took Betts's advice and moved to Jacksonville in 1968. The Jokers included bassist Joe Dan Petty, who would become a roadie for the Allman Brothers Band and later led his own group, Grinderswitch, signed to Capricorn Records.

2. Dickey Betts qtd. in Kirsten West, "Inside the Elusive Mr. Betts," *Hittin' the Note* 10, n.d., n.p., cited in Randy Poe, *Skydog: The Duane Allman Story* (San Francisco: Backbeat Books, 2006), 69.

3. Dickey Betts in Andy Aledort, "Big Brother: Dickey Betts Remembers Duane Allman," *Guitar World*, April 2007, reprinted at *Duane Allman Info*, https://www.duaneallman.info/bigbrother.htm.

4. Betts in Aledort, "Big Brother: Dickey Betts Remembers Duane Allman." See also Jas Obrecht, "Duane Allman: The Complete 1981 Dickey Betts Interview," *Jas Obrecht Music Archive*, November 29, 2010, http://jasobrecht.com/duane-allman-1981-dickey-betts-interview/

5. Poe, *Skydog*, 3.

6. Duane Allman qtd. in Poe, *Skydog*, 1.

7. See photo in Scott Freeman, *Midnight Riders: The Story of the Allman Brothers Band* (New York: Little, Brown, 1995), 250.

8. Bob Greenlee in Jas Obrecht, "Young Duane Allman: The Bob Greenlee Interviews," *Jas Obrecht Music Archive*, 2010, http://jasobrecht.com/young-duane-allman-bob-greenlee-interview/.

9. Michael Ray FitzGerald, "Boss Jocks: How Corrupt Radio Practices Helped

Make Jacksonville, Florida, One of the Great Music Cities," *Southern Cultures* 17, no. 4 (Winter 2011).

10. Alan Paul, *One Way Out: The Inside History of the Allman Brothers Band* (New York: St. Martins Griffin, 2014), 2.

11. Gregg Allman qtd. in Poe, *Skydog*, 14.

12. Gregg Allman qtd. in Dennis Elsas, "Gregg Allman Shares a Fillmore East Secret," Best Classic Bands, n.d., https://bestclassicbands.com/gregg-allman -interview-dennis-elsas-3-2-16/.

13. Bob Greenlee qtd. in Obrecht, "Young Duane Allman." See also Gregg Allman, *My Cross to Bear*, with Alan Light (New York: HarperCollins, 2012, 45.

14. Gregg Allman, qtd. in Paul, *One Way Out*, 2.

15. Gregg Allman, *My Cross to Bear*, 65.

16. It's not clear whether these dates were booked by Gunn, Allied Artists, or Nashville-based One Niters Inc., but apparently all three agencies booked the band at some point.

17. See chapter 2, "The Bitter Ind/31st of February."

18. John D. Loudermilk qtd. in Poe, *Skydog*, 32.

19. It was to Killen that Mae Axton brought the song "Heartbreak Hotel" in 1955 after plugging it herself to Elvis Presley in person at a hotel in Nashville (Mae Axton, *Country Singers as I Know 'Em* (Fort Worth, TX: Sweet Publishing, 1973), 253.

20. Allman, *My Cross to Bear*, 75.

21. Duane Allman qtd. in Freeman, *Midnight Riders*, 21.

22. Buddy Killen, telephone interview by the author, October 10, 2005.

23. David Brown, Facebook posting, July 30, 2019. See also Scott Cantor, "The Spotlights: 'Batman and Robin,'" *Duane Allman*, n.p., n.d., https://www. duaneallman.info/duanediscbatmanandrobin.htm.

24. Poe, *Skydog*, 38.

25. Michael Buffalo Smith, "Johnny Sandlin: Southern Producer, Engineer and Musician," *Gritz*, Spring 2004, reprinted at http://swampland.com/articles/ view/title:johnny_sandlin. Gregg Allman, however, writes that this merger of the two bands took place in St. Louis and that Hornsby, Sandlin, and bassist Mabron McKinley decided to give guitarist Hinton the heave-ho: "It didn't take long for them to get rid of Hinton and form a new band with us." Allman's recol- lection are often muddled (Allman, *My Cross to Bear*, 76).

26. Poe, *Skydog*, 70.

27. Poe, *Skydog*, 70–71.

28. The former site of the Scene, about a half mile from the author's home, is now the site of a strip mall.

29. John Meeks to Kirk West, letter published as "A Tale of the Second Com- ing," *Hittin the Note* 21, n.d, n.p.

30. Poe, *Skydog*, 70.

31. Second Coming drummer John Meeks wrote that Dale Betts's keyboard playing was insufficient (Meeks to West, n.d, n.p.)

32. Aledort, "Big Brother: Dickey Betts Remembers Duane Allman."

33. Reese Wynans in Poe, *Skydog*, 72.

34. Judy Seymour, who later married Ronnie Van Zant of Lynyrd Skynyrd, moved into the Green House with Dean Kilpatrick and Mary Hayworth after most of the Second Coming members had moved to the Gray House. Seymour let the Skynyrd boys hang out and rehearse there. They would also stop by the Gray House to visit with Second Coming members as well as Duane and Gregg Allman and ask advice ("Duane and Gregg Met Lynyrd Skynyrd," *Hittin' the Web with the Allman Brothers Band*, https://allmanbrothersband.com/modules.php?op=modload&name=XForum&file=viewthread&tid=2041).

35. Rick Whitney, "The Allman Brothers Band: Architectural Heritage—A Tale of Two Houses," *Hittin' the Note* 26 (2000), n.p.

36. Betts in Aledort, "Big Brother: Dickey Betts Remembers Duane Allman."

37. Unfortunately for Facemire, his program did not receive the kind of coverage most Big Ape shows enjoyed. The Big Ape's 50,000-watt clear-channel signal at AM 690, which could be heard from Daytona Beach to Virginia Beach, was reduced to 10,000 watts after dark because WTIX New Orleans had dibs on this frequency at night. In order not to impinge on TIX's territory, WAPE broadcast in an easterly direction from transmitters in Baldwin, due west of Jacksonville. Its nighttime signal was beamed directly at Jacksonville but could possibly be picked up in south Georgia (Tommy Register, telephone interview by the author, May 25, 2019). At night, WAPE transmitted "a pattern so tight that it simply didn't exist on the northern or southern sides of the metro [area]" (Scott Fybush, "Site of the Week 1/18/2013: Jacksonville, Florida, 2011 [Part 3], *Fybush.com*, January 18, 2013, https://www.fybush.com/site-of-the-week-1182013-jacksonville-florida-2011-part-3/).

38. Famed producer Luther Dixon, a Jacksonville native who wrote and produced several top-selling hits in the 1960s and had been A&R director at Scepter Records, was on Steady's staff ("Trefferson Bows Line with Khouri," *Billboard*, November 2, 1968, 86). See also "Second Coming's Disk to Hourglass," *Billboard*, April 26, 1969.

39. The Second Coming's version of "I Feel Free" can be heard at https://www.youtube.com/watch?v=EaY2MRZVa_M.

40. Allen Facemire, telephone interview by the author, October 1, 2017.

41. Richard Price, telephone interview by the author, June 4, 2019.

42. Paul, *One Way Out*, 22.

43. Paul, *One Way Out*, 22.

44. Freeman, *Midnight Riders*, 22. See also Poe, *Skydog*, 40.

45. Allman, *My Cross to Bear*, 77.

46. Gregg Allman qtd. in Freeman, *Midnight Riders*, 23.

47. *Cash Box*, October 28, 1967, 47. Boone himself had been born in Jacksonville in 1934.

48. Poe, *Skydog*, 47.

49. Poe, *Skydog*, 43.

50. Taj Mahal, "Statesboro Blues," *Taj Mahal*, Columbia Records, 1968.

51. Allman, *My Cross to Bear*. There are so many problems with Gregg Allman's recollections—one could compile a long list—that I would characterize him as perhaps the least reliable of all witnesses to what went on. Some of the things he claims to remember cannot possibly have happened—at least not in the time frames he places them in.

52. Poe, *Skydog*, 50–52.

53. Dave Kyle, "Remembering Duane Allman," *Vintage Guitar*, January 1997, reprinted at https://www.duaneallman.info/rememberingduaneallman.htm. See also Pete Carr qtd. in Poe, *Skydog*, 63.

54. John Einarson, *Desperados: The Roots of Country Rock* (Lanham, MD: Cooper Square, 2001). Galadrielle Allman writes that Gregg was working with Poco when Duane called him from Jacksonville on March 23, 1968 (Allman, *Please Be with Me* [New York: Spiegel and Grau, 2014], 163). Gregg Allman reiterates this time frame in his autobiography, but it is likely she got the information from him.

55. Larry Steele, *As I Recall: 1964–1987* (CreateSpace Independent Publishing Platform, 2016), 125.

56. Gregg Allman, *My Cross to Bear*, 82.

57. Paul Hornsby qtd. in Poe, *Skydog*, 64.

58. Geraldine Allman to Jo Jane Pitt, September 25, 1968, letter reprinted in Galadrielle Allman, *Please Be with Me*, 126–27.

59. Duane Allman to Donna Roosmann, September 4, 1968, letter reprinted in Galadrielle Allman, *Please Be with Me*, 130.

60. Meeks to West, n.d., n.p. See also Poe, *Skydog*, 73.

61. Gregg Allman, *My Cross to Bear*, 99–100.

62. Jim Clash, "Allman Brothers Band's Butch Trucks: 'Don't Call Lady Gaga Music,'" *Forbes*, April 4, 2016, https://www.forbes.com/sites/jimclash/2016/04/04/allman-brothers-bands-butch-trucks-dont-call-lady-gaga-music/#2a6fd4ce3a90.

63. Gregg Allman, *My Cross to Bear*, 111.

64. Rick Hall, *The Man from Muscle Shoals: My Journey from Shame to Fame* (Clovis, CA: Heritage Builders, 2015), 281–83. There is some discrepancy in the Allman lore as to whether Hall summoned Allman to Muscle Shoals (some say by telegram) or whether Allman, as Hall insists, showed up entirely uninvited and was, in fact, initially rebuffed by Hall.

65. Duane Allman to Donna Roosmann, in Galadrielle Allman, *Please Be with Me*, 132.

66. Duane Allman to Donna Roosmann, in Galadrielle Allman, *Please Be with Me*, 132.

67. Rick Hall, qtd. in Jerry Wexler, *The Rhythm and the Blues: A Life in American Music*, with David Ritz (New York: Knopf, 1993), 225. See also Hall qtd. in Poe, *Skydog*, 98.

68. Rick Hall in Paul, *One Way Out*, 8.

69. Rick Hall in Paul, *One Way Out*, 9.

70. Freeman, *Midnight Riders*, 37.

71. Freeman, *Midnight Riders*, 37. Regarding Gregg Allman's assessment of Duane's singing, see Gregg Allman, *My Cross to Bear*, 46.

72. Poe, *Skydog*, 97.

73. Hall, *Midnight Riders*, 286.

74. See entries from both Johnny Sandlin and Rick Hall in Paul, *One Way Out*, 10.

75. Hall in Paul, *One Way Out*, 10.

76. Wexler, *The Rhythm and the Blues*, 225.

77. Jerry Wexler qtd. in Freeman, *Midnight Riders*, 33.

78. Freeman, *Midnight Riders*, 33.

79. Butch Trucks qtd. in Phil W. Hudson, "Q&A: Butch Trucks of the Allman Brothers Band Talks Phil Walden, Reunion, Bruce Hampton," *Atlanta Business Chronicle*, December 15, 2016, https://www.bizjournals.com/atlanta/news/2016/12/15/q-a-butch-trucks-of-the-allman-brothers-band-talks.html.

80. Allman to Roosman in Galadrielle Allman, *Please Be with Me*, 142.

81. Jimmy Johnson in Jas Obrecht, "Duane Allman Remembered," *Guitar Player* 15, no. 10 (October 1981), reprinted at https://www.duaneallman.info/duaneallmanremembered.htm.

82. Duane Allman qtd. in Poe, *Skydog*, 89.

83. Paul Hornsby qtd. in Poe, Skydog, 97.

84. Johnny Sandlin qtd. in Paul, *One Way Out*, 16.

85. Duane Allman to Jo Jane Pitt, in Galadrielle Allman, *Please Be with Me*, 153–54.

86. Duane Allman qtd. in Poe, *Skydog*, 101.

87. There are at least three stories about how Gregg Allman got to Jacksonville (see Gregg Allman, *My Cross to Bear*, 11, 106–7; and Kim Payne in Paul, *One Way Out*, 27; see also Poe, *Skydog*, 106–7).

88. Gregg Allman is clearly conflating Trucks's cottage in Arlington with the Green House in Riverside, which were not only miles apart but across the river from each other. He notes that Ellen Hopkins lived "down the street" from Butch and that Berry and Linda and their daughter were staying there as well. The house where Hopkins et al. lived is in fact the Gray House (2844 Riverside Avenue), which is confirmed in the 1969 Jacksonville Residential Directory: Ellen Hopkins, Berry Oakley, Reese Wynans and Larry Reinhardt are listed

as living there in separate apartments (Whitney, The Allman Brothers Band, n.p.).

89. Gregg Allman, *My Cross to Bear*, 112.

90. Anthony Clark, "With Lipham's Closing, Gainesville Losing Link to Rock Royalty, *Gainesville Sun*, April 11, 2014, https://www.gainesville.com/article/LK/20140411/BUSINESS/604135191/GS/.

91. "Around J(action)ville," *Jacksonville Journal*, March 28, 1969.

92. Gregg Allman, *My Cross to Bear*, 115.

93. Richard Price, email correspondence with the author, October 6, 2017.

94. Betts in Paul, *One Way Out*.

95. Phil Walden in Paul, *One Way Out*, 63.

96. Marley Brant, *Southern Rockers: The Roots and Legacy of Southern Rock* (New York: Billboard Books, 1999), 13.

97. Arlene Weiss, "Gregg Allman's Thoughts on ABB Stating They're Not Southern Rock," *Hittin' the Web with the Allman Brothers Band*, n.d., https://allmanbrothersband.com/modules.php?op=modload&name=XForum&file=viewthread&tid=144753. See also Alan Paul, "Dickey Betts on the Term 'Southern Rock,'" AlanPaul.net, n.d. http://alanpaul.net/2016/10/dickey-betts-on-the-term-southern-rock/.

98. Michael Limnios, "Legendary Drummer Butch Trucks Talks about the Blues, Jazz, Allman Brothers and American Literature," Blues Network, October 27, 2016, http://blues.gr/profiles/blogs/legendary-drummer-butch-trucks-talks-about-the-blues-jazz-allman. See also Paul, *One Way Out*, 321–22.

99. Butch Trucks qtd. in John J. Moser, "Butch Trucks' Last Interview: The Complete Transcript," *Morning Call*, January 25, 2017, https://www.mcall.com/entertainment/lehigh-valley-music/mc-butch-trucks-last-interview-the-day-he-died-allman-brothers-co-founder-talked-with-lehigh-valley-mus-20170125-story.html.

100. Facemire telephone interview, May 28, 2019. See also Price telephone interview, June 4, 2019.

101. Reese Wynans, telephone interview by the author, May 21, 2016.

102. Facemire telephone interview, May 28, 2019.

103. Reese Wynans in Poe, *Skydog*, 108. Former 31st of February bassist David Brown also went with Scaggs at this time (see chapter 2, "The Bitter Ind/31st of February").

104. Patrick Snyder, "The Sorrowful Confessions of Gregg Allman," *Rolling Stone*, November 4, 1976, https://www.rollingstone.com/music/music-features/the-sorrowful-confessions-of-gregg-allman-108095/.

105. Jeff Giles, "How Scooter Herring's Arrest Broke up the Allman Brothers Band, *Ultimate Classic Rock*, May 28, 2016, https://ultimateclassicrock.com/allman-brothers-roadie-arrest/.

106. Jim Graves, telephone interview by the author, August 6, 2019.

107. David Browne, "Dickey Betts: The Lost Allman Brother" *Rolling Stone*, November 22, 2017, https://www.rollingstone.com/music/music-features/dickey-betts-the-lost-allman-brother-121021/.

Chapter 4. Cowboy

1. Bill Pillmore, telephone interview by the author, June 23, 2019.

2. "Legends of Southern Rock: Cowboy," *Swampland*, n.d., http://swampland.com/articles/view/title:legends_of_southern_rock_cowboy.

3. "Legends of Southern Rock: Cowboy," n.d.

4. Pillmore said the name "Cowboy" was his idea. Talton wanted to call it Easy (Pillmore telephone interview, June 23, 2019).

5. Scott B. Bomar, *Southbound: An Illustrated History of Southern Rock* (Lanham, MD, Backbeat Books, 2014), 71. See also Klemen Breznikar, "Cowboy Interview with Scott Boyer and Tommy Talton," *It's Psychedelic Baby*, April 14, 2015, https://www.psychedelicbabymag.com/2015/04/cowboy-interview-with-scott-boyer-and.html.

6. Bomar, *Southbound*, 71.

7. Bomar, *Southbound*, 73.

8. Matt Wake, "Scott Boyer Talks Cowboy, Recording with Allmans, Being Covered by Eric Clapton," AL.com, September 11, 2005, https://www.al.com/entertainment/2015/09/scott_boyer_talks_cowboy_capri.html.

9. Michael Buffalo Smith, "Pete Kowalke of Cowboy: The Gritz Interview," n.d., http://swampland.com/articles/view/title:pete_kowalke_of_cowboy_the_gritz_interview.

10. Bomar, *Southbound*, 71.

11. Tommy Talton, email correspondence with the author, April 18, 2019.

12. The Tampa group the Outlaws would follow much the same pattern later in the decade.

13. Luc Brunot, "Tommy Talton: We the People—Cowboy," *Bands of Dixie* 92, May 2013, reprinted at https://www.sweethomemusic.fr/Interviews/TaltonUS.php.

14. Breznikar, "Cowboy Interview with Scott Boyer and Tommy Talton."

15. Pillmore telephone interview, June 23, 2019.

16. Pillmore telephone interview, June 23, 2019.

17. Brunot, "Tommy Talton."

Chapter 5. Lynyrd Skynyrd: Bad-Boy Chic

1. Richard Price, telephone interview by the author, November 25, 2019.

2. Wayne G. Smith, telephone interview by the author, June 30, 2019.

3. Jacksonville guitarist Jimmy Pitman had also been with Strawberry Alarm Clock but left in 1969.

4. Don Dana, personal interview by the author, August 1997.

5. Larry Steele, *As I Recall, 1964–1987: Jacksonville's Place in American Rock History* (Scotts Valley, CA: CreateSpace Independent Publishing Platform, 2016). 446. Guitarist Jim DeVito, who was in Dougherty's band at the time, Sacred Cow, was sharing a room with Dougherty in Appleton, Wisconsin, when Dougherty took the call, affirms Dougherty's account (Jim DeVito, telephone interview by the author, August 16, 2017).

However, this interpretation seems unlikely to me. What seems more likely is that Van Zant was looking for an alternate lead singer to give him some relief onstage. This position would go to Rick Medlocke, who left his band Blackfoot and went with Skynyrd to Muscle Shoals, where he played drums for the group and also sang on three songs. Dougherty would go on to work with several former Skynyrd members as lead singer for the Allen Collins Band, who released one album in 1983.

6. Leon Wilkeson, qtd. in Mark Ribowsky, *Whiskey Bottles and Brand-New Cars: The Fast Life and Sudden Death of Lynyrd Skynyrd* (Chicago: Chicago Review Press, 2015), 41.

7. David Meyer, *Twenty-Thousand Roads: The Ballad of Gram Parsons and His Cosmic American Music* (New York: Random House, 2007), 72.

8. Barbara Ching, "Where Has the Free Bird Flown? Lynyrd Skynyrd and White Southern Manhood," in *White Masculinity in the Recent South*, ed. Trent Watts (Baton Rouge: Louisiana University Press, 2008), 253. See also J. Mike Butler, "'Luther King Was a Good Old Boy': The Southern Rock Movement and White Identity in the Post-Civil-Rights South," *Popular Music and Society* 2 (Summer 1999): 47.

9. I have never heard or read of Springsteen's having had any influence on Van Zant or his songwriting, but the similarities between the two are striking: both told story-songs using colorful characters, both touted themselves as working-class heroes, both had Dutch ancestry on their fathers' sides, and both had less-than-polished singing voices. There may be something in Dutch-American culture that embraces Calvinism and a work ethic that is sometimes envisioned as a panacea (James D. Bratt, *Dutch Calvinism in Modern America: A History of a Conservative Subculture* [Eugene, OR: Wipf and Stock, 1984], 127, 140).

10. Burns's father "worked his way up the corporate ladder" with the Hertz car-rental organization. The family moved to another—presumably nicer— house in 1967, eventually relocating to Marietta, Georgia, where the elder Burns founded a series of successful businesses. Both of Bob Burns's younger brothers are lawyers ("Robert Lewis Burns Sr." [obituary], 1932–2016, *Atlanta Journal-Constitution*, July 10, 2016, https://www.legacy.com/obituaries/atlanta/obituary.aspx?n=robert-lewis-burns-bob&pid=174591708&fhid=24392.

11. Scott Greene, "Larry 'L. J.' Junstrom: Larry Junstrom Recalls His Days with Lynyrd Skynyrd and Talks about His Band, .38 Special," *Swampland.com*, July 2003, http://swampland.com/articles/view/title:larry_lj_junstrom.

12. Steele, who died in 2017, has written a very detailed—and reliable—tome about his involvement in Jacksonville's music scene titled *As I Recall, 1964–1987: Jacksonville's Place in American Rock History*. He seems to be one of the few contemporaneous participants who remembers things clearly and at the same time seems unwilling to pay lip service to the common myths surrounding the more successful groups.

13. *If I Leave Here Tomorrow*, dir. Stephen Kijak (Passion Pictures/PolyGram Filmed Entertainment, 2015).

14. After a good deal of wrangling with diverging accounts, I have finally come to the conclusion that these are simply what should be called "colorful tales," often necessary to a life in show business. Others in the business call it "hype" (short for hyperbole).

15. Gary Rossington qtd. in Lee Ballinger, *Lynyrd Skynyrd: An Oral History* (New York: Avon Books, 1999), 5, 6.

16. Gene Odom, *Lynyrd Skynyrd: Remembering the Free Birds of Southern Rock*, with Frank Dorman (New York: Broadway Books, 2002), 18.

17. Odom, *Lynyrd Skynyrd*, 31.

18. The American Motorcycle Association purportedly released a statement shortly after a notorious Hollister, California, "motorcycle riot" in 1947. Executive Secretary E. C. Smith insisted that these "outlaw bikers" represented only "one percent" of the motorcycling community at most ("The AMA Responds," *Aging Rebel*, January 26, 2017, https://www.agingrebel.com/14987). See also William L. Dulaney, "A Brief History of 'Outlaw' Motorcycle Clubs," *International Journal of Motorcycle Studies* 1, no. 3 (November 2005), reprinted at https://web.archive.org/web/20180424010711/http://ijms.nova.edu/November2005/IJMS_Artcl.Dulaney.html.

19. Gary Rossington qtd. in Ballinger, *Lynyrd Skynyrd: An Oral History*, 9. It was far more typical for one band to play music for teens and another for the adults.

20. The Hour Glass played the Comic Book on Friday and Saturday, July 12 and 13, 1968; Larry Steele's group, the Male Bachs, opened on Friday, and the One Percent opened on Saturday. Both had been "house bands" at the Comic Book (Steele, *As I Recall*, 123–24).

21. Odom, *Lynyrd Skynyrd*, 48.

22. Steele, *As I Recall*, 144.

23. Tom Markham, telephone interview by the author, November 5, 2019.

24. Tom Rose, Magnum Studio: The Sound of the South," *Tom Rose Journalist*, http://tomrosejournalist.blogspot.com/2011/12/magnum-studio-sound-of-south.html.

25. Markham telephone interview, November 5, 2019.

26. Five of the six songs recorded under Markham and Sutton's auspices were included in MCA Records' *Skynyrd Collectybles* album in 2000. "He's Alive" was

omitted from this collection; however, a version recorded at Quinvy studio in Muscle Shoals in late 1970 is available on the 1991 *Lynyrd Skynyrd* box set.

27. Markham telephone interview, November 5, 2019. Some of Van Zant's tough-guy act, of course, was mere bravado. Skynyrd's later drummer, Artimus Pyle, who often worked alongside Burns, said Burns was actually the tougher of the two. Burns likely backed down out of deference to Van Zant's position as leader and surrogate big brother (Artimus Pyle, telephone interview by the author, November 21, 2019).

28. I was in the audience that night—I believe it was in April or May 1969— and didn't understand what the fuss was about. I asked a friend who Leonard Skinner was. I assumed this was a joke, but obviously the band intended to go through with the name change.

29. Odom, *Lynyrd Skynyrd*, 47–48.

30. Michael Buffalo Smith, "Skynyrd, The Allmans and Otis Redding: Alan Walden's Career in Rock and Soul," *Swampland.com*, January 2002, http://swampland.com/articles/view/title:alan_walden.

31. "Floyd and Walden Form Promo and Artist Management Pub. Co.," *Billboard*, November 21, 1970, 94.

32. Pat Armstrong, telephone interview by the author, July 9, 2019.

33. *If I Leave Here Tomorrow*, dir. Kijak. See also Ribowsky, *Whiskey Bottles and Brand-New Cars*, 49. This figure seems unlikely.

34. Gary Rossington qtd. in Ribowsky, *Whiskey Bottles and Brand-New Cars*, 139.

35. Markham telephone interview, November 5, 2019.

36. Five of the six songs would be licensed in 2000 to MCA Records for use in a collectors' set released on MCA called *Skynyrd Collectybles*.

37. "Quinvy Sound: The Natural Transition," *Billboard*, December 5, 1970, 48.

38. Ivy is mistaken here. Tom Markham and Jim Sutton of Shade Tree Records owned Lynyrd Skynyrd's first recording contract—the group may even have still been under contract to their Shade Tree operation at the time, but apparently Ivy was unaware of this.

39. Sir Shambling's Deep Soul Heaven, "Quin Ivy And His Norala And Quinvy Studios, Part 8, 1970," n.d., https://www.sirshambling.com/articles/quinvy_8/index.phphttps://www.sirshambling.com/articles/quinvy_8/index.php.

40. *Sir Shambling's*.

41. Bob Burns qtd. in Kristal Dixon, "Former Lynyrd Skynyrd Drummer Dies in Crash," *Cartersville (Ga.) Patch*, April 4, 2015, https://patch.com/georgia/cartersville/report-former-lynyrd-skynyrd-drummer-dies-crash-0.

42. Odom, *Lynyrd Skynyrd*, 55.

43. Steele, *As I Recall*, 194.

44. Greene, "Larry 'L. J.' Junstrom."

45. Odom, *Lynyrd Skynyrd*, 55.

46. Greg T. Walker in Michael Buffalo Smith, *From Macon to Jacksonville: More Conversations in Southern Rock* (Macon, GA: Mercer University Press, 2018), 88.

47. Alan Walden qtd. in Michael Buffalo Smith, "Skynyrd, the Allmans and Otis: Alan Walden's Career in Rock and Soul, *Swampland*, January 2002. http://swampland.com/articles/view/title:alan_walden.

48. Alan Walden qtd. in Mark Kemp, *Dixie Lullaby: A Story of Music Race and New Beginnings in a New South* (New York: Free Press/Simon and Schuster, 2004), 72.

49. *Juke*, pronounced *jook* (rhymes with "look"), is African American slang for drinking, dancing, and partying.

50. Scott B. Bomar, *Southbound: An Illustrated History of Southern Rock* (Milwaukee: Backbeat Books, 2014), 152.

51. Al Kooper, *Backstage Passes and Backstabbing Bastards* (New York: Billboard Books, 1998), 178.

52. *If I Leave Here Tomorrow*, dir. Kijak. See also Smith, "Skynyrd, the Allmans and Otis."

53. Kooper, *Backstage Passes and Backstabbing Bastards*, 191.

54. Ribowsky, *Whiskey Bottles and Brand-New Cars*, 81–82. For a better perspective on the fundamentalist-Christian view of rock as the devil's music, see Randall J. Stephens, *The Devil's Music: How Christians Inspired, Condemned, and Embraced Rock 'n' Roll* (Cambridge: Harvard University Press, 2018).

55. Matt Soergel, telephone interview by the author, June 25, 2019.

56. Leon Wilkeson qtd. in Ballinger, *Lynyrd Skynyrd: An Oral History*, 142.

57. Kooper, *Backstage Passes and Backstabbing Bastards*, 181.

58. Ballinger, *Lynyrd Skynyrd: An Oral History*, 1.

59. Ribowsky, *Whiskey Bottles and Brand-New Cars*, 21. See also Odom, *Lynyrd Skynyrd*, 35.

60. Alan Walden qtd. in Smith, "Skynyrd, the Allmans and Otis."

61. Leon Wilkeson qtd. in Ballinger, *Lynyrd Skynyrd: An Oral History*, 137.

62. Harry Doherty, "Lynyrd Skynyrd: Skyn Flick," *Melody Maker*, September 4, 1976, qtd. in Jeff Giles, "When Lynyrd Skynyrd Mixed Things up for 'Gimme Back My Bullets,'" *Ultimate Classic Rock*, February 2, 2016, https://ultimateclassicrock.com/lynyrd-skynyrd-gimme-back-my-bullets/.

63. Cameron Crowe, *One More from the Road* liner notes, MCA Records, 1976, reprinted at http://www.angelfire.com/tn/LSkynyrd/originallpliner.html.

64. C. Eric Banister, *Counting Down Southern Rock: The Best 100 Songs* (Lanham, MD: Rowman and Littlefield, 2016), 166.

65. Ronnie Van Zant qtd. in Susan Cross, "Guv'nah Wallace Meets Lynyrd Skynyrd," *Swank*, May, 1975, reprinted at *Susan Cross Writes*, https://susancrosswrites.blogspot.com/2014/11/interview-with-lynyrd-skynyrd-may-31.html.

66. Charlie Daniels qtd. in Kemp, *Dixie Lullaby*, 155.

67. Kemp, *Dixie Lullaby* , 155.

68. Leon Wilkeson qtd. in Zachary J. Lechner, ed., *The South of the Mind: American Imaginings of White Southernness, 1960–1980* (Athens: University of Georgia Press, 2018), 132.

69. Cross, "Guv'nah Wallace Meets Lynyrd Skynyrd."

70. Indeed, Van Zant once drunkenly referred to himself as "the Prince of Dixie." This led to a violent altercation between him and Outlaws singer-guitarist Henry Paul (Michael Buffalo Smith, "Henry Paul on the Outlaws, Blackhawk, and a Lifetime of Great Music," *Swampland*, n.d., http://swampland.com/articles/view/title:henry_paul_on_the_outlaws_blackhawk_and_a_lifetime_of_great_music).

71. Gary Rossington in Ribowsky, *Whiskey Bottles and Brand-New Cars*, 116. For the television appearance, see *The Old Grey Whistle Test*, BBC 4, November 11, 1975, https://www.youtube.com/playlist?list=PL7582840B288C9C80.

72. Ben Fong-Torres, *Hickory Wind: The Life and Times of Gram Parsons* (New York: St. Martins-Griffin, 1991), 182. See also "Gram Parsons: GP/Grievous Angel," gramparsons.com, n.d., https://gramparsons.com/discography/gp-grievous-angel/.

73. Cecil Kirk Hutson, "The Darker Side of Dixie: Southern Music and the Seamier Side of the Rural South" (PhD diss., Iowa State University, 1995), 285–86.

74. Nathaniel Carey and Doug Stanglin, "South Carolina Takes down Confederate Flag," *USA Today*, July 10, 2015, https://www.usatoday.com/story/news/nation/2015/07/10/south-carolina-confederate-flag/29952953/.

75. *If I Leave Here Tomorrow*, dir. Kijak. Johnny Van Zant even wears a Confederate soldier's uniform on the back cover of the band's 1993 album, *The Last Rebel*.

76. Hutson, "The Darker Side of Dixie," 296–97.

77. Keith Whitney, "Some Call Confederate Flag American Version of Swastika," *USA Today*, July 31, 2015, https://www.usatoday.com/story/news/politics/2015/07/31/confederate-flag-american-swastika/30948275/.

78. *If I Leave Here Tomorrow*, dir. Kijak.

79. Steve Newton, "Lynyrd Skynyrd and the Confederate Flag, *Georgia Straight*, August 27, 2015, https://www.straight.com/blogra/518196/lynyrd-skynyrd-and-confederate-flag.

80. Pat Armstrong, telephone interview by the author, August 16, 2018.

81. Ribowsky, *Whiskey Bottles and Brand-New Cars*, 129.

82. Ed King, *Ed King Forum*, December 1, 2009, http://edking.proboards.com/thread/70/ronnie.

83. Odom, *Lynyrd Skynyrd*, 159.

84. King, *Ed King Forum*.

85. Leon Wilkeson qtd. in Ballinger, *Lynyrd Skynyrd: An Oral History*, 142.

86. Cameron Crowe, "Lynyrd Skynyrd: Hell on Wheels Puts on the Brakes,"

Los Angeles Times, October 24, 1976, reprinted at http://www.theuncool.com/journalism/lynyrd-sknyrd-l-a-times/.

87. US. National Transportation Safety Board, "Aircraft Accident Report, 1 Company, Convair 248, N55 Gillsburg, Mississippi, October 20, 1977," June 19, 1978, 11., reprinted at http://libraryonline.erau.edu/online-full-text/ntsb/aircraft-accident-reports/AAR78-06.pdf.

88. Jordan Runtagh, "Remembering Lynyrd Skynyrd's Deadly 1977 Plane Crash," *Rolling Stone*, October 20, 2017, https://www.rollingstone.com/music/music-features/remembering-lynyrd-skynyrds-deadly-1977-plane-crash-2-195371/.

89. Scott K. Fish and Paul T. Riddle, "Artimus Pyle: Free Spirit," *Modern Drummer*, April 1983, https://www.moderndrummer.com/article/april-1983-artimus-pyle-free-spirit/. Pyle has written a screenplay about the crash, a movie of which is slated for release in March 2020. "Lynyrd Skynyrd Pic Set by Cleopatra Films with Drummer and Plane Crash Survivor Artimus Pyle, *Deadline.com*, June 24, 2016, http://cleorecs.com/home/lynyrd-skynyrd-pic-set-by-cleopatra-films-with-drummer-plane-crash-survivor-artimus-pyle-deadline-com/.

90. Eddie Mangum qtd. in Odom, *Lynyrd Skynyrd*.

91. Steve Garnaas, "Grand Jury Indicts Actress Linda Blair," *Florida Times Union*, March 12, 1979, reprinted at Skynyrd Frynds Forum, http://skynyrdfrynds.proboards.com/thread/846/grand-indicts-actress-linda-blair. See also "Linda Blair and Thirty-One Held in Drug Case," *New York Times*, December 21, 1977, 16.

92. Judy Jenness qtd. in Jaan Uhelszki, "Lynyrd Skynyrd: A Southern Ghost Story," Classic Rock, May 24, 2018, https://www.loudersound.com/features/lynyrd-skynyrd-a-southern-ghost-story.

93. Derek Hess to the author, personal message, July 13, 2019.

94. Hess message to the author, July 13, 2019.

95. Uhelszki, "Lynyrd Skynyrd: A Southern Ghost Story."

96. Randall Hall, telephone interview by the author, August 1, 2019.

97. Rachel Davis, "Bassist Couldn't Breathe, Emphysema Factor in Wilkeson Death," *Florida Times-Union*, September 8, 2001, reprinted at http://news.jacksonville.com/special/lynyrdskynyrd/bassistcouldntbreathe.html.

98. Qtd. in Runtagh, "Remembering Lynyrd Skynyrd's Deadly 1977 Plane Crash."

99. Tyler McCarthy, "Lynyrd Skynyrd Gets Candid about Departed Band Member, Plans after Farewell Tour," Fox News, October 22, 2018, https://www.foxnews.com/entertainment/lynyrd-skynyrd-gets-candid-about-departed-band-member-plans-after-farewell-tour.

100. Dave Everley, "Lynyrd Skynyrd Interview: The Last Stand," Classic Rock, June 25, 2019, https://www.loudersound.com/features/lynyrd-skynyrd-interview-the-last-stand.

101. Chuck Yarbrough, "Lynyrd Skynyrd's 'Free Bird' Flies toward Retirement with Farewell Tour," *Plain Dealer*, July 28, 2018, https://www.cleveland.com/music/2018/07/lynyrd_skynyrds_free_bird_flie.html.

Chapter 6. Blackfoot: Southern Metal

1. Greg T. Walker, telephone interview by the author, June 30, 2019.

2. Walker telephone interview, June 30, 2019.

3. Michael Buffalo Smith, "Legends of Southern Rock" Blackfoot," *Swampland.com.*, n.d., http://swampland.com/articles/view/title:legends_of_southern_rock_blackfoot/. See also Marty Jourard, "Gainesville Rock History: The Sixties and Seventies," Facebook, March 3, 2011, https://m.facebook.com/notes/gainesville-rock-history-the-60s-and-70s-bands-venues-stories/bands-bands-bands/159161717470226/?__tn__=C-R.

4. Walker telephone interview, June 30, 2019.

5. Walker telephone interview, June 30, 2019.

6. Rickey Medlocke in Paul Rees, "Rickey Medlocke: The Story of Southern Rock's Brightest Star," Classic Rock, October 28, 2016, https://www.loudersound.com/features/rickey-medlocke-the-story-of-southern-rocks-brightest-star.

7. Gene Odom, *Lynyrd Skynyrd: Remembering the Free Birds of Southern Rock* (New York: Broadway Books, 2002), 60–61.

8. Greg. T. Walker qtd. in Michael Buffalo Smith, *From Macon to Jacksonville: More Conversations in Southern Rock* (Macon, GA: Mercer University Press, 2018), 88.

9. Greg T. Walker, telephone interview by the author, August 27, 2019.

10. Guitarist Randall Hall has Super-8 footage of Burns and Medlocke both performing with Skynyrd at Jacksonville's Friendship Park in April 1972.

11. Walker in Smith, *From Macon to Jacksonville*, 88.

12. Walker in Smith, *From Macon to Jacksonville*, 88.

13. Scott B. Bomar, *Southbound: An Illustrated History of Southern Rock* (Milwaukee: Backbeat Books, 2014), 217.

14. Walker telephone interview, August 27, 2019.

15. Brian Rickman, "Why the 'New Blackfoot' Is Crap: How a Great Band Went Sour," Classic Rock 96.1, September 2, 2016, https://classicrock961.com/why-the-new-blackfoot-is-crap-how-a-great-band-goes-sour/.

16. Walker telephone interview, August 27, 2019.

17. Joe Tennis, "New Blackfoot Comes to Bristol Oct. 10," *Bristol Herald Courier*, October 5, 2015, https://www.heraldcourier.com/lifestyles/new-blackfoot-comes-to-bristol-oct/article_301b4fe6-6b81-11e5-b19d-3fe8f74169e8.html.

18. Walker telephone interview, August 27, 2019.

19. "Rickey Medlocke Biography," International Movie Database, n.d., https://www.imdb.com/name/nm1310712/bio?ref_=nm_ov_bio_sm.

20. Walker interview, August 27, 2019.

21. Walker interview, August 27, 2019.

22. Tennis, "New Blackfoot Comes to Bristol Oct. 10."

23. Tennis, "New Blackfoot Comes to Bristol Oct. 10."

24. Rickman, "Why the 'New Blackfoot' Is Crap." It's possible Medlocke and his business partner, Al Nalli, are simply keeping the trademark active—if a trademark falls into disuse it can be used by anyone—in the event Medlocke wants to use it himself it at a later date. This could just be a legal maneuver for keeping it on hold, so to speak.

Chapter 7. 38 Special: Holding on Loosely

1. Don Barnes qtd. in Scott B. Bomar, *Southbound: An Illustrated History of Southern Rock* (Milwaukee: Backbeat Books, 2014), 229.

2. Bomar, *Southbound*, 229.

3. John Wirt, "Classic .38 Special Songs Withstand the Test of Time," *Baton Rouge Advocate*, April 29, 2013, https://www.theadvocate.com/baton_rouge/entertainment_life/music/article_6e527b6b-ec37-54d2-9d70-c28c96a7133e.html.

4. "Battle of the Bands, Sponsored by Jacksonville Jaycees and Fuller Productions," n.d., n.p.

5. Gene Odom, *Lynyrd Skynyrd: Remembering the Free Birds of Southern Rock*, with Frank Dorman (New York: Broadway Books, 2002), 51. See also Larry Steele, *As I Recall, 1964–1987: Jacksonville's Place in American Rock History* (Scotts Valley, CA: CreateSpace Independent Publishing Platform, 2016), 142–43.

6. Fuller had engineered several recordings for Ocala's Royal Guardsmen, who had scored a couple of national hits on New York–based Laurie Records.

7. "In Profile: Veteran Mix Engineer Kevin Elson and His Work on the Current Kelly Clarkson Tour," *Pro Sound Web*, February 10, 2010, https://www.prosoundweb.com/topics/audio/in_profile_veteran_mix_engineer_kevin_elson_his_work_on_the_current_kelly_c/. See also "Kevin Elson: Biography," *People Pill*, n.d., https://peoplepill.com/people/kevin-elson/.

8. Steele, *As I Recall*, 228–29.

9. Cecil Kirk Hutson, "The Darker Side of Dixie: Southern Music and the Seamier Side of the Rural South" (PhD diss., Iowa State University, 1995, 137–40.

10. Ed King, *Ed King Forum*, December 1, 1999, http://edking.proboards.com/thread/52/jeff-carlisi.

11. Don Barnes qtd. in Brian Rademacher, "Interview with Don Barnes: 38 Special Still Rockin'," *Rock Eyez*, April 2008, http://www.rockeyez.com/interviews/int-don-barnes.html.

12. Rademacher, "Interview with Don Barnes."

13. Don Barnes qtd. in Bomar, *Southbound*, 235.

14. Don Barnes qtd. in Bomar, *Southbound*, 234.

15. Wirt, "Classic .38 Special Songs Withstand the Test of Time."

16. Van Zant qtd. in Bomar, *Southbound*, 234.

17. Matt Wardlaw, "How Survivor's Jim Peterik helped 38 Special and Sammy Hagar Write Big Hits," *Ultimate Classic Rock*, October 19, 2014, https://ultimateclassicrock.com/jim-peterik-interview/.

18. Don Barnes qtd. in Bomar, *Southbound*, 234.

19. C. Eric Banister, *Counting Down Southern Rock: The 100 Best Songs*. (Lanham, MD: Rowman and Littlefield, 2016), 73.

20. Don Barnes in Bomar, *Southbound*, 234–35.

21. Jim Peterik qtd. in Dave Paulson, "Story Behind the Song 'Hold on Loosely,'" *Nashville Tennessean*, February 21, 2015, https://www.tennessean.com/story/entertainment/music/2015/02/18/story-behind-song-hold-loosely/23646295/.

22. Jim Vallance, email correspondence with the author, August 14, 2019.

23. Michael Buffalo Smith, "There's Still Something Special about .38: The Don Barnes Interview," *Swampland.com*, February 2000, http://swampland.com/articles/view/title:don_barnes.

24. Steele, *As I Recall*, 525–27.

25. Don Barnes qtd. in "Don Barnes (38 Special)," *Wisconsin Music*, March 3, 2018, http://wisconsinmusic.net/2018/03/03/don-barnes-38-special/.

26. Jeff Carlisi and Dan Lipson, *Jam! Amp Your Team, Rock Your Business* (San Francisco: Jossey-Bass, 2009), 162–63.

27. Marley Brant, *Southern Rockers: The Roots and Legacy of Southern Rock* (New York: Billboard Books, 1999), 238–39.

Chapter 8. Molly Hatchet: Southern Spinal Tap

1. Dave Hlubek in Scott B. Bomar, *Southbound: An Illustrated History of Southern Rock* (Milwaukee: Backbeat Books, 2014), 221.

2. Dave Hlubek in Michael Buffalo Smith, *From Macon to Jacksonville: More Conversations in Southern Rock* (Macon, GA: Mercer University Press, 2018), 188.

3. Larry Steele, *As I Recall, 1964–1987: Jacksonville's Place in American Rock History* (Scotts Valley, CA: CreateSpace Independent Publishing Platform, 2016), 48–49.

4. "Dave Hlubek, Founding Member of Jacksonville Band Molly Hatchet, Dead at 66," *Florida Times-Union*, September 3, 2017, https://www.jacksonville.com/news/national/2017-09-03/dave-hlubek-founding-member-jacksonville-band-molly-hatchet-dead-66.

5. "Dave Hlubek, Founding Member of Jacksonville Band Molly Hatchet, Dead at 66." Grinderswitch was not a Jacksonville band but did include guitarist/vocalist Dru Lombar, who had led several bands including Jacksonville Beach teen band the Soul Searchers along with King James Version, a Christian-rock group that included bassist Leon Wilkeson.

6. Hlubek in Smith, *From Macon to Jacksonville*, 187.

7. Duane Roland qtd. in Smith, *From Macon to Jacksonville*, 201.

8. Hlubek in *Southbound*, 221–22. See also Danny Joe Brown in Smith, *From Macon to Jacksonville*, 183.

9. Pat Armstrong, telephone interview by the author, August 22, 2019.

10. Armstrong telephone interview, August 22, 2019.

11. Danny Joe Brown qtd. in Smith, *From Macon to Jacksonville*, 183.

12. Hlubek in Bomar, *Southbound*, 223.

13. Armstrong telephone interview, August 22, 2019.

14. Jeff Maysh, "The Scarface of Sex: The Millionaire Playboy Who Murdered His Way to the Top of Porn, *Daily Beast*, June 16, 2017, https://www.thedaily-beast.com/the-scarface-of-sex.

15. Armstrong, telephone interview, August 22, 2019.

16. Werman in Bomar, *Southbound*, 223.

17. "The Producers: Tom Werman, Chapter Seven," *Pop Dose*, May 21, 2009, http://popdose.com/the-producers-tom-werman-chapter-seven/.

18. Derek Kinner, "The War over Molly Hatchet," *Folio Weekly*, October 1, 2014, 10, reprinted at http://folioweekly.com/THE-WAR-OVER-MOLLY-HATCHET ,11040.

19. See liner notes by Gail Giddens from Hatchet's debut album, 1978.

20. Hlubek in Bomar, *Southbound*, 224.

21. Pat Armstrong, telephone interview by the author, September 25, 2019.

22. Kinner, "The War over Molly Hatchet."

23. Danny Joe Brown in Christopher Connelly, "Danny Joe Brown Gets Vindication," *Detroit Free Press*, August 17, 1981, 6C.

Perhaps a brief overview of music publishing is in order here. Song copyrights are almost always owned by music-publishing companies; this is a throwback to the days before sound recordings, when songs were primarily published and sold as sheet music. Many writers operate their own song-publishing companies, but it is still good practice is to assign the copyright to an established, full-service publisher who will "exploit" the property more extensively in return for 50 percent of the ensuing revenues the publisher generates. Obviously this isn't necessary if the writer is also the artist and already has his/her own recording contract. However, there are other, more esoteric, revenue streams a publisher can tap into, such as synchronization (film and television) fees and "plugging" the song (i.e., getting other artists to record it); hence there is still value in signing with an established publisher. A typical compromise is for a writer to copublish with an established publisher.

24. Armstrong telephone interview, September 25, 2019.

25. Brown qtd. in Smith, *From Macon to Jacksonville*, 186.

26. Armstrong telephone interview, September 25, 2019.

27. John Galvin in Smith, *From Macon to Jacksonville*, 193.

28. Hlubek in Bomar, *Southbound*, 226.

29. Philippe Archambeau, "Banner Thomas' interview," *Road to Jacksonville*,

November 2002, http://www.rtjwebzine.fr/rtjenglish/interviews/bthomas.
html.

30. Hlubek in Bomar, *Southbound*, 226.

31. Pat Armstrong, telephone interview with author, November 30, 2019.

32. Michael Smith, "Molly Hatchet: No Guts, No Glory," Allmusic, n.d., https:
//www.allmusic.com/album/no-gutsno-glory-mw0000837108.

33. Bomar, *Southbound*, 227.

34. Bomar, *Southbound*, 227.

35. "Interview with Dave Hlubek of Molly Hatchet," *Kaos2000*, n.d., link expired, reprinted in Bomar, *Southbound*, 227.

36. Perry had fronted a short-lived group alongside guitarist Ingram called
China Sky whom Armstrong also managed and had signed to his label, PARC
Records, marketed and distributed by Epic.

37. Riff West qtd. in Smith, *From Macon to Jacksonville*, 205.

38. Armstrong telephone interview, November 30, 2019.

39. Armstrong telephone interview November 30, 2019.

40. Brown qtd. in Smith, *From Macon to Jacksonville*, 185.

41. Bruce Crump qtd. in Kinner, "The War over Molly Hatchet."

42. Armstrong telephone interview, November 30, 2019.

43. Armstrong telephone interview, November 30, 2019.

44. Scott Sisson, telephone interview by the author, August 23, 2019.

45. Rebecca Sharpe in "Obituary: David Lawrence Hlubek, August 28, 1951–
September 2, 2017," Dignity Memorial, November 24, 2017, https://www.digni-
tymemorial.com/obituaries/jacksonville-fl/david-hlubek-7545753.

46. Aaron Hlubek qtd. in Kinner, "The War over Molly Hatchet."

47. Kinner, "The War over Molly Hatchet," 10.

48. Lisa Morgan, "Molly Hatchet Celebrates 40 Years at Stagecoach 2018,"
Coachella Valley Weekly, April 25, 2018, http://coachellavalleyweekly.com/molly
-hatchet-celebrates-40-years-stagecoach-2018/.

Chapter 9. Derek Trucks: Channeling Duane

1. Trucks now has his own line of medicine-bottle slides, manufactured by
Jim Dunlop.

2. David Fricke, "Derek Trucks Remembers Butch Trucks: 'He Left an Impression at All Times,'" *Rolling Stone*, January 31, 2017, https://www.rollingstone.
com/music/music-features/derek-trucks-remembers-butch-trucks-he-left-an-
impression-at-all-times-113703/.

3. Brian Braiker, "Derek Trucks Q&A: On Jamming with Legends and Covering Dylan," *Rolling Stone*, January 20, 2009, https://www.rollingstone.com/
music/music-news/derek-trucks-qa-on-jamming-with-legends-and-covering-
dylan-244577/. See also Derek Trucks, "How I Ended up on Stage with Bob Dylan
the First Time I Saw Him Live," *Ultimate Guitar*, July 4, 2017, https://www.

ultimate-guitar.com/news/general_music_news/derek_trucks_how_i_ended_up_on_stage_with_bob_dylan_the_first_time_i_saw_him_live.html.

4. Derek Hess in Michael Buffalo Smith, *From Macon to Jacksonville: More Conversations in Southern Rock* (Macon, GA: Mercer University Press, 2018), 71.

5. "Derek Hess: Drums, Percussion," Lynyrd Skynyrd Frynds, http://www.frynds.com/heartstrings/Chariot/Bios/DH.html.

6. Hess in Smith, *From Macon to Jacksonville*, 71.

7. Michael Rothschild, telephone interview by the author, August 31, 2019.

8. Of the four original members of the Derek Trucks Band, three are dead: drummer Chip Miller died in Jacksonville in 2005 at age fifty-three; bassist Meekins died in Jacksonville in 2013 at age sixty-three; and guitarist Baril died in Connecticut in 2019 at age sixty-three.

9. Rothschild telephone interview, August 31, 2019.

10. Rothschild telephone interview, August 31, 2019.

11. Fricke, "Derek Trucks Remembers Butch Trucks."

12. Susan Tedeschi qtd. in Steve Inskeep, "Susan Tedeschi and Derek Trucks, Partners in Music and in Life," NPR, March 1, 2019, https://www.npr.org/2019/03/01/697706005/susan-tedeschi-and-derek-trucks-partners-in-music-and-in-life.

13. Andy Tennille, "Finding His Path," *San Francisco Chronicle*, February 5, 2006, https://www.sfgate.com/entertainment/article/Finding-His-Path-2505242.php.

Chapter 10. Conclusion

1. David Gates, "White-Male Paranoia," *Newsweek*, March 29, 1993, 48–53.

2. Barbara Ching, "Where Has the Free Bird Flown? Lynyrd Skynyrd and White Southern Manhood," in *White Masculinity in the Recent South*, ed. Trent Watts (Baton Rouge: Louisiana State University Press, 2008), 251–65. See also Travis D. Stimeling, "To Be Polished More Than Extended': Musicianship, Masculinity and the Critical Reception of Southern Rock," *Journal of Popular Music Studies* 26, no. 1 (2014): 131.

3. Jason T. Eastman, "Rebel Manhood: The Hegemonic Masculinity of the Southern Rock Music Revival," *Journal of Contemporary Ethnography* 41, no. 2 (201): 189.

4. W. J. Cash, *The Mind of the South* (New York: Knopf, 1941), 50. See also "Masculinity," *Southern Rock and Civil Rights*, n.d., https://sites.google.com/site/southernrockcivilrights2/home/masculinity#_ftn1.

5. "You Got That Right." © 1978 Get Loose Music/Songs of Universal.

6. Jim Webb, *Born Fighting: How the Scots-Irish Shaped America* (New York: Broadway Books, 2004).

7. Walter Russell Meade, "The Jacksonians," *National Interest*, December 1, 1999, https://nationalinterest.org/article/the-jacksonian-tradition-939.

8. Jarrett Stepmann, Jarrett, "Trump Should Model His Foreign Policy after Andrew Jackson," *National Interest*, March 13, 2017, https://nationalinterest.org/feature/trump-should-model-his-foreign-policy-after-andrew-jackson-19771.

9. In 1975, the Lynyrd Skynyrd members were made honorary lieutenant colonels in the Alabama State Militia by none other than Governor George Wallace. Van Zant later called it a "bullshit gimmick thing" (Lee Ballinger, *Lynyrd Skynyrd: An Oral History* [Los Angeles: XT377 Publishing, 1999], 74–75).

10. Mark Kemp, *Dixie Lullaby: A Story of Music, Race, and New Beginnings in a New South* (Athens: University of Georgia Press, 2004), 87, 135.

11. Ted Ownby, "Freedom, Manhood and White-Male Tradition in 1970s Southern-Rock Music," in *Haunted Bodies: Gender and Southern Texts*, ed. Anne Goodwyn Jones and Susan V. Donaldson (Charlottesville: University of Virginia Press, 1998), 370. See also Mike Butler, "'Luther King Was a Good Ole Boy': The Southern-Rock Movement and White-Male Identity in the Post-Civil-Rights South," *Popular Music and Society* 23, no. 2 (Summer 1999): 41–61.

12. Al Kooper, *Backstage Passes & Backstabbing Bastards: Memoirs of a Rock 'n' Roll Survivor* (New York: Backbeat Books, 2008), 175.

13. Frederic Gomes Cassidy and Joan Houston Hall, *Dictionary of American Regional English IV* (Cambridge: Belknap Press of Harvard University Press, 2002), 531.

14. Jeff Carlisi, personal interview by the author, November 5, 2018.

15. Ed King qtd. in Kemp, *Dixie Lullaby*, 88–89.

16. Jaan Uhelszki, "Lynyrd Skynyrd: A Southern Ghost Story," Classic Rock, May 24, 2018, https://www.loudersound.com/features/lynyrd-skynyrd-a-southern-ghost-story.

17. Artimus Pyle, telephone interview by the author, May 1, 2019.

18. Paul, *One Way Out*, 321–22.

19. Charles E. Daniels, "Long Haired Country Boy," Epic Records, 1975. Song lyrics © 1975 by Kama Sutra Music.

20. David Allan Coe and Jimmy Rabbitt, "Longhaired Redneck," Columbia Records, 1976. Song lyrics © 1976 by Lotsa Music.

21. Indeed, rock 'n' roll itself, in its early forms, as exemplified by Elvis Presley, Chuck Berry, Buddy Holly, Gene Vincent, Buddy Knox, et al., *always* owed a great debt to country music—any country-music bar-band worth its salt can and probably does play "Johnny B. Goode." What is more, all of these artists have in fact been embraced by country fans, and many have been listed on the country & western best-seller charts.

22. There had been long-haired, loutish types in California who could qualify as "redneck hippies" for years or even decades by this point, mostly Hell's Angels and other "outlaw" bikers; however, the term "redneck" was peculiar to the South at this time.

BIBLIOGRAPHY

Primary Sources

Aledort, Andy. "Big Brother: Dickey Betts Remembers Duane Allman." *Guitar World*, April 2007. Reprinted at Duane Allman Info. https://www.duaneallman.info/bigbrother.htm.

Allman, Galadrielle. *Please Be with Me*. New York: Spiegel and Grau, 2014.

Allman, Gregg. *My Cross to Bear*. With Alan Light. New York: HarperCollins, 2012.

Archambeau, Philippe. "Banner Thomas' Interview." *Road to Jacksonville*, November 2002. http://www.rtjwebzine.fr/rtjenglish/interviews/bthomas.html.

Armstrong, Pat. Telephone interviews by the author. August 16, 2018, July 9, 2019, August 22, 2019, September 25, 2019, and November 30, 2019.

Axton, Mae Boren. *Country Singers as I Know 'Em*. Fort Worth, TX: Sweet Publishing, 1973.

"Battle of the Bands, Sponsored by Jacksonville Jaycees and Fuller Productions." 1965.

Berry, Chuck. "Rock and Roll Music." © 1957 by Arc Music.

Betts, Forrest. "Ramblin' Man." © 1973 by Forrest Richard Betts Music and Unichappell Music.

Braiker, Brian. "Derek Trucks Q&A: On Jamming with Legends and Covering Dylan." *Rolling Stone*, January 20, 2009. https://www.rollingstone.com/music/music-news/derek-trucks-qa-on-jamming-with-legends-and-covering-dylan-244577/.

Breznikar, Klemen. "Cowboy Interview with Scott Boyer and Tommy Talton." *It's Psychedelic Baby*, April 14, 2015. https://www.psychedelicbabymag.com/2015/04/cowboy-interview-with-scott-boyer-and.html.

Brown, David W. Personal message to the author. April 14, 2019.

———. Telephone interview by the author. April 12, 2019.

Browne, David. "Dickey Betts: The Lost Allman Brother." *Rolling Stone*, November 22, 2017. https://www.rollingstone.com/music/music-features/dickey-betts-the-lost-allman-brother-121021/.

Brunot, Luc. "Tommy Talton: We the People—Cowboy." *Bands of Dixie* 92 (May 2013). Reprinted at https://www.sweethomemusic.fr/Interviews/TaltonUS.php.

Cale, J. J. "Call Me the Breeze." © 1971 by Johnny Bienstock Music.

Carlisi, Jeff. Personal interview by the author. November 5, 2018.

Charles, Ray. *Brother Ray: Ray Charles' Own Story*. With David Ritz. New York: Da Capo, 1992.

Clash, Jim. "Allman Brothers Band's Butch Trucks: 'Don't Call Lady Gaga Music.'" *Forbes*, April 4, 2016. https://www.forbes.com/sites/jimclash/2016/04/04/allman-brothers-bands-butch-trucks-dont-call-lady-gaga-music/#2a6fd4ce3a90.

Coe, David Allan, and Jimmy Rabbitt. "Longhaired Redneck." © 1976 by Lotsa Music.

Conrad, Bill. *Country-Rock Journals*. New York: Knopf, 2015.

———. Personal interview by the author. March 27, 2019.

Dana, Don. Personal interview by the author. August 1997.

Daniels, Charles E. "Long Haired Country Boy." © 1975 by Kama Sutra Music.

DeVito, Jim. Telephone interview by the author. August 16, 2017.

Doss, Mack. Telephone interview by the author. April 19, 2015.

Dougherty, Jimmy. Personal interview by the author. August 1982.

Dowd, Tom. Personal interview by the author. 2002.

Escott, Colin. "Rickey Medlocke of Lynyrd Skynyrd Checks in with the Southern Rock Cruise Roundup." Southern Rock Cruise, April 5, 2017. https://southernrockcruise.com/news/ricky-medlocke-checks-in with-the-southern-rock-cruise-roundup.

Everley, Dave. "Lynyrd Skynyrd Interview: The Last Stand." Classic Rock, June 25, 2019. https://www.loudersound.com/features/lynyrd-skynyrd-interview-the-last-stand.

Facemire, Allen. Telephone interviews by the author. October 1, 2017, and May 28, 2019.

Fish, Scott K., and Paul T. Riddle. "Artimus Pyle: Free Spirit." *Modern Drummer*, April 1983. https://www.moderndrummer.com/article/april-1983-artimus-pyle-free-spirit/.

Fricke, David. "Derek Trucks Remembers Butch Trucks: 'He Left an Impression at All Times.'" *Rolling Stone*, January 31, 2017. https://www.rollingstone.com/music/music-features/derek-trucks-remembers-butch-trucks-he-left-an-impression-at-all-times-113703/.

Graves, Jim. Telephone interview by the author. August 6, 2019.

Greene, Andy. "Tom Petty on Past Confederate Flag Use: 'It Was Downright

Stupid."' *Rolling Stone*, July 14, 2015. https://www.rollingstone.com/politics/politics-news/tom-petty-on-past-confederate-flag-use-it-was-downright-stupid-177619/.

Greene, Scott. "Larry Junstrom Recalls His Days with Lynyrd Skynyrd and Talks about His Band, .38 Special." *Swampland.com*, July 2003, http://swampland.com/articles/view/title:larry_lj_junstrom.

Haggard, Merle. "The Fightin' Side of Me." © 1970 Tree Music.

Hall, Randall. Telephone interview by the author. August 1, 2019.

Hall, Rick. *The Man from Muscle Shoals: My Journey from Shame to Fame*. Clovis, CA: Heritage Builders, 2015.

Harrison, Jennifer. *Elvis as We Knew Him: Our Shared Life in a Small Town in South Memphis*. Bloomington, IN: iUniverse, 2003.

Herrin, Billy Ray. Telephone interviews by the author. March 12 and 13, 2019, and April 15, 2019.

Houk, Steve. "38 Special's Don Barnes: Fostering the Spirit of the Underdog." *Live for Music*, September 22, 2014. https://liveforlivemusic.com/features/38-specials-don-barnes-fostering-the-spirit-of-the-underdog/.

Hudson, Phil W. "Q&A: Butch Trucks of the Allman Brothers Band Talks Phil Walden, Reunion, Bruce Hampton." *Atlanta Business Chronicle*, December 15, 2016. https://www.bizjournals.com/atlanta/news/2016/12/15/q-a-butch-trucks-of-the-allman-brothers-band-talks.html.

"In Profile: Veteran Mix Engineer Kevin Elson and His Work on the Current Kelly Clarkson Tour." *Pro Sound Web*, February 10, 2010. https://www.prosoundweb.com/topics/audio/in_profile_veteran_mix_engineer_kevin_elson_his_work_on_the_current_kelly_c/.

Inskeep, Steve. "Susan Tedeschi and Derek Trucks, Partners in Music and in Life." NPR, March 1, 2019. https://www.npr.org/2019/03/01/697706005/susan-tedeschi-and-derek-trucks-partners-in-music-and-in-life.

Interview with Dave Hlubek of Molly Hatchet." *Kaos2000*, n.d. Link expired. Reprinted in Scott B. Bomar, *Southbound: An Illustrated History of Southern Rock*. Milwaukee: Backbeat Books, 2014.

Johnson, David W. Telephone interview by the author. April 5, 2019.

Killen, Buddy. Telephone interview by the author. October 10, 2005.

King, Ed. *Ed King Forum*, December 1, 2009. http://edking.proboards.com/thread/70/ronnie.

Kooper, Al. *Backstage Passes & Backstabbing Bastards: Memoirs of a Rock 'n' Roll Survivor*. New York: Backbeat Books, 2008.

Kyle, Dave. "Remembering Duane Allman." *Vintage Guitar*, January 1997. Reprinted at https://www.duaneallman.info/rememberingduaneallman.htm.

Limnios, Michael. "Legendary Drummer Butch Trucks Talks about the Blues, Jazz, Allman Brothers and American Literature." Blues Network, October

27, 2016. http://blues.gr/profiles/blogs/legendary-drummer-butch-trucks-talks-about-the-blues-jazz-allman.

Markham, Tom. Telephone interview by the author. November 5, 2019.

McCarthy, Tyler. "Lynyrd Skynyrd Gets Candid about Departed Band Member, Plans after Farewell Tour." Fox News, October 22, 2018. https://www.foxnews.com/entertainment/lynyrd-skynyrd-gets-candid-about-departed-band-member-plans-after-farewell-tour.

Meeks, John, to Kirk West. Letter published as "A Tale of the Second Coming." *Hittin' the Note* 21, n.d, n.p.

Moser, John J. "Butch Trucks' Last Interview: The Complete Transcript." *Morning Call*, January 25, 2017. https://www.mcall.com/entertainment/lehigh-valley-music/mc-butch-trucks-last-interview-the-day-he-died-allman-brothers-co-founder-talked-with-lehigh-valley-mus-20170125-story.html.

Murray, Larry. Telephone interviews by the author. March 25 and April 3, 2019.

Obrecht, Jas. "Duane Allman: The Complete 1981 Dickey Betts Interview." *Jas Obrecht Music Archive*, November 29, 2010. http://jasobrecht.com/duane-allman-1981-dickey-betts-interview/.

Old Grey Whistle Test. BBC 4, November 11, 1975. https://www.youtube.com/playlist?list=PL7582840B288C9C80.

Paul, Alan. "Dickey Betts on the Term 'Southern Rock.'" AlanPaul.net, n.d. http://alanpaul.net/2016/10/dickey-betts-on-the-term-southern-rock/.

Petty, Tom. "Rebels." © 1985 by Gone Gator Music.

Pillmore, Bill. Telephone interview by the author. June 23, 2019.

Price, Richard. Email correspondence with the author. October 6, 2017.

———. Telephone interviews by the author. June 4, 2019, and November 25, 2019.

Pyle, Artimus. Telephone interviews by the author. April 14, 2019, May 1, 2019, and November 21, 2019.

Register, Tommy. Telephone interview by the author. May 25, 2019.

Rickman, Brian. "Why the 'New Blackfoot' Is Crap: How a Great Band Went Sour." Classic Rock 96.1, September 2, 2016. https://classicrock961.com/why-the-new-blackfoot-is-crap-how-a-great-band-goes-sour/.

Rothschild, Michael. Telephone interview by the author. August 31, 2019.

Rowland, Marshall. Telephone interview by the author. 2002.

Sammons, Sylvia. Telephone interviews by the author. April 3 and 5, 2019.

Simpson, Hugh. Email correspondence with the author. April 1, 2019.

Sisson, Scott. Personal interview by author. November 29, 2018.

———. Telephone interview by the author. August 23, 2019.

Smith, Michael Buffalo. *From Macon to Jacksonville: More Conversations in Southern Rock*. Macon, GA: Mercer University Press, 2018.

———. "Henry Paul on the Outlaws, Blackhawk, and a Lifetime of Great Music." *Swampland*, n.d., http://swampland.com/articles/view/title:henry_paul_on_the_outlaws_blackhawk_and_a_lifetime_of_great_music.

———. "Johnny Sandlin: Southern Producer, Engineer and Musician." *Swampland.com*, Spring 2004. http://swampland.com/articles/view/title:johnny_sandlin.

———. "Legends of Southern Rock: Blackfoot." *Swampland*, n.d. http://swampland.com/articles/view/title:legends_of_southern_rock_blackfoot/.

———. "Molly Hatchet: No Guts, No Glory." Allmusic, n.d. https://www.allmusic.com/album/no-gutsno-glory-mw0000837108.

———. "Pete Kowalke of Cowboy: The *Gritz* Interview." *Swampland*, n.d. http://swampland.com/articles/view/title:pete_kowalke_of_cowboy_the_gritz_interview.

———. "Skynyrd, the Allmans and Otis: Alan Walden's Career in Rock and Soul. *Swampland*, January 2002. http://swampland.com/articles/view/title:alan_walden.

———. "There's Still Something Special about .38: The Don Barnes Interview." *Swampland.com*, February 2000. http://swampland.com/articles/view/title:don_barnes.

Smith, Wayne G. Telephone interview by the author. June 30, 2019.

Snyder, Patrick. "The Sorrowful Confessions of Gregg Allman." *Rolling Stone*, November 4, 1976. https://www.rollingstone.com/music/music-features/the-sorrowful-confessions-of-gregg-allman-108095/.

Soergel, Matt. Telephone interview by the author. June 25, 2019.

Spangler, Kevin, and Ron Currens. "Butch Trucks, the Different Drummer." *Hittin' the Note* 15, n.p., n.d.

Steele, Larry. *As I Recall: 1964–1987*. CreateSpace Independent Publishing Platform, 2016.

Talton, Tommy. Email correspondence with the author. April 18, 2019.

Trevett, Ryan. Personal interview by the author. March 11, 2019.

Truck, Butch. "First Blog." *The World According to Butch Trucks*. July 13, 2011, http://thebutchtrucks.blogspot.com/2011/07/first-blog.html.

Trucks, Derek. "How I Ended up on Stage with Bob Dylan the First Time I Saw Him Live." *Ultimate Guitar*, July 4, 2017. https://www.ultimate-guitar.com/news/general_music_news/derek_trucks_how_i_ended_up_on_stage_with_bob_dylan_the_first_time_i_saw_him_live.html.

Vallance, Jim. Email correspondence with the author. August 14, 2019.

Van Zant, Ronnie. "Jacksonville Kid." © 1977 by Songs of Universal.

Van Zant, Ronnie, and Steve Gaines. "You Got That Right." © 1977 by Get Loose Music and Songs of Universal.

Van Zant, Ronnie, Gary Rossington, and Ed King. "Sweet Home, Alabama." ©
1974 by Songs of Universal.

Wake, Matt. "Scott Boyer Talks Cowboy, Recording with Allmans, Being Covered by Eric Clapton." AL.com, September 11, 2005. https://www.al.com/entertainment/2015/09/scott_boyer_talks_cowboy_capri.html.

Walker, Greg T. Telephone interviews by the author. June 30, 2019, and August 27, 2019.

Weiss, Arlene. "Gregg Allman's Thoughts on ABB Stating They're Not Southern Rock." *Hittin' the Web with the Allman Brothers Band*, n.d. https://allmanbrothersband.com/modules.php?op=modload&name=XForum&file=viewthread&tid=144753.

Weissman, Dick. Telephone interviews by the author. April 3 and 6, 2019.

West, Kirsten. "Inside the Elusive Mr. Betts." *Hittin' the Note* 10, n.d., n.p.

Wexler, Jerry. *The Rhythm and the Blues: A Life in American Music*. With David Ritz. New York: Knopf, 1993.

Whitney, Rick. "The Allman Brothers Band: Architectural Heritage—A Tale of Two Houses." *Hittin' the Note* 26 (2000): n.p.

Wynans, Reese. Telephone interview by the author. May 21, 2016.

Secondary Sources

Abbott, Lynn, and Doug Seroff. *The Original Blues: The Emergence of the Blues in African American Vaudeville*. Jackson: University Press of Mississippi, 2017.

"AMA Responds." Aging Rebel. January 26, 2017, https://www.agingrebel.com/14987.

"Around J(action)ville." *Jacksonville Journal*, March 28, 1969.

Atlas, Jacoba. "Gram Parsons: The Burrito Ego Man." *Melody Maker*, April 3, 1973. Cited in John F. Stanislawski, "Grievous Angel: Gram Parsons and the Country-Rock Movement." PhD diss., University of Illinois–Urbana, 2014.

Ballinger, Lee. *Lynyrd Skynyrd: An Oral History*. Los Angeles: XT377 Publishing, 1999.

Banister, C. Eric. *Counting Down Southern Rock: The 100 Best Songs*. Lanham, MD: Rowman and Littlefield, 2016.

"The Best Southern Rock Bands of All Time," *Ranker*, n.d. https://www.ranker.com/list/southern-rock-bands-and-musicians/reference.

Bockris, Victor. *Keith Richards: The Biography*. New York: Da Capo, 2003.

Bomar, Scott B. *Southbound: An Illustrated History of Southern Rock*. Milwaukee: Backbeat Books, 2014.

Brant, Marley. *Southern Rockers: The Roots and Legacy of Southern Rock*. New York: Billboard Books, 1999.

Bratt, James D. *Dutch Calvinism in Modern America: A History of a Conservative Subculture*. Eugene, OR: Wipf and Stock, 1984.

Butler, J. Michael. "Lord, Have Mercy on My Soul: Sin, Salvation and Southern Rock." *Southern Cultures* 9, no. 4 (December 2003): 73–87.

———. "'Luther King Was a Good Ole Boy': The Southern-Rock Movement and White-Male Identity in the Post-Civil-Rights South." *Popular Music and Society* 23, no. 2 (Summer 1999): 41–61.

Carey, Nathaniel, and Doug Stanglin. "South Carolina Takes down Confederate Flag." *USA Today*, July 10, 2015, https://www.usatoday.com/story/news/nation/2015/07/10/south-carolina-confederate-flag/29952953/.

Carlisi, Jeff, and Dan Lipson. *Jam! Amp Your Team, Rock Your Business*. San Francisco: Jossey-Bass, 2009.

Cash, W. J. *The Mind of the South*. New York: Knopf, 1962.

Ching, Barbara. "Where Has the Free Bird Flown? Lynyrd Skynyrd and White Southern Manhood." In *White Masculinity in the Recent South*, edited by Trent Watts, 251–65. Baton Rouge: Louisiana State University Press, 2008.

Clark, Anthony. "With Lipham's Closing, Gainesville Losing Link to Rock Royalty. *Gainesville Sun*, April 11, 2014. https://www.gainesville.com/article/LK/20140411/BUSINESS/604135191/GS/.

Connelly, Christopher. "Danny Joe Brown Gets Vindication." *Detroit Free Press*, August 17, 1981, 6C.

Country Aircheck, May 26, 2015. https://www.countryaircheck.com/pdfs/current052615.pdf.

Cross, Susan. "Guv'nah Wallace Meets Lynyrd Skynyrd." *Swank*, May 1975. Reprinted at *Susan Cross Writes*, https://susancrosswrites.blogspot.com/2014/11/interview-with-lynyrd-skynyrd-may-31.html.

Crowe, Cameron. "Lynyrd Skynyrd: Hell on Wheels Puts on the Brakes." *Los Angeles Times*, October 24, 1976. Reprinted at http://www.theuncool.com/journalism/lynyrd-sknyrd-l-a-times/.

———. *One More from the Road* liner notes. MCA Records, 1976. Reprinted at http://www.angelfire.com/tn/LSkynyrd/originallpliner.html.

"Dave Hlubek, Founding Member of Jacksonville Band Molly Hatchet, Dead at 66." *Florida Times-Union*, September 3, 2017. https://www.jacksonville.com/news/national/2017-09-03/dave-hlubek-founding-member-jacksonville-band-molly-hatchet-dead-66.

Davis, Ennis Armon. *Jacksonville*. Charleston: Arcadia, 2015.

Davis, Rachel. "Bassist Couldn't Breathe, Emphysema Factor in Wilkeson Death." *Florida Times-Union*, September 8, 2001. Reprinted at http://news.jacksonville.com/special/lynyrdskynyrd/bassistcouldntbreathe.html.

"Derek Hess: Drums, Percussion." Lynyrd Skynyrd Frynds. N.d. http://www.frynds.com/heartstrings/Chariot/Bios/DH.html.

"Distinguish Jacksonville: The Silent Film Industry." February 27, 2007. https://www.metrojacksonville.com/article/2007-feb-distinguish-jacksonville-the-silent-film-industry.

Dixon, Kristal. "Former Lynyrd Skynyrd Drummer Dies in Crash." *Cartersville (GA) Patch*, April 4, 2015. https://patch.com/georgia/cartersville/report-former-lynyrd-skynyrd-drummer-dies-crash-o.

"Don Barnes (38 Special)." *Wisconsin Music*, March 3, 2018. http://wisconsin-music.net/2018/03/03/don-barnes-38-special/.

"Duane and Gregg Met Lynyrd Skynyrd." Hittin' the Web with the Allman Brothers Band. https://allmanbrothersband.com/modules.php?op=modload&name=XForum&file=viewthread&tid=2041.

Dulaney, William L. "A Brief History of 'Outlaw' Motorcycle Clubs." *International Journal of Motorcycle Studies* 1, no. 3 (November 2005). Reprinted at https://web.archive.org/web/20180424010711/http://ijms.nova.edu/November2005/IJMS_Artcl.Dulaney.html.

Dunlop, Ian. *Breakfast in Nudie Suits*. Huntingdon, UK: Clarksdale Books, 2011.

Eastman, Jason T. "Rebel Manhood: The Hegemonic Masculinity of the Southern Rock Music Revival." *Journal of Contemporary Ethnography*, 41, no. 2 (2012).

Eastman, Jason T., and Douglas P. Schrock. "Southern-Rock Musicians' Construction of White Trash." *Race, Gender & Class* 15, no. 1 (January 2008): 205–19.

Ehler, Jay. "Gram Parsons Sweeps out the Ashes." *Crawdaddy*, October 1973, 74.

Einarson, John. *Desperados: The Roots of Country Rock*. New York: Cooper Square, 2001.

———. *Hot Burritos: The True Story of the Flying Burrito Brothers*. Minneapolis: Jawbone Books, 2008.

Elsas, Dennis. "Gregg Allman Shares a Fillmore East Secret." Best Classic Bands, n.d. https://bestclassicbands.com/gregg-allman-interview-dennis-elsas-3-2-16/.

Erickson, Lori. "Maintaining Dutch Heritage." *American Profile*, April 23, 2000. https://americanprofile.com/articles/maintaining-dutch-heritage/.

"First Use of Drums on the Grand Ole Opry." *Musicweird*, n.d. http://music-weird.blogspot.com/2014/08/the-first-drums-on-grand-ole-opry.html. Retrieved March 20, 2019.

FitzGerald, Michael Ray. "Boss Jocks: How Corrupt Radio Practices Made Jacksonville One of the Great Music Cities." *Southern Cultures* 17, no. 4 (Winter 2011): 6–23.

———. "NE Florida Music Scene More Than Lynyrd Skynyrd." *Jacksonville Business Journal*, July 15, 2002. https://www.bizjournals.com/jacksonville/stories/2002/07/15/story1.html.

———. *Swamp Music*. Jacksonville: Hidden Owl, 2019.

Fletcher, Dorothy K. "By the Wayside: The Big Bad Smell: Jacksonville's Age-Old Problem Finally Conquered. Jacksonville.com (*Florida Times-Union*), January 30, 2010. https://www.jacksonville.com/community/riverside/2010-01-30/story/by_the_wayside_the_big_bad_smell_jacksonvilles_age_old_problem_.

———. *Historic Jacksonville Theatre Palaces, Drive-ins and Movie Houses.* Charleston, SC: History Press, 2015.

Fong-Torres, Ben. *Hickory Wind: The Life and Times of Gram Parsons.* New York: Knopf, 1990.

Freeman, Scott. *Midnight Riders: The Story of the Allman Brothers Band.* New York: Little, Brown, 1995.

Fybush, Scott. "Site of the Week 1/18/2013: Jacksonville, Florida, 2011 (Part 3). Fybush.com, January 18, 2013, https://www.fybush.com/site-of-the-week-1182013-jacksonville-florida-2011-part-3/.

Garnaas, Steve. "Grand Jury Indicts Actress Linda Blair." *Florida Times Union*, March 12, 1979.

Gates, David. "White-Male Paranoia." *Newsweek*, March 29, 1993, 48–53.

Giddens, Gail. *Molly Hatchet* (album), liner notes, 1978.

Giles, Jeff. "How Scooter Herring's Arrest Broke up the Allman Brothers Band. Ultimate Classic Rock, May 28, 2016. https://ultimateclassicrock.com/allman-brothers-roadie-arrest/.

Gomes, Frederic Cassidy, and Joan Houston Hall. *Dictionary of American Regional English IV*. Cambridge: Belknap Press of Harvard University Press, 2002.

Gordon, Robert. *It Came from Memphis.* New York: Simon and Schuster, 1995.

Griffin, Sid. *Gram Parsons: A Music Biography.* Pasadena, CA: Sierra Books, 1985.

Hajdu, David. *Positively Fourth Street: The Lives and Times of Joan Baez, Bob Dylan, Mimi Baez Farina, and Richard Farina.* London: Bloomsbury, 2002.

Hilburn, Robert. "Tom Petty Tries His Hand at Southern Rock." *Los Angeles Times*, March 31, 1985. https://www.latimes.com/archives/la-xpm-1985-03-31-ca-18746-story.html.

Hoskyns, Barney. *Waiting for the Sun: A Rock 'n' Roll History of Los Angeles.* Milwaukee: Backbeat Books, 2009.

Hutson, Cecil Kirk. "The Darker Side of Dixie: Southern Music and the Seamier Side of the Rural South." PhD diss., Iowa State University, 1995.

If I Leave Here Tomorrow. Directed by Stephen Kijak. Passion Pictures/PolyGram Filmed Entertainment, 2015.

"Jacksonville's Place in Film History." City of Jacksonville, n.d. http://www.coj.net/departments/sports-and-entertainment/film-and-television/film-history-in-jacksonville.

Jancelewicz, Chris. "Female Country Singers Have Far Less Radio Time, and It's Not Changing Any Time Soon." *Global News*, August 13, 2017. https://globalnews.ca/news/3625516/country-music-radio-women-men/.

Johnson, David W. "Crediting Hickory Wind." Folklinks, n.d. http://www.folklinks.com/hickory_wind.html.

———. "His Talent Died in the Desert." *Harvard Journal*, July-August 1994.

Jourard, Marty. "Gainesville Rock History: The Sixties and Seventies." Facebook, March 3, 2011. https://m.facebook.com/notes/gainesville-rock-history-the-60s-and-70s-bands-venues-stories/bands-bands-bands/159161717470226/?__tn__=C-R.

Kahn, Andy. "Grateful Dead Cover Three Merle Haggard Songs at Show in 1971." *JamBase*, April 8, 2016.

Kealing, Bob. *Calling Me Home: Gram Parsons and the Roots of Country Rock*. Gainesville: University Press of Florida, 2012.

Kemp, Mark. *Dixie Lullaby: A Story of Music, Race, and New Beginnings in a New South*. New York: Free Press/Simon and Schuster, 2004.

"Kevin Elson: Biography." People Pill, n.d. https://peoplepill.com/people/kevin-elson/

Kinner, Derek. "The War over Molly Hatchet." *Folio Weekly*, October 1, 2014, 10. Reprinted at http://folioweekly.com/THE-WAR-OVER-MOLLY-HATCHET,11040.

Lechner, Zachary J., ed. *The South of the Mind: American Imaginings of White Southernness, 1960–1980*. Athens: University of Georgia Press, 2018.

"Legends of Southern Rock: Cowboy." *Swampland*, n.d. http://swampland.com/articles/view/title:legends_of_southern_rock_cowboy.

"Linda Blair and Thirty-One Held in Drug Case." *New York Times*, December 21, 1977, 16.

Malone, Bill C. *Country Music, U.S.A.* Austin: University of Texas Press, 1968.

Marin, Carol. "Listening Closely to Merle Haggard." *Chicago Tribune*, July 23, 2003. https://www.chicagotribune.com/news/ct-xpm-2003-07-23-0307230214-story.html.

"Masculinity." Southern Rock and Civil Rights. n.d. https://sites.google.com/site/southernrockcivilrights2/home/masculinity#_ftn1.

Mather, Olivia Carter. "Cosmic American Music: Place and the Country Rock Movement, 1965–1974." PhD diss., University of California–Los Angeles, 2006.

Maysh, Jeff. "The Scarface of Sex: The Millionaire Playboy Who Murdered His Way to the Top of Porn. *Daily Beast*, June 16, 2017. https://www.thedailybeast.com/the-scarface-of-sex.

Meade, Walter Russell. "The Jacksonians." *National Interest*, December 1, 1999. Reprinted at https://nationalinterest.org/article/the-jacksonian-tradition-939.

Medlocke, Rickey Biography." *International Movie Database*, n.d. https://www. imdb.com/name/nm1310712/bio?ref_=nm_ov_bio_sm.

Meyer, David N. *Twenty-Thousand Roads: The Ballad of Gram Parsons and His Cosmic American Music*. New York: Random House, 2007.

Miller, Blair. *Almost Hollywood: The Forgotten Story of Jacksonville, Florida*. Lanham, MD: Rowman and Littlefield, 2012.

Moon, Tom. *One Thousand Recordings to Hear before You Die*. New York: Workman, 2008.

Morgan, Lisa. "Molly Hatchet Celebrates 40 Years at Stagecoach 2018." *Coachella Valley Weekly*, April 25, 2018. http://coachellavalleyweekly.com/molly-hatchet-celebrates-40-years-stagecoach-2018/.

Neal, Jocelyn R. *The Songs of Jimmie Rodgers: A Legacy in Country Music*. Bloomington: Indiana University Press, 2009.

Nelson, Richard Allen. "Movie Mecca of the South: Jacksonville, Florida, as an Early Rival to Hollywood." *Journal of Popular Film and Television* 8, no. 3 (Fall 1980): 38–51.

Newton, Steve. "Lynyrd Skynyrd and the Confederate Flag." *The Georgia Straight*, August 27, 2015. https://www.straight.com/blogra/518196/lynyrd-skynyrd-and-confederate-flag.

Obrecht, Jas. "Duane Allman Remembered." *Guitar Player* 15, no. 10 (October 1981). Reprinted at https://www.duaneallman.info/duaneallmanremembered.htm.

———. "Young Duane Allman: The Bob Greenlee Interview." *Jas Obrecht Music Archive*, n.d. http://jasobrecht.com/young-duane-allman-bob-greenlee-interview/.

Obstfield, Raymond, and Sheila Burgener. *Twang! The Ultimate Book of Country-Music Quotations*. New York: Henry Holt, 1997.

Odom, Gene. *Lynyrd Skynyrd: Remembering the Free Birds of Southern Rock*. With Frank Dorman. New York: Broadway Books, 2002.

Ownby, Ted. "Freedom, Manhood and White-Male Tradition in 1970s Southern-Rock Music." In *Haunted Bodies: Gender and Southern Texts*, edited by Anne Goodwyn Jones and Susan V. Donaldson. Charlottesville: University of Virginia Press, 1998.

"Panel Faults Skynyrd Crew." *Rolling Stone*, July 13, 1978, 23.

Patrick, Donovan. "Unsung Jagger Rolls His Own Way." *Brisbane Times*, August 12, 2009. https://www.brisbanetimes.com.au/entertainment/unsung-jagger-rolls-his-own-way-20090812-ehlr.html.

Paul, Alan. *One Way Out: The Inside History of the Allman Brothers Band*. New York: St. Martins Griffin, 2014.

Paulson, Dave. "Story behind the Song Hold on Loosely." *Nashville Tennessean*, February 21, 2015. https://www.tennessean.com/story/entertainment/music/2015/02/18/story-behind-song-hold-loosely/23646295/.

Perone, James E. "Gram Parsons: Grievous Angel." In *The Golden Age of the Singer-Songwriter, 1970–1973*. Santa Barbara, CA: Praeger, 2012.

Poe, Randy. *Skydog: The Duane Allman Story*. Milwaukee: Backbeat Books, 2006.

"The Producers: Tom Werman, Chapter Seven." *Pop Dose*, May 21, 2009. http://popdose.com/the-producers-tom-werman-chapter-seven/.

Rademacher, Brian. "Interview with Don Barnes: 38 Special Still Rockin'." *Rock Eyez*, April 2008. http://www.rockeyez.com/interviews/int-don-barnes.html.

Rees, Paul. "Rickey Medlocke: The Story of Southern Rock's Brightest Star." Classic Rock, October 28, 2016. https://www.loudersound.com/features/rickey-medlocke-the-story-of-southern-rocks-brightest-star.

Ribowsky, Mark. *Whiskey Bottles and Brand-New Cars: The Fast Life and Sudden Death of Lynyrd Skynyrd*. Chicago: Chicago Review Press, 2015.

"Richards Leads Parsons Tributes." *Billboard*, July 11, 2004. https://www.billboard.com/articles/news/67393/richards-leads-parsons-tributes.

Roberts, Randall. "Tom Petty and the Heartbreakers, an L.A. Band, Stare at 'Hypnotic Eye.'" *Los Angeles Times*, July 18, 2014. https://www.latimes.com/entertainment/music/la-et-ms-tom-petty-hypnotic-eye-20140720-column.html.

Rumble: The Indians Who Rocked the World. Directed by Stevie Salas. Rezolution Films, 2018.

Runtagh, Jordan. "Remembering Lynyrd Skynyrd's Deadly 1977 Plane Crash. *Rolling Stone*, October 20, 2017. https://www.rollingstone.com/music/music-features/remembering-lynyrd-skynyrds-deadly-1977-plane-crash-2-195371/.

Rushing, J. Taylor. "Waycross' Forgotten Son." *Florida Times-Union*, July 20, 2005. Retrieved March 20, 2019, from http://buffettnews.com/forum/viewtopic.php?t=38274.

Sanchez, Daniel. "Hounded by Debt, Allman Brothers Butch Trucks May Have Committed Suicide." *Digital Music News*, January 27, 2017. https://www.digitalmusicnews.com/2017/01/27/allman-brothers-butch-trucks-commits-suicide/.

Schramm, Darianne. "Los Angeles through the Eyes of Tom Petty." *Journiest*, n.d. https://www.journiest.com/pt-tom-petty-top-spots-2497662720.html.

Scoppa, Bud. Liner notes to *Return of the Grievous Angel: A Tribute to Gram Parsons*. Almo Sounds, April 1999. Reprinted at http://www.furious.com/perfect/gramparsons/budscoppa.html.

———. Review of *Grievous Angel*. *Rolling Stone*, March 28, 1974.

Sharpe, Rebecca. Comment in "Obituary: David Lawrence Hlubek, August 28, 1951–September 2, 2017." *Dignity Memorial*, November 24, 2017.

https://www.dignitymemorial.com/obituaries/jacksonville-fl/david-hlubek-7545753.

Sims, Judy. "Ex-Byrd Gram Solos: He's No Longer in a Hurry." *Rolling Stone*, March 1973, 14.

Stanislawski, John. "Gram Parsons and the Country-Rock Movement." PhD diss., University of Illinois, Urbana, 2014.

Stephens, Randall J. *The Devil's Music: How Christians Inspired, Condemned, and Embraced Rock 'n' Roll*. Cambridge: Harvard University Press.

Stepmann, Jarrett, "Trump Should Model His Foreign Policy after Andrew Jackson." The National Interest, March 13, 2017. https://nationalinterest.org/feature/trump-should-model-his-foreign-policy-after-andrew-jackson-19771.

Stimeling, Travis D. "To Be Polished More Than Extended': Musicianship, Masculinity and the Critical Reception of Southern Rock." *Journal of Popular Music Studies* 26, no. 1 (2014): 121–36.

"Ten Details about the Fatal Plane Crash That Was the Death of Lynyrd Skynyrd as We Knew It." History Collection, August 1, 2018. https://history-collection.co/10-details-about-the-tragic-crash-that-was-the-death-of-lynyrd-skynyrd-as-we-knew-it/5/.

Tennille, Andy. "Finding His Path." *San Francisco Chronicle*, February 5, 2006. https://www.sfgate.com/entertainment/article/Finding-His-Path-2505242.php.

Tennis, Joe. "New Blackfoot Comes to Bristol Oct. 10." *Bristol Herald Courier*, October 5, 2015. https://www.heraldcourier.com/lifestyles/new-blackfoot-comes-to-bristol-oct/article_301b4fe6-6b81-11e5-b19d-3fe8f74169e8.html.

Trefferson Bows Line with Khouri." *Billboard*, November 2, 1968, 86.

Uhelszki, Jaan. "Lynyrd Skynyrd: A Southern Ghost Story." *Classic Rock*, May 24, 2018. https://www.loudersound.com/features/lynyrd-skynyrd-a-southern-ghost-story.

U.S. National Transportation Safety Board. *Aircraft Accident Report, 1 Company, Convair 248, N55 Gillsburg, Mississippi, October 20, 1977*. June 19, 1978, 11. Reprinted at http://libraryonline.erau.edu/online-full-text/ntsb/aircraft-accident-reports/AAR78-06.pdf.

Walker, Jason. *God's Own Singer*. London: Helter Skelter, 2002.

Wardlaw, Matt. "How *Survivor*'s Jim Peterik Helped 38 Special and Sammy Hagar Write Big Hits." Ultimate Classic Rock, October 19, 2014. https://ultimateclassicrock.com/jim-peterik-interview/.

Webb, Jim. *Born Fighting: How the Scots-Irish Shaped America*. New York: Broadway Books, 2004.

"Welcome to the Home of the Georgia Bulldog Club of Jacksonville: America's Largest Bulldog Club." *Georgia Bulldog Club of Jacksonville*, 2019. https://jaxbulldogs.com/.

Whitely, Sheila, ed. *Sexing the Groove: Popular Music and Gender*. New York: Routledge, 1997.

Whitney, Keith. "Some Call Confederate Flag American Version of Swastika." *USA Today*, July 31, 2015. https://www.usatoday.com/story/news/politics/2015/07/31/confederate-flag-american-swastika/30948275/.

"Why Are Dutch-Americans So Different from the Dutch?" *Economist*, May 24, 2018. https://www.economist.com/united-states/2018/05/24/why-are-dutch-americans-so-different-from-the-dutch.

"Winter Film Capital of the World: The Early Cinematic History of Jacksonville." *Coastal*, June 7, 2018. https://thecoastal.com/featured/jax-cinematic-past/.

Wirt, John. "Classic .38 Special Songs Withstand the Test of Time." *Baton Rouge Advocate*, April 29, 2013. https://www.theadvocate.com/baton_rouge/entertainment_life/music/article_6e527b6b-ec37-54d2-9d70-c28c96a7133e.html.

Yarbrough, Chuck. "Lynyrd Skynyrd's 'Free Bird' Flies toward Retirement with Farewell Tour." *Plain Dealer*, July 28, 2018, https://www.cleveland.com/music/2018/07/lynyrd_skynyrds_free_bird_flie.html.

INDEX

Acid-rock, viii, 2. *See also* Underground
    music
ACP Records (Atlantic Coast Produc-
    tions), 34, 35
Alaimo, Steve, 35, 36, 37, 52, 53, 66
Albert, Howie, 35
Albert, Ron, 35
Alias, 13, 98
Alice Marr, 121, 122
Allen Collins Band, 13, 82, 99–102, 121,
    172n5
Allman, Devon, 65
Allman, Duane, x, 5, 15, 30, 33, 35–37,
    39–59, 61–64, 66–69, 71, 85, 145–46,
    150, 165n6, 168n54
Allman, Galadrielle, 52, 168n54
Allman, Geraldine, 52
Allman, Gregg, x, 5, 15, 35–37, 40–43,
    49–53, 55, 59–60, 62, 64, 66, 68, 69,
    71–72, 85, 98, 147, 166n25, 167n34
Allman Betts Band, 65
Allman Brothers Band, xi, 1, 5, 6, 12, 13,
    14, 29, 31, 36, 37, 39–65, 68, 70, 76, 86,
    95, 107, 118, 120, 133, 135, 136, 145,
    147, 156, 159n7, 160n16, 164n57
Allman Joys, x, 5, 14, 33, 39, 42, 43, 51,
    81, 107
Almanac, 43, 49
APB (Artimus Pyle Band), 101, 103
Ardent Studios, 34
Armstrong, Pat, 85–86, 94, 109, 122,
    125, 133–38, 140–42
Artimus Pyle Band. *See* APB

Ascot Records, 25
Atco Records, 5, 36–37, 55–56, 60, 66, 70,
    111, 113–15
Atkins, Charles, 41
Atlanta Rhythm Section, 89, 106, 131
Atlantic Coast Productions. *See* ACP
    Records
Atlantic Records, 19, 36, 54, 102
Axe, 114–17
Axton, Hoyt, 11, 12, 106, 132, 162n9
Axton, Mae Boren, 11, 12, 18, 42, 105,
    161n30, 162n9, 166n19

Bakersfield sound, 3, 27
Barber, Adrian, 60
Baril, Greg, 145, 147, 183n8
Barnes, Don, 14, 15, 73, 119, 120–23,
    125–31
Barth, Bobby, 114–17
Beachcomber Lounge, 33, 34, 42, 51, 81
Beaches Coliseum, 59, 61. *See also* Jack-
    sonville Beach Auditorium
Beatles, the, 9, 23, 25–26, 32, 54
Berry, Chuck, 2, 9, 125, 184n21
Betts, Dale, 62–63, 65
Betts, Dickey, viii, ix–x, 5, 29, 39–40,
    43–47, 49, 58–63, 65, 71, 149, 156,
    165n1
Bianco, Fred, 133, 134
Big Brother and the Holding Company,
    9, 52
Big People, 131
Big Tree Records, 111

Billingsley, JoJo, 98
Bitter Ind, 30, 31–38, 107. *See also*
    Thirty-First of February
Black Bear Angel, 76, 82, 86, 98
Blackfoot, 64, 87–88, 105–17
Black Oak Arkansas, 4, 9, 93, 111, 123
Blind Blake (Arthur Phelps), 12
Blondheim, Philip (Scott MacKenzie),
    22
Blues Messengers, the, ix, 44
Bolles School/Bolles Academy, 16,
    19–24, 33, 134, 148
Bomar, Scott B., 69, 70, 73, 140, 159n1
Borden, Barry "B. B.," 140
Boyer, Scott, 30–37, 52–53, 66–74
Braddock, Bobby, 19
Bradenton, Fla., viii, 39, 44, 63, 75, 78,
    165n1
Bradley's Barn (recording studio), 35, 42
Bramblett, Randall, 71–73
Bramlett, Bonnie, 4, 7, 9, 71, 151
Brant, Marley, 60, 129
Brennan, Bill, 12
Bristow, Carol, 98, 102, 125
Brookins, Steve, 118, 119, 122, 129
Brothers and Sisters (album), 6, 53, 60,
    62
Brown, Danny Joe, 134, 137–45
Brown, David, 30, 31–37, 43, 52–53, 63,
    66, 72, 73
Brownsville Station, 111
Brusco, Charlie, 102, 138
Buchanan, Bob, 20
Buffalo Springfield, 25, 26, 51, 52
Burns, Bob, 30, 78, 80, 83, 85–86, 88, 95,
    104, 109–10, 132, 174n27, 178n10
Byrds, the, 3, 18, 20–26, 30, 31, 33, 35

Cale, J. J., 8, 150
California country-rock, 2–5, 15, 18,
    25–26, 28–30, 51, 61–62, 70–71, 73
Camelots, the, 119–20
Capps, Bobby, 130
Capricorn Records, x, 1, 37, 53, 56, 60,
    63, 69, 70, 71, 73, 74, 89, 90, 165n1
Capricorn Studios, 60, 65, 70

Captain Beyond, 63
Carl, Max, 129, 130
Carlisi, Jeff, xiii, ix, 14, 79, 96, 119, 120,
    121–25, 128–32
Carlton, Jim, 24
Carr, Pete, 50, 55
Carter, Clarence, 54, 71
Cash, W. J., 153
Chappelle, Pat, 11
Charles, Jimmy, 64–65
Charles, Ray, 6, 11, 12, 18–19
Chauncey, Danny, 60, 129, 130
Ching, Barbara, 152
Civil War, 94
Clapton, Eric, viii, 30, 60, 71, 119, 132,
    149, 150, 151
Clark, George, 67, 69
Clarke, Michael, 25
Classics IV, the, vii, 12, 31, 62, 107, 164n3
CMC International Records, 117, 130,
    143
Cobb, J. R., 89, 107, 135
Cocaine. *See* Drugs
Coe, David Allan, 157
Cogburn, Dorman, 98
Collins, Allen, 13, 78, 80–82, 85, 86, 88,
    92, 98–103, 109–10, 115, 119–20, 124,
    143
Collins, Kathy, 99
Columbia Records, 20, 25, 34, 89,
    130–31, 149, 151
Comic Book Club, x, 33, 51, 81, 82, 108
Confederate flag controversy, 6, 30, 62,
    91, 94–95
Conley, Arthur, 54
Connor, Ingram "Coon Dog," 17, 19
Conrad, Bill, 22, 27
Convertibles, the, 73
Corneal, Jon, 19
*Country and Western Meets Rhythm and
    Blues* (album), 19
Country Frolics (television program),
    106, 161n32
Country-rock. *See* California
    country-rock
Cowboy, xi, 4, 13, 30, 37, 66–74

Cow Ford, 9, 31
Cream, 44, 48, 60, 119
Criteria Recording Studios, 35, 36, 66
Cross Country, 110
Crowe, Cameron, 96
Crump, Bruce, 133, 134, 137, 138, 140–44

"D.I.V.O.R.C.E." (song), 51
Dana, Don, 34, 76
Daniels, Billy, 11
Daniels, Charlie, 2, 3, 93, 125, 157
Davis, Jesse Ed, 50
Daybreakers, the, vii
Daytona Beach, Fla., x, 12, 33, 35, 39,
    40–42, 50, 52, 68, 80, 134, 167n37
Decoys, the, 37, 73, 74
Delaney and Bonnie, 4, 7, 9, 71, 151
Derek and the Dominators, 147
Derek Trucks Band, 13, 73, 147, 148–49,
    151, 183n7
DeVito, Jim, 7, 172n5
Dial Records, 5, 14, 42
Dickinson, Jim, 34
Dillards, the, 26
Doeschler, Rick, 78
Doomsday Refreshment Committee,
    viii, 119
Doss, Mack, 39–40
Dougherty, Jimmy, 76, 82, 98–100,
    172n5
Dowd, Tom, 10, 36, 96, 147, 149
Dowdy, Toby, 106, 161n32
Driscoll, Phil, 98, 101
Drugs, 2, 27, 60, 64, 98, 103, 138, 140,
    153, 155
Dub's Steer Room, 108
Duncan, Finlay, 35
Dunlop, Ian, 24
Durden, Tommy, 42, 161n32
Dylan, Bob, 23, 26, 32, 34, 35, 78, 147

Eagles, the, 3, 6, 18, 28, 30, 70
Easy Rider (film), 155
Eat a Peach (album), 5, 60
Ebenezer Baptist Church, 94
Echoes, the, 32

Einarson, John, 51
Elson, Kevin, 120–22, 134
Englewood High School, 32, 66, 85
Epics, the, 120
Erlichman, Marty, 25
Escorts, the, 42

Facemire, Allen, 48, 62–64
FAME (Florence, Alabama, Music En-
    terprises), 50, 53–57
Farrar, Jimmy, 139–40, 143, 144
"Fightin' Side of Me, The" (song), 28
Fillmore East, 56, 61, 70, 133
Fisher, Margaret, 27
Five Men-Its, 43, 50
Fletcher, Dorothy, 160n24
Flirtin' with Disaster (album), 136, 153
Florence, Alabama, Music Enterprises.
    See FAME
Florida School for the Deaf and Blind,
    11
Florida State University, 32, 66
Floyd, Eddie, 86–87
Flying Burrito Brothers, 3, 18, 25, 30
Folk-rock, 31–33, 70, 71
Forest Inn, 48, 58, 75, 81, 84
Forum, the, 44
"Four Walls of Raiford" (song), 123
Frazetta, Frank, 135
Freaks. See Hippies
Free Bird (band), 98
"Free Bird" (song), 83, 87, 88
Fresh Garbage (band), 88, 107–8
Frogwings, 149
Funocchio's, 89
Furay, Richie, 25

Gaines, Steve, 96
Gainesville, Fla., 3, 6, 48, 59, 66, 78, 108,
    110, 111, 117, 119, 122
Galvin, John, 138, 140, 142, 144
Gator Country, song, 134, 136
Gator Country, band, 143–44
Gauvin, Mickey, 25
Gibbs, DeWitt, 108, 110
Gillsburg, Miss., 97, 125

Glass, Paul, vii–x
Goble, Claude, 17
"God Rest His Soul" (song), 36, 53
Grand Ole Opry, 39, 192
Graves, Jim, 64, 145
Graves, Judson, 24
Gray House, x, 46, 48, 53, 57, 59, 85, 167n34, 169n88
Greasers, 28
Great Southern, 3
Great Speckled Bird (newspaper), 1
Green, Steve, 142
Green House, 46, 48, 85, 167n34, 169n88
Greenlee, Bob, 41
Grey, JJ, 7, 151
Grievous Angel (album), 23
Griffin, David, 81, 82, 119
Griffin, Sid, 24
Grondin, Jack, 122, 127, 129–30
Groom Lake (feature film), 116
Gunn, Toby, 42
Guralnick, Peter, 6

Haggard, Merle, 28, 30, 157
Haines, Connie, 12
Hall, Jimmy, 74, 77–78, 96, 131, 147
Hall, Randall, 38, 100, 102–3, 178n10
Hall, Rick, 50, 54–57
Hardy, Oliver, 10
Hargrett, Charlie, 107, 108, 110, 113–14, 116–17
Hartman, Dan, 125–26
Harwood, Barry Lee, 96–99, 143
Hazlewood, Lee, 26
"Heartbreak Hotel" (song), 12, 18, 42, 106, 166n19
Hearts and Flowers, 3, 18, 26
Hell-of-a-fellow archetype, 153
Henderson, Nancy, 125
Hensley, Ken, 113–14
Herrin, Billy Ray, 17, 30
Herring, John "Scooter," 64
Hess, Derek, 99, 147
Hickory Wind (music store), 30
"Hickory Wind" (song), 20, 23
Higgins, Bertie, 43

Highway Call (album), 71
Hillbillies, 18, 39, 154–55
Hillbilly boogie, 2
Hillcrest district, 78, 118
Hillman, Chris, 3, 18, 25–28
Hinton, Eddie, 43, 50, 53
Hippies, 2, 6, 28–29, 46–48, 54, 154–55, 158
Hlubek, Dave, 14, 78, 80, 116, 132–40, 142–44
Hodges, Alex, 122
Holland, Steve, 133, 137, 140, 143–44
Holly, Buddy, 2, 25, 184n21
Hombres, the, 4
"Honky-Tonk Nighttime Man" (song), 30
Hood, David, 111
Hopkins, Ellen, 53, 57, 59, 169n88
Hornsby, Paul, 50, 52, 55, 61, 73–74
Hour Glass, the, x, 5, 36–37, 43, 49–53, 55, 69, 73, 81, 85
House Rockers, the, 41
Hoyt Hi-fi, x
Hustlers, Inc., 85–86
Hutson, Cecil Kirk, 94

Idlewild South (album), 5, 60
Idlewild South (house), 37
Illusions, the, 34, 76
Ingram, Bobby, 134, 138, 140–44
International Submarine Band, 18–19, 25–26, 29
Iron Butterfly, 52, 63
Ivy, Quin, 87, 87–88

Jackson, Andrew, 154
Jacksonians, 93, 154
Jacksonville Beach Auditorium, 59, 61. *See also* Beaches Coliseum
Jacksonville Jam, 58–59
Jacksonville Jaycees, 119–20
Jean Ribault High School, 31
Jefferson Airplane, 44, 46, 48
Jennings, Waylon, 29, 157
Jesters, the, viii, 39, 59
Johnny Van Zant Band, 13, 101, 130, 142

Johnson, Bob, 86
Johnson, David (producer), 88
Johnson, David W. (author), 20, 24
Johnson, James Weldon, 11
Johnson, Jay, 116, 136
Johnson, Jimmy, 50, 56, 88–89, 111, 116
Johnson, Johnny "Jaimoe," 57–58
Johnson, Rick "Hurricane," 102
Joiner, Frank, 89
Jokers, the, 39
Joplin, Janis, 9, 153
Journeymen, the, 19, 22
Junstrom, Larry, 78, 80, 86, 88, 104

Kaufman, Phil, 27
"Keep on Smilin'" (song), 8
Kemp, Mark, 93, 154
Killen, Buddy, 42–42, 166n19
Kilpatrick, Dean, 85, 97, 167n34
King, Martin Luther, vii, 36, 53, 94,
   172n8, 184n11
King James Version (band), 89, 180n5
Kingston Trio, 3–4, 19, 165n12
Kinner, Derek, 135, 138
Knight, David, 108
Knowbody Else, 4
Kooper, Al, 89–91, 94–96, 101, 122, 154,
   156, 158
Kowalke, Pete, 66–67, 69, 70, 74
Krantz, Dale, 9, 99, 101, 102, 125

Laid Back (album), 37, 71
Lake Shore Middle School, 78–80, 82,
   132
Landslide Records, 148
LaVilla district, 11, 161n29
LaVoie, Kent "Lobo," 19, 96
Leadon, Bernie, 3, 18, 26–28
Leavell, Chuck, 37, 61, 71, 73, 147
Legends, the, 19, 24
Les Paul guitars, vii, 4, 5, 29
LHI Records, 26
Limp Bizkit, 13, 76
Lindsey, Tim, 101, 132, 144
Lipham Music, 59
Lipsky, Tom, 117

"Little Black Egg" (song), 42
Little Black Eggs, the (band), 80
"Livin' in the Country" (song), 67
Load, the (band), 48–49, 59, 62, 64, 75,
   78
Lombar, Dru, 73, 89, 140, 180n5
"Long-Haired Country Boy" (song), 2,
   157
Longhairs. See Hippies
Loud and Proud Records, 117
Loudermilk, John D., 42
LSD, 2, 95
Lundgren, Erik, 101, 142
Lynyrd Skynyrd, airplane crash, 97–99,
   102, 104
Lynyrd Skynyrd, drug use, 98
Lyons, Ken, 120, 121–22, 125

MacKenzie, Scott (Philip Blondheim),
   22
Macon, Ga., x, 37, 53, 55–57, 60, 63, 65,
   68–70, 74, 85–87, 89–90, 122, 134
Mahal, Taj, 50
Malone, Bill C., 159n3, 5
Manganiello, Lou, 110
Markham, Tom, 82–83, 87, 135
Marshall, Rocco, 102
Martin, John W., 11
Martinique, the, 33
McCormack, Phil, 142–44
McEuen, Bill, 49–50, 55
McKinley, Mabron, 49, 166n25
McTell, "Blind Willie," 50
Meaux, Huey P., 4
Medlock, Paul "Shorty," 106–7, 112
Medlocke, Rickey, 14, 88–89, 105,
   106–11, 114–17, 119, 172n5
Meekins, Buzzy, 136, 138, 142, 144, 147,
   183n8
Meeks, John, ix, 44, 58, 62, 63–64
"Melissa" (song), 36, 53
Messina, Jim, 51
Meyer, David, 17, 24, 27, 28, 77
"Michelle" (song), 83
"Midnight Rider" (song), 5, 60
Miles, Floyd, 41

Miller, Harold "Chip," 73, 147, 183n8
Miller, Linda (Linda Oakley), 51, 53,
    169n88
Mills, Rodney, 127, 130
Minaret Records, 35
*Modern Sounds in Country and Western
    Music* (album), 19
Mods, the, 78
Mofro, 7, 13, 151. *See also* Grey, JJ
Molly Hatchet, 111, 116, 123, 132–44, 153
Monroe, Bill, 2, 29
Monument Records, 4
Moreland, Ace, 73, 146, 147
Mose Jones, 90
Mother's Finest, 115, 140
MTV (Music Television), 103, 113, 126,
    139
Mudcrutch, 6, 147
Murray, Larry, 3, 18, 26, 28
Murray Hill district, 79, 92
Muscle Shoals, Ala., 87–88, 109–11, 116,
    121
Muscle Shoals Sound (recording stu-
    dio), 71, 88, 116
My Back Yard, 78
My Cross to Bear (book), 166n13, 15, 20,
    25
"My Cross to Bear" (song), 59

Nalli, Al, 111, 114, 115, 117
Nallie, Reen, 111
Nashville, 4–5, 9, 17–18, 27, 29, 35, 40,
    42, 63, 103–4, 130, 161n32, 166n16,
    166n19
Nathan B. Forrest High School, 85, 119,
    120
Naval Air Station Jacksonville, Fla., vii
Naval Air Station Lemoore, Calif., vii
Navy brats, 14, 92, 120, 132
"Need All My Friends" (song), 83
Neil, Fred, 22
Nelson, Willie, 29, 63, 157
Niblick, Kenny, 133–34
Nightcrawlers, the, 42
Nitty Gritty Dirt Band, 29, 49
Nix, Robert, 89, 107, 131, 135

Noble Five, 48, 80
No Reservations (album), 111
Normandy Club, viii
Norm Vincent Recording, 82–83
Nuese, John, 24–25
Nu-Sounds, the, vii

Oakley, Berry, viii, ix, x, 43–48, 51, 53,
    57–62, 64, 71
Oakley, Linda, 51
O'Connor, Nancy, 108
Odom, Bunky, 148
Odom, Gene, 80–81
Offord, Eddie, 114
"Okie from Muskogee" (song), 28, 157
One Percent, xi, 75–76, 81–84, 108,
    173n18, 173n20
Orange Park High School, vii
Orlando, Fla., 30, 37, 67, 98, 109, 120,
    136, 139
Outlaw country, 157
Outlaws, the, 4, 64, 123, 135, 136, 138,
    171n12, 176n70
Owens, Buck, 24–26
Ownby, Ted, 160n14, 184n11

Palatka, Fla., ix, 34
Parker, Jimmy, 78
Parsons, Gram, 3, 15, 16–30, 31, 33, 70,
    77, 94, 107, 134
Parsons, Robert, 19, 23
Paul, Alan, 29, 40, 49, 54
Paulus Music, vii, 133
Paxon High School, 107, 108
Pegasus recording studio, 38
Pelkey, Bill, 120–22
Peter, Paul and Mary, 3, 4, 19, 32
Peterik, Jim, 126–28, 130
Petty, Joe Dan, 165n1
Petty, Tom, 6–7, 59, 119
Phelps, Arthur ("Blind Blake"), 12
Phillips, John, 19, 22, 163n28
Phil Walden Artists and Promotions,
    85, 87
Pickett, Wilson, 54
Pillmore, Bill, 66–67, 69, 71, 73–74

Pinera, Mike, 63
Pinske, Mark, 108
Pitman, Jimmy, 42, 171n3
"Please Be with Me" (song), 30, 71
Poco/Pogo, 3, 18, 51, 70
Poe, Randy, 32, 36, 40, 44, 52, 55
Ponte Vedra Beach, Fla., 17, 20
Powell, Billy, 14, 79–80, 90, 92, 98–99, 102–4, 120, 122, 124, 132
Presley, Elvis, 2, 12, 18, 25, 67, 107, 161n32, 166n19, 184n21
Price, Richard, 48–49, 59, 62, 64, 75
Pyle, Artimus, 30, 95, 97, 99, 102, 103, 124, 156, 174n27, 177n89

Quinvy Studio, 87–88. *See also* Ivy, Quin

"Ramblin' Man" (song), 5–6, 8, 29–30, 62, 65, 71, 93
Reach for the Sky (album), 70
Rebel flag. *See* Confederate flag controversy
"Rebels" (song), 7
Red Jumpsuit Apparatus, 13
Redneck hippies, 6, 14
Reinhardt, Larry, 44, 46, 48, 62–64, 165n1
Renzler, Leonard, 44, 46
Ribowsky, Mark, 104
Richbourg, John ("John R"), 41
Riverside district, 46–48, 67–68, 85, 123, 134, 169n88
Robert E. Lee High School, 47, 84–85, 119, 132
Roberts, Danny, 147
Roberts, Marcus, 13
Rockin' into the Night (album), 126–28
Rodgers Agency, 89
Roemans, the, 43
Roland, Duane, 133–34, 137, 140–44
Rolling Stones, the, 5, 9, 26, 49, 81, 136, 147, 152–53
Roosman, Donna, 52, 54, 57
Rose Hill Cemetery, 64
Ross, Gary, 101
Rossington, Gary, 9, 78–81, 85–86, 92, 94–95, 98–99, 101–5, 115, 116, 124–25, 132, 143, 147
Rossington Band, 101, 116, 132
Rossington Collins Band, 9, 13, 98–99, 101, 125, 143, 147
Rothschild, Michael, 148
Rowland, Marshall, 12
Rudge, Peter, 124–26
Russell, Leon, 43

Safe at Home (album), 26
Sammons, Sylvia, 20
Sandlin, Johnny, 37, 50, 52–53, 55, 57, 69–71, 73–74
Scaggs, Boz, 37, 63
Scene, the, 44, 46
Sciabarasi, Ron, 64, 108
Scots-Irish settlers, 154–55. *See also* Hillbillies
Scottsville Squirrel Barkers, 18
Second Coming, the, 36, 44–49, 52–54, 57–60, 62–64, 68, 75, 78, 108
Seymour, Judy (Judy Van Zant), 30, 85, 98, 103, 115, 127, 149, 167n34
Shade Tree Records, 82–83, 87, 135, 174n38
Shantytown, 118
Shapiro, Bradley, 35–36, 52–53, 66
Shilos, the, 20, 33, 70
Simpson, Hugh, 23
Singleton, Charlie "Hoss," 11
Singleton, Shelby, 35, 43
SIOGO (album), 113
Sir Douglas Quintet, 4
Sisson, Scott, 14, 77, 143
Skinner, Leonard, 83–85
Sky Man (Duane Allman), 67
Sledge, Percy, 54, 56, 87
Smith, Dallas, 49–50
Smith, Michael Buffalo, 89, 110, 133, 140, 147
Smith, Wayne, 75
Snively, Avis, 17
Snively, John, 17
Snow, Hank, 18–19, 26
Snyder, John, 148

Soergel, Matt, 91
Sokoloff, Ira, 109
Sons of Satan, 118, 119, 122
Soul Stew Revival, 151
Sound Lab recording studio, 62, 108
Sound Pit studio
Sounds of the South Records, 135
Spector, Larry, 26
Spector, Mark, 126, 128
Spires, Jack "Jakson," 107–11, 114, 116, 143
"Spooky" (song), vii, 31
SSS International Records, 35. *See also* Singleton, Shelby
Stafford, Jim, 19, 24, 96
Standard Productions, 119. *See also* Sons of Satan
Starr, Ruby, 9, 111
"Statesboro Blues" (song), 50, 145, 147
Steady Records, 48, 62–63
Steele, Larry, 51, 78, 80, 82, 88, 122, 129
Stewart, Bill, 71–74
Stills, Stephen, 25, 147
Stimeling, Travis D., 8
Stone, Butch, 111
Stone, Henry, 35
Strawberry Alarm Clock, 76, 90, 171n3
Studio One, 89, 92, 96, 100, 101, 130
Summer of Love, 47, 158
Sun Studio, 124
Sutton, Jim, 82–83, 87, 174n37
Swamp Cabbage, 7
Swamp rock, 7
Sweethearts of the Rodeo (album), 31
"Sweet Home, Alabama" (song), 91–92, 122, 124, 134
Sweet Rooster, viii, 120–22

"Take It Easy" (song), 6, 30
Talton, Tommy, 30, 37, 67, 69–74, 120
Tangerine (band), 107–8
Tedeschi, Susan, 149–51
Tedeschi Trucks Band, 7, 150–51
Terry Parker High School, 66, 134
Thevis, Mike, 135
Thirty-Eight Special, viii, xi, 9, 12–14,

73, 78, 96, 99, 104, 111, 118–31, 132, 133, 134, 135, 157
Thirty-First of February, 30, 31–38, 52–53, 57, 63
Thomas, Banner, 116, 133, 137–39, 142–44
Thomas, James "Jet," 24
Thomas, Mickey, 77–78
Three-guitar army, 91, 144
Thunderbeats, the, 44, 164n1
Tickner, Eddie, 20
Tiffany System, 35, 43. *See also* Thirty-First of February
Tillotson, Johnny, 12
"Train, Train" (song), 113
Tredinnick Youth Center, 32
"Truck Drivin' Man" (song), 25–26
Trucks (band), 64
Trucks, Chris, 145
Trucks, Claude "Butch," 29, 30–38, 42, 52, 53, 57–59, 62, 64–66, 68, 145, 147, 149
Trucks, Derek, 13, 38, 64, 73, 145–51
Trucks, Duane, 145
Tuscaloosa, Ala., 37, 52, 61, 71, 73

U.S. Navy, 11, 14–15, 18, 77, 132, 133
Ugly Jellyroll, 63
Ultra-Fix, 64
Underground Circus (radio program), 48
Underground music, viii, 2, 44, 48. *See also* Acid-rock
Untils, the, 41
Us, 78

Valenti, Dino, 35, 165n12
Vallance, Jim, 128
Vanguard Records, 31, 35–36, 52–53, 66
Van Zant (band), 101
Van Zant, Donnie, 80, 101, 118–19, 121–22, 125–28, 130–31
Van Zant, Johnny, 80, 101–3, 105, 121, 130
Van Zant, Judy. *See* Seymour, Judy
Van Zant, Lacy, 92
Van Zant, Marion "Sister," 118

Van Zant, Ronnie, 8, 15, 30, 51, 62, 75, 76, 78, 80, 82, 86, 93, 102, 103, 104, 108, 118, 122–25, 134, 154, 155, 158, 167n34

Walden, Alan, 85–89, 90, 92, 109
Walden, Phil, 1, 37, 53–56, 60, 69–70, 85–86, 89, 90, 122, 124, 133, 138
Walker, Greg T., 107–11, 114, 116–17
Wallace, George, 93, 154
WAPE-AM, vii, 12, 22, 48, 83
Warnock, Raphael, 94
Watts, Debra Jean, 102
Waycross, Ga., 3, 15, 16–18, 22, 26, 28, 30, 85, 107
Weck, Henry, 111
Weissman, Dick, 22–23
Werman, Tom, 135, 136, 139, 140
We the People (band), 67, 120
West Side Story (Ace Moreland's band), 146
West, Ralph "Riff," 139, 141, 143, 144
Wet Willie, 1, 4, 7, 8, 73, 74, 77, 96, 131, 147
Wexler, Jerry
Wheeler, Steve
"Whipping Post" (song)
White, Tony Joe
Whitney, Rick, 54–56

Who, the, 113, 125, 153, 156
Wilkeson, Leon, viii, 14, 76, 79–80, 89, 91–93, 96, 98, 99, 102–4, 110, 119–20, 124, 132, 156, 180n5
Williams, Hank, 2, 27, 40
Williams, Hank Jr., 29, 63, 94, 157
Willowbranch Park, 46, 48, 68
Will the Circle Be Unbroken (album), 29
Winter Haven, Fla., 17, 19, 23, 39
Winter Park, Fla., 67, 74
WJAX-AM, 12, 22
WLAC-AM, 40–41
WMBR-TV, 106, 160n23
Woodstock Youth Center, ix
"Workin' for MCA" (song), 90
WQIK-AM, 12
Wright, Betty, 36, 66
WSM-AM, 39
Wynans, Reese, 44, 49, 58–59, 62–64
Wynn, Tom, 67, 69

Yellowcard, 13
Young, Monty, 48, 62
Younger Brothers Band, 100
Yuno, 13

Zambito, Jerry, 100
Zoo, the (band), 36–37, 53

MICHAEL RAY FITZGERALD is a media historian and scholar with a master's degree in mass communication/media history from the University of Florida and a doctorate from the University of Reading (UK). He is the author of *Native Americans on Network TV*. He is also a former musician, songwriter, and studio owner.